T3-BSE-947

# Mergers and Acquisitions in the U.S. Banking Industry

## Evidence from the Capital Markets

Gabriel A. Hawawini

Yamaichi Professor of Finance
Euro-Asia Centre
INSEAD, Fontainebleau, France

Itzhak Swary

Associate Professor of Banking
Faculty of Management
Tel Aviv University, Israel

1990
North-Holland
Amsterdam · New York · Oxford · Tokyo

ELSEVIER SCIENCE PUBLISHERS B.V.
Sara Burgerhartstraat 25
P.O. Box 211, 1000 AE Amsterdam, The Netherlands

*Distributors for the U.S.A. and Canada:*
ELSEVIER SCIENCE PUBLISHING COMPANY, INC.
655 Avenue of the Americas
New York, N.Y. 10010, U.S.A.



**Library of Congress Cataloging-in-Publication Data**

Hawawini, Gabriel A.
Mergers and acquisitions in the U.S. banking industry: evidence from the capital markets / Gabriel Hawawini, Itzhak Swary.
p. cm.
Includes bibliographical references and index.
ISBN 0-444-88639-7
1. Bank mergers--United States. 2. Capital market--United States.
I. Swary, Itzhak, 1946- II. Title.
HG2491.H37 1990
332. 1'6--dc20 90-39691
CIP

ISBN: 0 444 88639 7



Printed in The Netherlands

# FOREWORD

The findings reported in this book are the result of a research project on mergers and acquisitions in the U.S. banking industry that was funded by a most generous grant from the Prochnow Educational Foundation in Madison, Wisconsin. We wish to thank Mr. Thomas Mudge, Mr. Robert Klockars and Ms. Joan Pfister for their useful comments and most of all, for the patience and understanding they displayed when we told them on several occasions that we needed additional time to complete the final manuscript.

The empirical work that provides the foundation of this book was undertaken while the first author was a Visiting Professor at the Wharton School of the University of Pennsylvania during the academic year 1987–1988. During that same year, the second author was a Visiting Professor at the Graduate School of Business Administration at New York University. We have benefited from numerous comments made by colleagues on earlier drafts of the manuscript for which we are most grateful. We thank Professor Donald Fraser (Texas A&M University) for providing some of the newspaper information we needed in order to perform the tests reported in Chapter VII.

This empirical work could not have been completed on time without the help and valuable contributions of Dr. Ik-Hwan Jang who was completing his doctorate thesis at New York University at that time. In addition to this help with the empirical work, Dr. Ik-Hwan Jang assisted with comments and advice at every stage of the research.

A number of people transformed our handwritten notes into a readable manuscript. Mrs. Jocelyne Billot of INSEAD in Fontainebleau typed several versions of the manuscript and the word processing center of the Wharton School of the University of Pennsylvania produced all the tables. We thank them for their patience and the quality of their work.

September 1990

Gabriel Hawawini
Itzhak Swary

# BIOGRAPHICAL SKETCHES

*Gabriel Hawawini*, Yamaichi Professor of Finance, has been on the faculty of INSEAD (European Institute of Business Administration) since 1982 and is currently serving as Associate Dean and Director of the Euro-Asia Centre. Prior to joining INSEAD he taught at New York University, Columbia University and the City University of New York. During 1987/1988 he was a Visiting Professor at Wharton School of the University of Pennsylvania. He received his MBA (1974) and Ph.D. (1977) degrees from New York University.

Dr. Hawawini's principal areas of research include international banking, portfolio management and security valuation. He has published widely on these topics in various professional journals and is the author of numerous monographs and books, the most recent of which is *The Transformation of the European Financial Services Industry: From Fragmentation to Integration* (Salomon Brothers Centre/New York University, 1989).

He has served as a consultant to a number of international institutions, banks and corporations in the United States, Europe, the Middle East and Japan.

*Itzhak Swary* is Associate Professor of Accounting, Finance and Banking, the Director of the Joseph Kasierer Institute for Research in Accounting, Faculty of Management, Tel Aviv University and a Visiting Professor at the Graduate School of Business Administration, New York University.

He received his B.A. (1970) from Tel Aviv University, M.A. in economics (1973) from the Hebrew University of Jerusalem and Ph.D. (1979) from the University of Rochester. He also certified as a C.P.A. (Israel) in 1971.

Dr. Swary published numerous papers in leading banking and finance journals. In addition to the book co-authored with G. Hawawini, he is the author of *Capital Adequacy Requirements and Bank Holdings Companies* (UMI, 1980).

His current research interests include dividend policy, corporate bankruptcy, market-related empirical studies, taxation under inflation, and banking issues.

Dr. Swary has served as Assistant Director of the Open Market Operations Department, the Bank of Israel, and Deputy to the Income Tax Commissioner, the Ministry of Finance of Israel. He is currently a member of the Board of Directors of the Tel Aviv Stock Exchange and a consultant to several large banks in Israel, a member of the Banking Committee of the Examiner of Banks, the Bank of Israel, and a member of the Committee of Accounting and Reporting Standards, the Institute of Certified Public Accountants in Israel.

# CONTENTS

# LIST OF TABLES

CHAPTER I

# INTRODUCTION: OVERVIEW AND REVIEW

## 1. Purpose of the study

There is strong evidence indicating that corporate takeovers generate net aggregate gains, resulting in benefits to acquired-firm shareholders and no losses to acquiring-firm shareholders. [1] A number of hypotheses have been advanced to explain the sources of these gains. These include (i) the potential reduction in production or distribution costs resulting from the adoption of more efficient technology (synergy), (ii) the removal of the target firm's inefficient management, including management that does not adopt policies that maximize the wealth of shareholders, and (iii) the creation of monopoly power in the product market which may lead to higher product prices and profits.

Identifying the sources of gains to merging firms is crucial to policymakers, especially in such a highly regulated industry as banking. Though studies of market reactions to takeover activities have been found to be inconsistent with the creation-of-monopoly-power hypothesis, there seems to be some evidence consistent with the synergy hypothesis. However, merger gains are most likely due to more than a single factor; for example, the elimination of a target firm's inefficient management and the synergies resulting from the combination of two or more independent management teams. In Chapter II we examine a number of hypotheses that seek to explain the merger phenomenon and its effect on the shareholder wealth of merging firms. We also discuss the relevance of these hypotheses to the case of the banking industry.

This study focuses on takeover activities in the banking industry. Evidence from studies on takeovers in other industries may not be

[1] Jensen and Ruback (1983) provide a comprehensive review of this literature.

applicable to the banking sector since banks operate in a different environment (and under a different set of constraints) than non-banking firms. This is due to the regulatory framework within which banks operate, a framework which has the potential to strongly affect the incentives for horizontal bank mergers. In addition, regulators are directly involved in the process of bank mergers. These mergers are the subject of antitrust laws and must be processed and approved by bank regulators.

Strong regulatory intervention can determine the incentives for bank mergers by affecting the potential economies of scale, by imposing constraints on risk taking, and by determining potential bidders and alternative targets. It should be emphasized that, unlike most other industries, banking services do not cover a nationwide market. This is due to the nature of banking services and the limitations imposed by government agencies on interstate banking.

The purpose of this study is to examine the merger phenomenon in the banking industry by answering the following questions:
(1) What are the incentives for banks to merge?
(2) Has the prohibition of interstate banking prevented banks from diversifying and has it increased the rate of bank failures by restricting (geographical) diversification opportunities?
(3) Are bank mergers wealth-creating activities and how are the gains/losses from a merger distributed between the acquiring and acquired bank shareholders?
(4) How can the changes in shareholder wealth resulting from bank mergers be explained and are there differences between interstate and intrastate mergers?
(5) What are the implications of the study's findings for regulatory policy?

The rest of this chapter is organized as follows: in Section 2 we discuss the unique framework in which bank mergers occur, while also identifying the exceptional characteristics of the banking industry. Section 3 provides a review of previous studies on horizontal mergers, antitrust intervention and bank mergers. An overview of the structure of the study is given in Section 4.

## 2. The structure and regulation of the banking industry

This section provides an overview of the structure and regulation of the banking industry in order to identify the potential incentives for horizontal bank mergers. The issues we examine are (1) economies of scale and scope, (2) concentration, competition and performance, (3) interstate banking, (4) safety and diversification, and (5) the regulation of bank mergers.

### *2.1. Economies of scale and scope*

Mergers are usually considered a common and important means to achieve economies of scale (if they exist). Most recent studies on economies of scale, in which financial institutions are generally modeled as providers of multiple products, have reached a similar conclusion: except at relatively low output levels, there do not appear to be economies of scale. [2] The author of the most recent review of literature on economies of scale and scope examined 134 different studies and concluded that, "first, overall economies of scale appear to exist only at low levels of output with diseconomies of scale at large output levels. Second, there is no consistent evidence of global economies of scope. Third, there is some evidence of cost complementarities (product-specific economies of scope) in production. Finally, these results appear to be generally robust across the three types of institutions [commercial banks, savings and loan associations and credit unions], as well as across different data sets and product and cost definitions" (Clark (1988)).

Accordingly, there is no evidence to suggest that larger banking organizations have a cost advantage over smaller banks. It should also follow that mergers between financial firms which increase the scale of operations should yield little or no cost savings. Note that

[2] See, for example, Benston, Berger, Hanweck and Humphrey (1983), Clark (1984), Gilligan and Smirlock (1984), Gilligan, Smirlock and Marshall (1984), Berger, Hanweck and Humphrey (1987). Mester (1987) provides an excellent review of these studies. These studies differ, however, in their findings on economies of scope.

the above findings were obtained under a regulatory framework within which incentives both for banks to remain small as well as to become large exist, not necessarily reflecting the operating cost function. Small banks have a lower reserve requirement, a lighter tax burden, and a higher percentage of insured deposits than larger banks (since the average deposit at a small bank is smaller than that of a larger bank). However, under the same framework, large banks have the ability to make large loans to a single borrower (a loan to a single borrower cannot exceed ten percent of a bank's equity capital). Furthermore, previous studies were conducted during the period of restricted geographic expansion and thus our whole understanding of economies of scale could change with the removal of these barriers. A bank holding company (BHC) might enjoy economies of scale on a nationwide market and *not* in a local market. Hence the necessity to compare interstate mergers to intrastate mergers. [3] A related issue is the recognition that the scope of business of different banks is not identical and economies of scale should be studied for each group of banks separately. The most common distinction is between retail and wholesale banking where this characteristic is proxied by size, with large banks tending to be involved in wholesale activities.

### 2.2. *Concentration, competition and performance*

There is some concern that interstate mergers and acquisitions may lead to an increase in the concentration of banking resources, since mergers reduce the number of banks and give rise to larger banking organizations. This concern is based on the common perception that mergers will significantly reduce competition in the banking industry. Economic theory holds that the probability of non-competitive pricing and market power can be inferred from the number and size distribution of firms in the market. [4] In addition, the linked-oligopoly hypothesis holds that increased multimarket contact among geographically diversified bank holding companies

[3] Relaxation of geographic restrictions in banking will primarily affect the local market for retail financial services since wholesale banking is already regional in scope.

[4] See Bain (1959) pp. 98–101, 295 and Stigler (1964).

may lead to a lessening of local market competition. In other words, BHCs operating in several different geographical markets are likely to lessen competition in local markets out of fear that their rivals might retaliate in other markets (see Alexander (1985)).

However, for an uncompetitive pricing policy to be effective, at least two conditions must exist (Shull (1974)). First, barriers to entry must be imposed by regulators and, second, the demand market must show some kind of imperfection. Johnson and Meinster (1975) do provide some evidence of changes in pricing policy following a merger in the banking industry. But it is possible that with the removal of interstate barriers, the mere threat of a new entry into a banking market (potential competition) could diminish the ability of banks to behave collusively. In this respect, Whitehead and Luytjes (1984) concluded, in their study of intrastate expansion in Florida, that "the empirical evidence presented *does not support* the hypothesis that market extension activities by banking organizations have reduced competition" (p. 10).

Regarding the relationship between bank market shares and profitability, a number of studies [5] report that there exists a significant positive correlation between market share and performance, although the magnitude of market share impact on profitability is quite low. Once again, these studies were conducted in the presence of interstate barriers. Such conclusions may change if re-examined in light of interstate banking. In a recent study, Evanoff and Fortier (1988) attempt to control for the effect of entry barriers on the structure-performance paradigm in the banking industry and conclude that entry barriers have significant influence. They state that "in those markets characterized by significant entry barriers, profits are also shown to be influenced by market structure as proposed by the traditional paradigm. However, this effect is not present in markets with lower entry barriers".

Finally, it should be pointed out that there exist banking regulations that prohibit mergers and acquisitions which reduce competi-

[5] See, for example, Edwards (1964), Kaufman (1966), Ware (1972), Rhoades (1982), (1985a) and Graddy and Kyle (1979).

tion in local banking markets. But there is evidence (see Rose, Kolari and Riener (1985)) suggesting that more services are offered by larger institutions and by banks with a branching status (as compared to unit banks).

### *2.3. Interstate banking*

Historically, the McFadden Act of 1927 and the Banking Act of 1933 prohibited interstate branching by making all branching subject to state authority. Nevertheless, bank holding companies were unregulated, thus enabling investors to operate banks in more than one state.

The Douglas Amendment to the Bank Holding Company Act of 1956 (BHC Act) prohibited bank holding companies from acquiring banks in more than one state. But no state took advantage of its right to allow acquisitions by out-of-state BHCs until 1975. In that year, Maine passed legislation allowing unrestricted entry by out-of-state BHCs. In 1982, Massachusetts adopted a New England regional reciprocal law. Litigation followed quickly, with the future of regional pacts subject to considerable debate. On June 10, 1985, the Supreme Court of the United States delivered its opinion on the North East Bankrop case (North East Bankrop Inc. vs. Board of Governors of the Federal Reserve System). The court ruling upheld regional banking with regional barriers to entry providing some reduction in the constraints on merger activities. By the end of 1988, 42 states had enacted some provisions allowing for entry by out-of-state BHCs. A state-by-state update on the status of interstate banking as of February 1989 is given in the appendix to this chapter.

Legislation that established interstate barriers had a major effect on the structure and organization of the banking industry. This is because it (i) defined the market for banking services, (ii) constrained bank investment opportunities, and (iii) prevented the exploitation of economies of scale via diversification and economies of scope of services (assuming these economies do exist). However, banking organizations have employed several devices in recent years to circumvent the restrictions which prohibit the provision of banking services across state borders. These include:

(a) The use of the loophole whereby interstate banking acquisitions made by BHCs are grandfathered if they were undertaken before the 1956 BHC Act.

(b) The Garn-St-Germain Depository Institution Act of 1982 which grants out-of-state banking organizations the opportunity to bid for large failed banks as well as problem or failed thrifts.

(c) The International Banking Act of 1978 and the Edge Act which allow for limited interstate banking through international banking provisions.

(d) Chapter 4(c) (8) of the BHC Act which allows BHCs to own certain non-bank subsidiaries that are closely related to banking without imposing any geographic restrictions.

(e) The use of the non-bank "loophole" as a means to cross state lines. A non-bank bank is an institution which, in order to avoid federal regulation under the BHC Act, offers either demand deposits or commercial loans, but not both.

The use of the above devices by banking organizations to circumvent interstate restrictions has been limited since they are usually costly to implement. Nevertheless, they have allowed some banks to undertake interstate mergers. From a research viewpoint, this fact is significant because it provides a sample of interstate bank mergers which can be analyzed and compared to intrastate bank mergers.

### 2.4. *Safety and diversification*

Commercial banks are private firms, and consequently their safety and potential gains from diversification can be analyzed with the same tools employed to examine the behavior of firms in other industries. The most commonly used valuation model assumes a "linear" relationship between the returns on any two financial assets. [6] This property implies that, given any two return streams (investments), the market value of the combined stream is equal to

[6] Ross (1978) shows that an arbitrage argument under any competitive market leads to this property.

the sum of the separated streams. Therefore, firms have no incentive to diversify. However, as Long (1974) points out, this model is only useful so long as bankruptcy costs are non-existent.

In banking, as has been noted by Kahane (1977) and Buser, Chen and Kane (1981), bank regulators are primarily concerned with maintaining bank "safety and soundness". Consequently, regulators impose solvency standards on banks through capital adequacy requirements and by implicitly defining the upper bounds of acceptable probabilities of ruin (or bank risk). Such policies effectively impose a risk of ruin constraint on a bank's portfolio choice (in return–risk space), which may become more binding as earnings variability increases. As pointed out by Buser, Chen and Kane (1981), capital requirements, bank activity and portfolio composition, as well as bank examinations, can all be thought of as regulatory taxes which create increasing deadweight losses on the value of the banking firm as bank risk increases. [7] In extreme cases, regulators may close a bank if the risk of ruin is perceived to be too high. In such a case, "the residual value of its lost charter serves as the firm's cost of bankruptcy" (Buser, Chen and Kane (1981, p. 57)). And to the extent that there is some finite probability that regulators will close a bank, while the charter still has "residual" value to the shareholders, the value of the banking firm will fall with an increase in its earnings variability.

A direct implication of the above analysis is that banks have an incentive to diversify in order to reduce the variability of their earnings. In other words, banks can achieve real gains by decreasing the variability of the random portion of their cash flows. One way to achieve this objective is to diversify via a bank merger. This suggested framework is consistent with the empirical observation that banks are generally well diversified on both sides of their balance

[7] The regulations imposed by the FDIC can be thought of as risk-sensitive implicit insurance premiums which complement explicit fixed premium insurance; these implicit premiums (and deadweight losses) increase with the riskiness of the bank.

sheets. [8] We should expect, then, that unrestricted geographic expansion will provide banks with improved diversification opportunities. By acquiring banks in new markets, BHCs would be geographically more diversified and less susceptible to deterioration due to local economic conditions. [9] This hypothesis is tested in Chapter IV.

### *2.5. The regulation of bank mergers*

The two major federal regulations affecting bank mergers are the Bank Merger Act and the Bank Holding Company Act.

The Bank Merger Act of 1960 (BM Act of 1960) requires that applications for mergers and acquisitions by banks be processed through bank regulators, who hand down either approval or denial orders. The Antitrust Department of the Department of Justice has only advisory responsibility. Bank merger activities were exempted from the Sherman Act and the Clayton Act reviews. However, in 1963, the Supreme Court ruled that the Clayton Act did indeed apply to bank mergers. [10] Prior to this antitrust interpretation of bank merger activity, the extensive regulatory environment of the banking industry was cited as justification for exemption of banks from the provision of the antitrust law. The Supreme Court decision supplies an additional barrier of entry for banks. Following this ruling, the 1966 amendments of the BM Act of 1960 specified provisions for bank mergers in relation to antitrust laws.

The federal regulation of bank mergers can be summarized as follows:

[8] Most studies in this area treat the individual bank as an investor maximizing expected utility in order to obtain the desired incentive to diversify. See, for example, Pyle (1972), Blair and Heggestad (1978), Klein (1971) and Kahane (1977).

[9] Another motive for bank diversification can be traced to the "economic theory of agency". This theory is based on the relative risk aversion of the principal and the agent. See Harris and Raviv (1978), Marshall et al. (1984) and the discussion in Chapter II, Section 9.

[10] U.S. vs. The Philadelphia National Bank, 374 U.S. 321.356 (1963). The court stated that the case would be eligible for the application of antitrust laws.

(1) The federal regulator responsible for bank mergers has regulatory authority over the final form of the bank resulting from the merger (irrespective of the agency that regulated the bank prior to the merger). Thus, while the approval agency of a BHC is the Federal Reserve Board (FRB), the responsible authority will be either the Comptroller of the Currency or the Federal Deposit Insurance Corporation (FDIC) if a BHC elects to have a subsidiary bank acquire a target bank.

(2) The BHC Act requires approval by the Board of Governors of the Federal Reserve System of any action that causes a bank to become a subsidiary of a BHC. Application to merge with, or acquire another bank, is made by the acquiring bank to the responsible banking agency on forms that require the disclosure of various information. This information is explicitly stated in Chapter 3(c) of the BHC Act of 1956 and its 1970 Amendment and includes:
   (a) the financial history and condition of the company or companies and the banks concerned;
   (b) prospects after the merger, if the merger is permitted;
   (c) the character of management;
   (d) how the proposed merger will affect the needs and welfare of the communities and the areas concerned;
   (e) whether or not the effect of such an acquisition, merger, or consolidation would be to expand the size or extent of the bank involved beyond limits consistent with adequate and sound banking, the public interest and the preservation of competition in the field of banking. (70. Stat.133 (1956), 3.c.)

(3) The general criterion for an agency's decision on a bank merger is summarized in the BHC Act of 1956 and the BM Act of 1960. These acts specify that a merger shall not be approved unless the agency "finds that the anti-competitive effects of the proposed transaction are clearly outweighed in the public interest by the probable effect of the transaction in meeting the convenience and needs of the community to be served."

Finally, the processing of bank merger applications proceeds as follows:

(1) An acquiring BHC must prepare and organize all information required by regulators.

(2) When a BHC submits its official application to the FRB, a public notification is required. This requirement is satisfied through a public notice and by offering an opportunity for written comments on the application.

The FRB's decision also takes into consideration the opinions of involved bank regulators. Specifically, if the primary supervisor of the bank to be acquired recommends disapproval of the application (within 30 calendar days from the date on which notice is given), the FRB is required to hold a hearing on the application and afford all interested parties a reasonable opportunity to testify. At the conclusion of such a hearing, the FRB grants or denies the application on the basis of the records made at the hearing.

The following passages quote several FRB denial orders by category:

(1) Banking competition:
... was denied by the Board since the BHC's acquisition would adversely affect both existing and potential competition between the proposed subsidiary and future area banking competition in general, notwithstanding whatever benefits might follow in the way of expanded banking facilities and convenience in the area ... 628 F2d 1133, 1980.

(2) Financial and managerial resources:
... was denied by the Board since prospects of the BHC's acquisition would result in a 2–1 debt to equity ratio, and under these circumstances the applicant would not be able to render any significant banking service not presently possible under the existing ownership ... FRBul 198, 1966.

(3) Benefit to community:
... was denied by the Board since the applicant, the largest holding company in the state, had failed to show how the acquisition would increase the services the proposed subsidiary could perform and how the acquisition would benefit the community. The applicant's acquisition can extend to those situations where present competitive advantage to the applicant would increase without foreseeable compensating benefit to the public ... FRBul 288, 1970.

Finally, the Justice Department has 30 calendar days after FRB's approval in which to challenge a bank acquisition proposal based on antitrust considerations. Therefore, the FRB approval order states that the transaction shall not be made until 30 calendar days after the effective date of the order, and no later than 90 calendar days unless the period is extended for good cause by the FRB upon applicant request.

The ways in which the FRB has interpreted and implemented the BM Act and the BHC Act with respect to bank mergers has been a controversial issue.[11] Loeys (1986) reached the conclusion that the Board of Governors of the Federal Reserve System approves many more merger applications than would be implied by a strict application of the Justice Department merger guidelines. Frequently, the FRB cites specific factors as mitigating the anti-competitive effect of increases in market concentration. In his survey, Loeys found that of the ten factors that the FRB has used most often, only three appear to have had a decisive mitigating influence. These are competition from thrift institutions, the weak financial condition of one of the merging banks, and prior common control of the merging banks.

In June of 1982, the Department of Justice issued new merger guidelines replacing those issued in 1968. These guidelines focus on market structure and the possible change in structure as a result of proposed mergers. To implement this policy, the guidelines use the Herfindahl-Hirshman Index (HHI) as a summary measure of market structure.[12] The main objective of the new guidelines is to reduce the uncertainty associated with enforcement of the antitrust laws. DiClemente and Fortier (1984) examine the implementation of the new guidelines and conclude nevertheless that "the bank regulatory

[11] Eisenbeis (1975) found that "some agencies are more strict than others in their approach to mergers. The Justice Department, at least based upon its advisory opinions, took the hardest line, followed in turn by the Federal Reserve, FDIC and Comptroller of Currency" (pp. 103, 104).

[12] The HHI is the sum of squares of market shares of each of the firms in the relevant market.

agencies and the Justice Department differ somewhat in their actual enforcement policy with respect to mergers of depository institutions" (p. 19).

## 3. Review of previous studies

This section presents a brief review of relevant empirical studies on the following topics: horizontal mergers, antitrust actions and bank mergers.

### *3.1. Horizontal mergers*

Horizontal mergers, by nature, are liable to be anti-competitive. The market concentration doctrine predicts that a horizontal merger is more likely to have collusive and anti-competitive effects, the greater the merger induces changes in industry concentration. The market power (concentration) hypothesis is the basis of antitrust rules and bank regulations. It presupposes that mergers increase product prices and thereby benefit the merging firms and other competing firms in the industry. Furthermore, this hypothesis predicts negative abnormal returns for rival firms at the time the antitrust lawsuit is filed, as the complaint causes a reduction in the probability of an increase in output prices.

However, empirical studies by Eckbo (1983), Stillman (1983) and Eckbo and Wier (1985) reject this prediction on the basis of their findings on the merger-induced abnormal performance of competitors of merging firms that were challenged with violations of Chapter 7 of the Clayton Act. [13] Moreover, these authors conclude that, although challenged, horizontal mergers were not anti-competitive. Eckbo (1985) also studied firm- and industry-specific characteristics (such as concentration), concluding that the positive abnormal returns to competitors of the target firms are not positively correlated

[13] Chapter 7 of the Clayton Act prohibits one corporation from acquiring the stock or assets of another, if the effect of such acquisition is to substantially lessen competition or if it indicates a trend to create a monopoly.

with the change in concentration implied by the horizontal mergers and, additionally, are not correlated with the pre-merger level of concentration. Nevertheless, the evidence also indicates that the gains are not only available to firms involved in the merger, but appear to be shared with rivals in the industry. In this respect, the structure of the industry plays an important role. Whalem and Mugel (1986) examine the linked-oligopoly effect of large BHC acquisitions, using stock market data. They conclude that "the results of this study suggest that acquisition-related increases in multi-market linkage among BHCs do not lead to mutual forbearance". Therefore, interstate banking is unlikely to have a material adverse impact on competition.

### 3.2. Antitrust actions

Evidence indicates that merger gains do not result from the acquisition of market power. Given this finding, it is of interest to examine the effects of antitrust actions on merging firms.

Ellert (1976), Wier (1983), and Eckbo (1983) found that anti-merger law enforcement imposes substantial and abnormal losses on merging firm shareholders. Their findings indicate that shareholders of both bidding firms and target firms involved in law suits which were later decided against them, earn, on average, negative abnormal returns. The authors interpret these findings as implying that enforcement agencies impose costly constraints on dependent firms. Evidence presented by Stillman (1983) and Eckbo (1983) that the competitors of losing defendants bear no abnormal losses, further confirms the conclusion that acquisition is not collusive.

### 3.3. Bank mergers

Early studies have indirectly examined the effects of acquisition on merging banks. Smith (1971) and Hobson, Masten and Severiens (1978) found that the profitability of acquired banks was not significantly greater than that of non-merging banks. The performance of acquired banks, however, was significantly different from that of non-merging banks according to a number of accounting-based performance measures. These studies used a cross-sectional comparison of (average) performance variables between acquired banks and "matched-pair" independent banks. Another group of studies examined the effect of acquisition on the acquiring BHC's profitability following the merger. Incentives for bank acquisitions are based on the perceived resultant changes in the earnings of the acquired banks and in the valuation of these earnings. Piper and Weiss (1971), Varvel (1975) and Frieder (1980) found mixed results on this issue.

Since the above mentioned studies are based solely on accounting data they suffer from well known biases (Schwert (1981)). Furthermore, the studies were conducted over a relatively long period of time and are therefore limited in their ability to capture the significant effects of mergers and acquisitions. Finally, these studies did not address a number of important issues such as the motives and incentives for bank mergers and the bank characteristics most likely to produce successful mergers.

More recent studies, however, have directly addressed these issues. Hannan and Rhoades (1987) examined the relationship between the likelihood of a bank being acquired and the various characteristics of the bank and the market in which it operates. They used a number of variables in their study, including market concentration, capital-asset ratio, rate of return on equity and on assets, growth in the market for banking services, and a large sample of firms involved in acquisitions during the period 1971–1982. Hannan and Rhoades concluded by stating "we have not found any results consistent with the belief that poorly managed firms are more likely to be acquired than better managed firms", and, "we find no support for the notion that the market for corporate control disproportionately eliminates poorly managed firms".

Finally, James and Wier (1987a) examined the effects of competition on acquirer wealth in the market for bank acquisitions, using stock market data. They found that "the gains to acquirers are positively related to the number of alternative target firms and negatively related to the number of other potential bidders in the market". Other studies of the market reaction to the announcement of bank mergers were performed by Neely (1987), Trifts and Scanlon (1987) and de Cossio, Trifts and Scanlon (1987). They all report a substantial rise in the stock price of target banks and a relatively smaller drop in the stock price of bidding banks in interstate and intrastate mergers during the week the merger proposal is announced. Cornett and De (1989) found a significant and positive stock market reaction to announcements of interstate bank mergers *for both* bidding and target banks. They conclude by stating that "... it has been verified that the results are robust to various factors such as the size of participating banks and the type of financing used in the transaction".

## 4. Overview of the study

Chapter II presents a survey of a number of hypotheses that attempt to explain why firms in general, and banks in particular, merge. These hypotheses are then tested in Chapters V and VI by analyzing the stock price behavior of merging banks and their competitors during the weeks surrounding the merger announcements and the regulatory decision to either approve or deny proposed mergers.

The sample of banks used and the methodology employed to carry out the tests are discussed in Chapter III. Chapter IV identifies the major causes of bank failure and investigates whether the prohibition of interstate banking, which prevents banks from taking advantage of geographical diversification, is a factor that has contributed to the recent rise in the number of bank failures.

Chapter V further examines the market reaction of bank stock prices to merger announcements, while Chapter VI investigates the reasons for stock market reactions to bank merger announcements. This exercise allows us to differentiate between alternative hypotheses of bank mergers. Chapter VII examines the stock market reaction to the announcement of interstate banking legislation in three states: Texas, Arizona and Virginia. The last chapter contains concluding remarks.

## Appendix

A state-by-state update on interstate banking legislation (February 1989)

1. *Alabama.* Since July 1987, Alabama has permitted regional, reciprocal banking with Arkansas, the District of Columbia, Florida, Georgia, Kentucky, Louisiana, Maryland, Mississippi, North Carolina, South Carolina, Tennessee, Virginia, and West Virginia.
2. *Alaska.* Alaska has enacted legislation permitting unrestricted, national interstate banking.
3. *Arizona.* Arizona has enacted legislation permitting unrestricted, national interstate acquisitions. Banks applying for a charter after May 1, 1984, may not be acquired by an out-of-state bank until five years after the application date or 1992, whichever is earlier.
4. *Arkansas.* Regional reciprocal banking is allowed with Alabama, Florida, Louisiana, Maryland, Mississippi, Missouri, North Carolina, Oklahoma, South Carolina, Tennessee, Texas, Virginia, West Virginia, and the District of Columbia. Any Arkansas banking institution being acquired must have been in existence for at least ten years.
5. *California.* California has passed legislation that permits regional banking on a reciprocal basis with Alaska, Arizona, Colorado, Idaho, Nevada, New Mexico, Oregon, Texas, Utah, and Washington. Nationwide banking on a reciprocal basis begins January 1, 1991.
6. *Colorado.* Regional reciprocal banking is permitted with Arizona, Nebraska, New Mexico, Oklahoma, Utah, and Washington. National banking on a reciprocal basis begins January 1, 1991.
7. *Connecticut.* Regional, reciprocal banking is permitted with Maine, Massachusetts, New Hampshire, Rhode Island, and Vermont.
8. *Delaware.* Regional, reciprocal banking is permitted with the District of Columbia, Maryland, New Jersey, Ohio, Pennsylvania, and Virginia. Delaware banks subject to acquisition must have been in existence for at least five years. National banking on a reciprocal basis begins July 1, 1990.

9. *District of Columbia.* Although unrestricted national interstate banking is permitted, companies that seek to acquire banks here must agree to substantial investments in the city.
10. *Florida.* Interstate banking on a regional, reciprocal basis is approved with Alabama, Arkansas, the District of Columbia, Georgia, Louisiana, Maryland, Mississippi, North Carolina, South Carolina, Tennessee, Virginia, and West Virginia. Florida banks subject to acquisition must have been in existence for at least two years.
11. *Georgia.* Authorized regional, reciprocal banking with Alabama, the District of Columbia, Florida, Kentucky, Louisiana, Maryland, Mississippi, North Carolina, South Carolina, Tennessee, and Virginia. Georgia banks subject to acquisition must have been in existence for at least five years.
12. *Hawaii.* There is no interstate banking legislation currently under consideration.
13. *Idaho.* National, unrestricted banking became effective January 1, 1988.
14. *Illinois.* Illinois allows cross-border banking with Indiana, Kentucky, Michigan, Missouri, and Wisconsin. Acquiring institutions must have a capital-to-assets ratio of at least 7 percent. Illinois banks chartered after July 1, 1982, that are the target of an acquisition must have been in existence for at least ten years. National, reciprocal interstate banking is permitted effective December 1, 1990.
15. *Indiana.* Regional, reciprocal banking is authorized with Illinois, Kentucky, Michigan, Missouri, Ohio, Pennsylvania, Tennessee, Virginia, West Virginia, and Wisconsin. Acquisitions are prohibited if the acquiring bank holding company holds more than 12 percent of total bank deposits in the state. National reciprocity begins July 1, 1992.
16. *Iowa.* A regional, reciprocal interstate banking bill will be considered during the 1990 legislative session.
17. *Kansas.* The legislature asked a study committee to review the possible effects of interstate banking in the Kansas banking market. This committee recommended that interstate banking should not be authorized at this time.
18. *Kentucky.* Kentucky's legislation allows for national, reciprocal

interstate banking. Acquisitions are prohibited if the acquiring bank holds more than 15 percent of total bank deposits in the state.

19. *Louisiana.* Banks based in Alabama, Arkansas, the District of Columbia, Florida, Georgia, Kentucky, Maryland, Mississippi, North Carolina, Oklahoma, South Carolina, Tennessee, Texas, Virginia, and West Virginia have been able to acquire Louisiana banks since July 1, 1987. Louisiana banks subject to acquisition must have been in existence for at least five years. National reciprocity begins July 1, 1989.
20. *Maine.* Maine allows unrestricted, national interstate banking.
21. *Maryland.* Regional, reciprocal banking exists with Alabama, Arkansas, Delaware, the District of Columbia, Florida, Georgia, Kentucky, Louisiana, Mississippi, North Carolina, Pennsylvania, South Carolina, Tennessee, Virginia, and West Virginia. In addition, any out-of-state bank holding company may establish a single-office, limited-purpose bank, which, after June 30, 1988, can be converted into a full-service bank with limited branching privileges.
22. *Massachusetts.* Currently, Massachusetts authorizes regional, reciprocal banking with Connecticut, Maine, New Hampshire, Rhode Island, and Vermont. A bill that establishes national, reciprocal banking effective July 1, 1990, is being considered by the Senate Banking Committee. A bill is also expected in the House, requiring all acquiring institutions to maintain a 7.5 percent capital-to-assets ratio.
23. *Michigan.* National, reciprocal banking became effective on October 10, 1988.
24. *Minnesota.* Legislation has been enacted in Minnesota that permits regional, reciprocal banking with Idaho, Nebraska, South Dakota, Washington, Wisconsin, and Wyoming, plus Colorado, Illinois, Iowa, Kansas, Missouri, Montana, and North Dakota as and when their laws permit reciprocity.
25. *Mississippi.* Mississippi has passed legislation authorizing regional, reciprocal banking with Alabama, Arkansas, Louisiana, and Tennessee, after July 1, 1988. Florida, Georgia, Kentucky, Missouri, North Carolina, South Carolina, Texas, Virginia, and

West Virginia will be included in the region, effective July 1, 1990.

26. *Missouri.* Cross-border banking is authorized with states contiguous to Missouri. The region includes Illinois, Kentucky, Nebraska, Oklahoma, and Tennessee.
27. *Montana.* There was no legislative session scheduled during 1989.
28. *Nebraska.* Legislation was passed authorizing regional, reciprocal interstate banking with the north-central states of Colorado, Minnesota, Missouri, South Dakota, Wisconsin, and Wyoming. Under the terms of this bill, an out-of-state holding company may not control more than 11 percent of total state deposits or control more than nine banks in Nebraska.
29. *Nevada.* National reciprocal interstate banking became law on January 1, 1989. The establishment of *de novo* offices by out-of-state institutions will be permitted after July 1, 1990.
30. *New Hampshire.* As of September 1, 1987, regional, reciprocal banking became effective with Connecticut, Massachusetts, Maine, Rhode Island, and Vermont.
31. *New Jersey.* National, reciprocal banking became effective on January 1, 1988.
32. *New Mexico.* National, unrestricted interstate banking will be authorized on January 1, 1990. New Mexico banks subject to acquisition must have been in existence for at least five years. The aggregate sum of all deposits of the acquiring company and its subsidiaries may not exceed 40 percent of the total deposits in all financial institutions in New Mexico.
33. *New York.* National, reciprocal interstate banking legislation allows out-of-state bank holding companies to acquire commercial banks and state-chartered savings banks.
34. *North Carolina.* North Carolina allows regional, reciprocal banking with Alabama, Arkansas, the District of Columbia, Florida, Georgia, Kentucky, Louisiana, Maryland, Mississippi, South Carolina, Tennessee, Texas, Virginia, and West Virginia. North Carolina banks subject to acquisition must have been in existence for at least five years.
35. *North Dakota.* An interstate banking bill will likely be submitted for consideration during the 1989 session.

36. *Ohio.* National reciprocity became effective on October 16, 1988. An acquiring out-of-state banking institution cannot control more than 20 percent of the aggregate deposits held by all the other financial institutions in Ohio.
37. *Oklahoma.* Effective July 1, 1987, Oklahoma permitted national, reciprocal interstate banking. Any Oklahoma banking institution subject to acquisition must have been in existence for at least five years. Further acquisitions are barred for four years after the initial acquisition. Finally, no multibank bank holding company may control more than 11 percent of aggregate deposits held in all Oklahoma financial institutions.
38. *Oregon.* Oregon permits interstate banking with states in the twelfth Federal Reserve District: Alaska, Arizona, California, Hawaii, Idaho, Nevada, Utah, and Washington. No reciprocity requirement exists. On July 1, 1989, national unrestricted banking goes into effect.
39. *Pennsylvania.* Cross-border banking is authorized with Delaware, the District of Columbia, Indiana, Kentucky, Maryland, New Jersey, Ohio, Virginia, and West Virginia. Nationwide, reciprocal banking begins March 4, 1990.
40. *Rhode Island.* Legislation allows national, reciprocal banking as of January 1, 1988.
41. *South Carolina.* South Carolina permits interstate banking with Alabama, Arkansas, the District of Columbia, Florida, Georgia, Indiana, Kentucky, Louisiana, Maryland, Mississippi, North Carolina, Tennessee, Virginia, and West Virginia. South Carolina institutions subject to acquisition must have been in existence for at least five years.
42. *South Dakota.* An act that authorizes national, reciprocal interstate acquisitions of South Dakota banks was signed on February 17, 1988.
43. *Tennessee.* Tennessee's regional banking legislation operates on a reciprocal basis with Alabama, Arkansas, Florida, Georgia, Indiana, Kentucky, Louisiana, Mississippi, North Carolina, South Carolina, Virginia, and West Virginia. Tennessee banking institutions subject to acquisition must have been in existence for at least five years.

44. *Texas.* Texas permits nationwide, interstate acquisitions with no reciprocity requirement.
45. *Utah.* Nationwide, unrestricted banking became effective on January 1, 1988. Currently, out-of-state bank holding companies are authorized to purchase industrial loan companies and convert them into commercial banks.
46. *Vermont.* Regional, reciprocal banking is authorized with Connecticut, Maine, Massachusetts, New Hampshire, and Rhode Island effective December 31, 1987. National reciprocity will become effective on February 1, 1990.
47. *Virginia.* On a reciprocal basis, Virginia authorizes interstate banking with Alabama, Arkansas, the District of Columbia, Florida, Georgia, Kentucky, Louisiana, Maryland, Mississippi, North Carolina, South Carolina, Tennessee, and West Virginia. Virginia banking institutions subject to acquisition must have been in existence for at least two years.
48. *Washington.* National, reciprocal interstate banking went into effect July 1, 1987.
49. *West Virginia.* As of December 31, 1987, national, reciprocal interstate banking was permitted in West Virginia. Acquisitions will be prohibited if the combined institutions would hold more than 20 percent of the state's deposits.
50. *Wisconsin.* Legislation has been enacted that allows regional, reciprocal banking with Illinois, Indiana, Kentucky, Michigan, Minnesota, Missouri, and Ohio. Wisconsin institutions subject to acquisition must have been in existence for at least five years.
51. *Wyoming.* During 1987, Wyoming passed legislation permitting unrestricted, national interstate banking.

Source: *Salomon Brothers Inc., Stock Research – Commercial Banks* (February 9, 1989)

CHAPTER II

# WHY DO FIRMS MERGE? ALTERNATIVE HYPOTHESES OF BANK MERGERS

## 1. Motives for merging

The decision to acquire another firm, like any other investment decision, should be primarily motivated by the desire to increase the market value of the acquiring firm's shareholders. In this case, the management of the acquiring firm is said to display a wealth-maximizing behavior. The increase in the stockholders' wealth of the acquiring firm could be the result of value created by the merger. It could also result from a wealth transfer from bondholders to shareholders with no change in the total market value of the firm. In the latter case, shareholders gain what bondholders lose. Alternatively, the management of the acquiring firm may be motivated by the desire to increase the acquiring firm's size regardless of whether the acquisition is a wealth-creating activity. Under such conditions, the management of the acquiring firm displays a non-wealth-maximizing behavior. In some cases the rationale for (conglomerate) merger is management's desire to reduce risk (see Amihud and Lev (1981)) in order to improve its own utility.

Several hypotheses have been advanced to explain why firms engage in merger activities. This chapter presents a review of these hypotheses, most of which assume that the acquirer's objective is to maximize shareholder wealth. Others, such as the manager-utility-maximization hypothesis, assume that the acquirer displays a non-wealth-maximizing behavior. In this case, the merger is not motivated by a desire to increase the wealth of the shareholders of the acquiring firm, but rather to increase manager utility (e.g. by growth or risk reduction). This is the manager-utility-maximization hypothesis. It is discussed in Section 2. Another non-wealth-maximizing hypothesis of mergers is Roll's (1986) hubris hypothesis, according to which managers systematically overpay to acquire target firms. The reasons they do so are explained in Section 3.

Hypotheses that assume that the acquirer wishes to increase shareholder wealth are consistent with wealth-maximizing behavior. Shareholder wealth will increase as a result of an acquisition only if (a) the future cash-flow stream generated by the combination exceeds the sum of the future cash-flow streams of the two individual firms, and/or (b) the risk to the merged firms is reduced.

Note, first, that the future cash-flow stream generated by the merged firms will exceed the sum of the future cash-flow streams of the two individual firms if:

(1) The acquirer has privileged information indicating that the target firm is undervalued. If the acquirer can purchase the target for less than its true value, then the shareholders of the acquiring firm will benefit from the merger. This acquisition motive is known as the *information hypothesis.* It is discussed in Section 4.
(2) The acquirer can raise the price of its product after the merger. This would be possible if the acquirer succeeds in reducing price competition in the product market by acquiring some of its competitors. This acquisition motive is known as the *market power hypothesis.* It is discussed in Section 5.
(3) The acquirer can reduce the cost of its product after the merger. This would be possible if the merger generates synergies via economies of scale and scope, reduced distribution and marketing costs, divestiture of redundant assets, etc... This acquisition motive is known as the *synergy hypothesis.* It is discussed in Section 6.
(4) The acquirer can reduce the tax liability of the combined firms below their aggregate non-merged tax liabilities. This can be considered an extension of the "synergy hypothesis". However, it is "financial" synergy rather than cost-reducing synergy. It is known as the *tax hypothesis.* It is discussed in Section 7.
(5) The acquirer removes inefficient management from the target firm and improves the performance of that firm. This acquisition motive is known as the *inefficient-management hypothesis.* It is discussed in Section 8.

Regarding the risk dimension, the merged firms may reduce their combined risk if the merger creates diversification gains. This will be the case if the risk of the combined firms is less than the weighted average of the risks of the two individual firms prior to the merger. This acquisition motive is known as the *diversification hypothesis.* It is discussed in Section 9.

## 2. The manager-utility-maximization hypothesis

The large modern corporation is characterized by the separation of ownership and management. Owners (shareholders) usually have little control over management. Thus, in this context, managers may act to maximize their own utilities rather than serve the interests of shareholders.

If manager utility depends on firm size, risk or managers' compensation rather than the firm's value, then managers will maximize the firm's growth, reduce its risk or expropriate the firm rather than maximize shareholder wealth. But why would manager utility be a function of firm size? One reason may be that large firms pay higher salaries to their managers. And in fact there is empirical evidence showing a positive relationship between the level of manager remuneration and firm sales (Penrose (1959), Baumol (1967)), whereas no relationship has been found between the level of manager remuneration and changes in firm market value. Another reason that manager utility is not directly related to firm value is that non-monetary rewards (power, prestige, perquisites) are usually easier to obtain in larger firms. Finally, large firms may provide managers with a greater degree of job security.

What does the manager-utility-maximization hypothesis predict regarding changes in the stock price of target and bidding firms when a merger proposal is announced? If the acquisition is perceived by the market as an unprofitable investment undertaken for the sole purpose of enlarging the bidder's size, then the stock price of the bidding firm should drop to reflect the losses associated with an unprofitable investment. And the higher the premium paid to acquire the target firm, the steeper the drop in the price of the bidding firm's shares. Actually, carried to its logical extreme, the manager-utility-maximization hypothesis predicts no net aggregate wealth creation: the gains realized by the target-firm shareholders should be equal to the losses incurred by the bidding-firm shareholders. This entails a wealth transfer from the bidding-firm shareholders to the target-firm shareholders. More precisely, we should observe a *net reduction* in aggregate wealth to account for the wealth transferred to third parties in the form of fees and commissions (to advisors, lawyers, bankers and brokers) as well as for any indirect costs that result from the time and effort devoted by the managers of the bidding firm to acquire the target and, in the case of unfriendly takeovers, by the managers of the target firm to fend off an unwelcome bid. The manager-utility-maximization hypothesis is tested in Chapter V, Sections 3 and 4.

## 3. The hubris hypothesis

The hubris hypothesis is another behavioral hypothesis of firm mergers. According to Roll (1986, 1988), though target firms are correctly valued, managers of bidding firms believe that they are capable of uncovering "bargains". Consequently, bidders invariably end up paying too much for the firms they acquire. Nevertheless, managers of bidding firms persist in taking over target firms. Roll (1988) believes that "the *individual* decision makers in the bidding firm are infected by overweening pride and arrogance (hubris), and thus persist in a belief that their own valuation of the target is correct, despite objective information that the target's true economic value is lower".

Another reason for bidders paying too much for target firms is the so-called "winner's curse". In a bidding contest involving only a few bidders the winner usually ends up paying too much for the object being auctioned. This situation is a positive valuation error. Roll argues that "if the market price (of a target firm) fully reflects value, only positive valuation errors will be observed because a valuation below the market price will not elicit a bid". The implication of this phenomenon is that the stock price of bidding firms should drop, and that of target firms should rise, when a merger proposal is announced. Furthermore, mergers should not create any net aggregate wealth to shareholders. Instead they should only produce a wealth transfer from bidding-firm shareholders to target-firm shareholders. The dollar gains accruing to target-firm shareholders must be equal to the dollar losses incurred by bidding-firm shareholders.

Note that the stock price implication of the hubris hypothesis is similar to that of the manager-utility-maximization hypothesis. Both hypotheses are based on the premise of a non-wealth maximizing behavior and/or an error in valuation on the part of the bidder. And since the reason for this behavior is recognized by the market, both hypotheses suggest a zero net aggregate wealth creation which reflects a transfer of wealth from bidding-firm to target-firm shareholders. More precisely, these hypotheses predict a net reduction of aggregate wealth to account for the direct and indirect costs of the merger. Consequently, it is not always possible to differentiate empirically between the manager-utility-maximization hypothesis and the hubris hypothesis.

What is the empirical evidence? A recent paper by Bradley, Desai and Kim (1988) reports that "a successful tender offer increases the combined value of the target and acquiring firms by an average of 7.40 percent", a conclusion that does not support the wealth-transfer phenomenon implied by both the manager-utility-maximization and hubris hypotheses. A similar result is presented in Dennis and McConnell (1986). Recently, it has been suggested by several authors (Pettway and Trifts (1985), Giliberto and Varaiya (1989)) that winning bidders overpay for acquiring failed banks through auctions organized under the Purchase and Assumption Policy of the FDIC, a conclusion that is consistent with the winner's curse phenomenon.

## 4. The information hypothesis

According to the information hypothesis, the shares of some firms are incorrectly valued by the market because relevant information about those firms is not available to the public. Suppose that a potential bidder has information indicating that a potential target is undervalued. Clearly, the target becomes a desirable acquisition for the potential bidder. When the bidder announces its proposed merger with the target, the market price of the target increases immediately to reflect the information revealed by the bidder's takeover announcement. The bidder's share price, however, is not affected by the announcement, unless the merger proposal reveals information about the bidder beyond the fact that the bidder has uncovered an undervalued target firm.

Note that the information hypothesis is consistent with a stock market that is efficient in the semi-strong form (a market in which stock prices reflect all *publicly* available information), but inefficient in the strong form (that is, a market in which stock prices do not reflect *private* information). Because the stock market is semi-strong efficient, once the bidder announces its intention to take over the target, the market price of the target firm rises immediately to reflect what is now new public information. The takeover announcement signals to the market that the target firm is undervalued. However, the price of the target firm does not necessarily rise to the level of its "true" value, because the announced price may or may not be equal to what the bidder believes the target firm is worth.

How credible is the information hypothesis in the context of bank mergers? And how does the bidding bank obtain information on the target bank not available to the market? One possible mechanism that would allow for the acquisition of privileged information is the correspondent-respondent relationship that may exist between a bidder and a potential target. Large banks usually act as correspondent banks to smaller respondent banks. Correspondent banks provide various kinds of services at low prices to the respondent banks. This special relationship can facilitate correspondent banks (the bidder) acquiring inside information on the respondent bank (the potential target). This scenario is consistent with the fact that bidding banks are generally much larger than their targets (see Chapter III, Table 1D). Another characteristic of the banking sector relevant to the information hypothesis is that banks are labor-intensive. If the labor market is inefficient, the stock market may not be able to value banks correctly (Keenan (1982)). If the bidding bank can value the potential target's labor better than the market, then the value of labor becomes capitalized at the moment the merger proposal is announced.

The information hypothesis cannot be tested directly since we do not know whether bidding banks have access to privileged information about target banks. One possible indirect test is to check whether bidders and targets do have a correspondent-respondent relationship. But even if such a relationship does not exist, this does not imply a rejection of the information hypothesis, since the inside information could have come from other sources. Another indirect test of the information hypothesis is provided by observing the stock price reaction of the target bank when a proposed merger is cancelled. According to the information hypothesis, the price of a target bank rises when a merger proposal is announced because the announcement reveals that the target bank is undervalued. If the merger is then cancelled, the price of the target bank should be unaffected since the cancellation of the merger does not modify the fact that the target bank was undervalued. However, if after cancellation of the proposed merger, the price of the target bank drops toward its pre-merger-announcement level, this would indicate that the market believes that the merger must be completed in order to generate gains to the shareholders of the target bank. In this case, the original rise in the price of the target bank was not caused by the revelation of undervaluation, but rather resulted from the belief that the value of the target bank would increase via synergies, increased market power, and similar sources of gains that can be realized only through a merger.

Early work by Dodd and Ruback (1977), Bradley (1980) and Firth (1980) provided some evidence that supports the information hypothesis. They reported a permanent rise in the price of target firms even in the case of unsuccessful tender offers. But Bradley, Desai and Kim (1983) later showed that the targets of unsuccessful tender offers experience a permanent rise in value only because the original unsuccessful offer was later followed by a successful one. When an unsuccessful offer was not followed by a successful offer within 5 years, the original rise in price was completely reversed.

Bank mergers provide an ideal situation to test the information hypothesis because a merger proposal may be denied by regulators. Thus, if we observe a drop in the price of target banks toward their pre-merger-announcement level when the Federal Reserve issues a denial order, we can reject the information hypothesis. We perform this and other tests in Chapter V.

## 5. The market-power hypothesis

According to the market-power hypothesis, horizontal mergers create monopolistic power by reducing the number of competing firms in an industry. The reduction in the number of competitors allows the merged firms to raise their product price. The reduction in the number of competitors will also lower the cost of monitoring rival firms in the industry (Stigler (1964)). "The fewer the members of the industry, the more 'visible' are each producer's actions, and the higher is the probability of detecting members who try to cheat on the cartel by increasing output. The higher this probability, the lower the expected gains from cheating, and the more stable (and profitable) is the cartel in the short run" (Eckbo (1983, 1985)).

How can this hypothesis be tested? One approach suggested by Eckbo (1983) and Stillman (1983) is to examine the price reaction of other firms in the industry when two rivals announce their intention to merge. If the merger creates market power that translates into higher product prices and lower monitoring costs, then all the remaining firms in the industry should benefit and not just the two merging firms. Thus, the merger announcement should increase the share price of the merging firms as well as the share price of their rivals in the industry. We perform this type of test in Chapter VI, Section 8, for horizontal mergers in the banking industry.

## 6. The synergy hypothesis

Mergers create synergetic gains if the production, administrative and marketing costs of the merged firms are smaller than the sum of these costs for the two individual firms before their merger. Everything else being the same, lower aggregate costs mean increased profits and higher stock prices to bidders, unless competition among bidders pushes the price of the target up to the point where the acquisition price of the target fully reflects the present value of the expected synergetic gains. Thus the entire present value of the expected synergetic gains will accrue to the shareholders of the target firm. In any case, the merger should create a positive net aggregate wealth equal to the present value of the expected synergetic gains minus the transaction costs paid to third parties in order to carry out the merger.

An issue of direct relevance to the synergy hypothesis is whether economies of scale and scope are achievable in banking and, if so, what is the optimal size of a bank. As already mentioned in Chapter I, empirical evidence indicates that economies of scale occur only for relatively small banks (less than $100 million in deposits) and that there is no consistent indicator of economies of scope. In light of this evidence, we can formulate two testable hypotheses:

*The relative-size-effect hypothesis*
"The smaller the target bank relative to the bidding bank, the higher the potential synergetic gains".

*The absolute-size-effect hypothesis*
"The smaller the bidding bank (irrespective of the target bank's size) the higher the potential synergetic gains".

The first hypothesis can be justified on the grounds that since the potential for economies of scale is relatively small, there is a greater opportunity for exploiting potential benefits of scale economies whenever the acquiring bank takes over a bank that is significantly smaller. The second hypothesis is based on the fact that the optimal size of a bank is attained at a relatively small size ($100 million in deposits).

Another relevant issue regarding the relevance of the synergy hypothesis in banking is that of intrastate versus interstate mergers. Everything else being the same, we should expect intrastate mergers to offer a greater potential for synergetic gains than interstate mergers. This should be the case because economies of scale are more likely to be achieved when the merging banks operate in the same geographical market. This hypothesis, as well as the two size hypotheses, are tested in Chapter VI.

## 7. The tax hypothesis

According to the tax hypothesis, a merger will create wealth to stockholders whenever the tax liability of the combination is smaller than the sum of the tax liabilities of the two individual firms. This situation may occur if one firm has generated a loss and the other a profit. The first pays no taxes but the second does. However, the tax paid by the second will be smaller if the two firms merge because the aggregate net profit for the combined firms will be smaller than the profit of the second firm.

Another situation that may produce a smaller tax liability for merged firms occurs whenever the merged firm can borrow more funds than the sum of the borrowings of the two pre-merger firms. This will happen if the merged firms are perceived to be less risky when combined than when separated. If there is increasing borrowing power for the combined firm, there is an accompanying decrease in tax liability since debt is a tax deductible expense. It is doubtful, however, if this phenomenon is actually at work in the banking industry. We do not test this hypothesis in this study.

## 8. The inefficient-management hypothesis

This hypothesis suggests that mergers provide a mechanism to remove poor management from target firms. The potential gains associated with acquiring a badly managed firm and improving its performance provide the incentive for acquirers to dislodge inefficient and entrenched management via takeovers.

According to Jensen and Ruback (1983), a distinction should be made between the inefficient-management hypothesis and the synergy hypothesis. Synergetic gains require the completion of a merger in order to achieve a reduction in production and marketing costs. However, improving the performance of a firm through better management does not require that it merges with another firm. Poor management can be removed by other devices than a takeover (for example, proxy fights), though takeovers may be the least costly alternative.

This distinction between the synergy hypothesis and the inefficient-management hypothesis can be tested empirically by looking at the stock price reaction of target firms that are the subject of a tender offer extended by a bidder who already owns over 50 percent of the target's shares. Dodd and Ruback (1977) report that the average price of these target firms increases by the same magnitude as the average price of target firms which are not owned by bidders. Since the bidders already control their target, the rise in the price of these firms cannot be attributed to synergetic gains or increased market power. Instead, it is the anticipation of better management of existing facilities that may explain the increase in the price of these target firms.

A test of the inefficient-management hypothesis in the banking industry has been performed by Hannan and Rhoades (1987), as reported in Chapter I. As mentioned above, these authors analyzed a sample of 1,046 Texas banks in existence in 1970, out of which 201 were acquired during the period 1970–1982. They conclude that their "results yield no support for the hypothesis that poorly managed firms, measured in a number of different ways, are more likely to be acquired than other firms". However, though this study shows that poorly managed banks are not privileged candidates for a takeover attempt, it does not indicate whether the shareholders of poorly-managed target banks achieve higher than average returns on their holding when a merger proposal is announced. Such higher than average returns can be expected in an efficient capital market. In fact, this would reflect the present value of the future benefits to be achieved by removing poor managers and improving the bank's performance. In Chapter VI we present a test of the inefficient-management hypothesis using a capital market approach along the lines described above.

Another empirical study that should be mentioned in the context of managerial performance in the banking industry was released in June 1988 by the Comptroller of the Currency (New York Times: June 21, 1988). It found that "the primary cause of bank failure is mismanagement, inept chief executives and directors who are either inexperienced in banking or lax in their supervision of a bank's affair". Chapter IV investigates this statement by examining whether bank failures can be attributed to unfavorable economic conditions or poor management. It is found that poor management alone cannot explain bank failures.

## 9. The diversification hypothesis

The value additivity principle implies that, in a perfect capital market, given any two return streams (corporations), the market value of the combined stream (merged company) is equal to the sum of the separated streams (companies). Therefore, firms have no incentive to diversify.

In banking, however, we do observe that banks extensively diversify both their asset (loans) and liabilities (deposits) portfolios. This behavior is usually explained by two factors. The first is the fact that regulators impose solvency standards on banks through capital adequacy requirements and implicitly define the upper bounds of acceptable probabilities of bankruptcy. The second is that the bank investment in goodwill is substantially lost should it fail. The bank's goodwill is represented by the quasi-rent resulting from the bank-customer relationship.

These factors imply, for banks, some kind of market value maximization under safety-first constraint on the probability of bankruptcy (see, for example, Swary (1980), Kahane (1977), and Blair and Heggestad (1978)). Under such an objective function, which is consistent with the observed behavior of commercial banks, the market value of merging banks with low correlation between their future cash flow streams is greater than the sum of the market values of the banks before their merger.

Finally, diversification should benefit shareholders in a situation characterized by an agency relationship between principals (the shareholders) and their agent (the firm's manager) (Jensen and Meckling (1976)). Several authors have shown that in order to maximize the value of their firm, shareholders (principals) should link manager (agent) compensation to firm performance (Harris and Raviv (1978, 1979) and Shavell (1979)). Under such conditions both owners and managers gain from risk-reducing diversification. Managers gain because the risk attached to their incentive contracts is reduced. Owners gain because the value of their firm is now more closely related to managerial effort. This lowers owners' cost of monitoring manager performance. And since managers bear less risk, they provide a given level of effort at a lower cost. This hypothesis was examined by Amihud and Lev (1981) and by Amihud, Dodd and Weinstein (1986) who provide evidence consistent with the hypothesis that managers do diversify in order to decrease their "employment risk". The evidence presented in these studies indicates that: (i) manager-controlled firms engage in more conglomerate acquisitions than owner-controlled firms; and (ii) the operations of manager-controlled firms are more diversified than the operations of owner-controlled firms. Saunders, Strock and Travlos (1987) reached similar conclusions for the banking industry.

Various tests of the diversification hypothesis are presented in Chapters V and VI. Chapter V compares the variability of the stock price of bidding banks before merger announcement and after merger approval. The diversification hypothesis predicts a decline in variability after merger approval. Chapter VI compares the case of market reaction to the announcement of a merger involving two banks whose returns exhibit low correlation, with the case of market reaction to the announcement of a merger involving two banks whose returns exhibit high correlation. The diversification hypothesis predicts a stronger market reaction in the former case (low correlation) than in the latter (high correlation).

## 10. Summary and concluding remarks

This chapter has presented a number of hypotheses that attempt to explain the market reaction of target and bidding banks when a proposed merger is announced. The two hypotheses that assume a non-wealth creating behavior on the part of bidders (the manager-utility-maximization and the hubris hypotheses) predict that the share price of target banks will rise, and that of bidding banks will drop with no net aggregate wealth creation. The other hypotheses, which assume a wealth-creating behavior on the part of bidders, predict that the share price of target banks will rise and that of bidding banks will *not* drop. The assumption is that the market for corporate control is efficient and hence competition among potential bidders will drive the share price of a target bank up to the point where target shareholders receive all the wealth created by the merger.

Note that in any merger attempt, the bidder plays an active role and the target is passive. This means that the merger announcement is an unexpected external event for the target and that any change in its share price can be safely attributed to the fact that a merger may occur. This is not the case for the bidding firm. A change in its share price may be attributed to the fact that it has announced a merger, or to the fact that the merger announcement reveals information about the bidding firm which may be unrelated to the merger. For example, a merger may reveal that the bidder is financially stronger than the market had thought. This favorable revelation may drive up the share price of the bidder irrespective of the merger conditions. However, a merger may also reveal that the bidder does not have internal investments, an unfavorable revelation that may drive down the share price of the bidder irrespective of the merger. According to Roll (1988), "the problem is that the bid is a 'polluted' information item. The bidding firm is an activist, unlike the target firm, and its actions can be interpreted in the market as conveying more than just information about the takeover *per se*".

# CHAPTER III

# DATA AND METHODOLOGY

In this chapter we describe our sample and explain the methodology we employ to carry out our empirical tests. The first section presents the sample properties and the various sources of data. The second section examines the characteristics of the sample of target and bidding banks. The last section covers research design and methodology.

## 1. Sample properties and sources of data

The sample properties, the sources of the data and their use in this study are summarized in Table 1A. The sample consists of 452 banks that had publicly traded common stocks over the period beginning January 5, 1968 and ending June 26, 1987. Daily rates of return were obtained from the CRSP daily tape (see note a, Table 1A) and the OTC daily tape (see note b, Table 1A). The former provides data up to December 1986 and the latter from December 1972 to December 1985. Data unavailable on tapes were collected from the various issues of the Standard and Poor's Daily Stock Price Record. The CRSP daily tape provided data for a subsample of 75 banks whose shares traded either on the New York Stock Exchange or the American Stock Exchange. The balance came from the OTC daily tape which provides data for banks trading on the Over-the-Counter market. The sample includes practically all publicly traded banks and most of the largest banks (banks with assets exceeding $300 million in 1978 and $400 million in 1983). Weekly rates of returns are computed for each bank as compounded daily returns for each calendar week, or using end-of-week daily bid prices plus dividends adjusted for stock splits and stock dividend.

A few banks had a complete set of 1016 weekly returns from the week ending January 5, 1968 to the week ending June 26, 1987. The other banks in the sample had only a subset of return data.

Table 1A
Sample properties and data sources.

| | | |
|---|---|---|
| 1. Closing Friday stock prices (or last day of trade if not Friday) and cash dividends for a comprehensive sample of 452 banks from 1/5/68 to 6/26/87 | – CRPS [a] tape up to 12/86<br>– OTC [b] tape from 12/72 to 12/85<br>– Standard & Poor's Daily Stock Prices Record prior to 12/72 and past 12/85 | Calculate weekly stock returns and abnormal stock returns |
| 2. Rate of returns on the market value weighted index of all common stock listed on the NYSE and ASE | – CRPS tape | Calculate weekly returns on the market portfolio |
| 3. State in which bank is located | – Moody's banking Manual<br>– Keefe Bank Book | Analysis of interstate versus intrastate price behavior |
| 4. Total number of banks and number of failed banks in each state and the size of their deposits for the period 1982–1986 | – Statistical Abstract of the United States<br>– FDIC [c] Annual Reports | Study of the distribution of failed banks over the 5-year period from 1982 to 1986 |
| 5. Announcement date of mergers and term of the offer (cash vs. securities) | – Keefe Bank Book<br>– Well Street Journal<br>– Predicasts: F&S Index of Corporate Change | Analysis of stock price reaction to announcements related to bank mergers for a sample of 123 targets and 130 bidders |
| 6. Announcement date of regulators' decision | – Federal Reserve Bulletin | Same as above (see item 5) |

In addition to stock returns, we collected the following set of data:

(1) the state and region in which each bank in the sample is located;

Table 1A (continued)

| | | |
|---|---|---|
| 7. Book value of total assets and book value of equity for all banks in the sample | – Keefe Bank Book<br>– Moody's Banking Manual<br>– Statistical Abstract of the United States | Independent variables to explain the cross-sectional behavior of abnormal returns during the weeks surrounding the announcements of bank mergers |
| 8. Return of shareholders' equity (ROE) for the banks in the sample and for the largest banks in each state | – FDIC [c] Annual Reports<br>– Moody's Banking Manual | Same as above (see item 7) |
| 9. Concentration ratio in states (share of deposits of 5 largest banks) | – Statistical Information of the Financial Services Industry<br>– American Banks Association (Third Edition: 1984) | Independent variable (see item 7) |
| 10. Date of enactment of interstate banking legislation and major dates preceding enactment in Arizona, Texas and Virginia | – Federal Reserve Bank of Chicago<br>– Wall Street Journal Index<br>– The Houston Post | Analysis of the reaction of bank stock prices to announcements related to interstate banking legislation in Virginia |

[a] CRPS – Center for Research in Securities Prices of the University of Chicago.
[b] OTC – Over-the-counter (made available by the University of Chicago).
[c] FDIC – Federal Deposit Insurance Corporation.

(2) the total number of banks and the number of failed banks in the period 1981–1986 in each state and the size of their deposits (see Chapter IV);
(3) the announcement (or press) date of mergers, the term of the offer (cash, securities or both), and the announcement date of the Federal Reserve decision (approval or denial of the merger) (see Chapter V);
(4) the book value of the total assets of all banks in the sample at the end of each calendar year from 1968 to 1986;

(5) the book value of total assets, the book value of equity and the return on equity of the subsample of banks involved in mergers, measured at the end of the calendar year preceding the merger announcement week (see Chapter VI);
(6) the date of the enactment of interstate banking legislation and major dates preceding the enactment in three states: Arizona, Texas and Virginia (see Chapter VII).

The sources of all these data and their use in the following chapters of the study are summarized in Table 1A.

## 2. Characteristics of the sample of target and bidding banks

Only a subset of the sample of 452 banks were involved in a merger: 78 different banks made 130 bids to acquire 123 target banks over the $16\frac{1}{2}$ year period beginning in January 1971 and ending in June 1987. Note that the subset of banks *not* involved in a merger are used in the empirical work performed in Chapters VI and VII. In Chapter VI we examine the market reaction of banks *not* involved in a merger when a bidding bank announces its intention to acquire a target bank. As we will see in Chapter VI, the market reaction of these uninvolved banks can shed some light on the motives for bank mergers. In Chapter VII we examine the market reaction of banks when a state announces major legislation related to interstate banking. In this case, the entire sample of 452 banks is used in the empirical analysis. Note that seven cases in which the bidding banks were involved in another transaction within a five-week period were excluded from the final sample. In what follows, we describe the subsample of banks that were involved in a merger.

### *2.1. Distribution of target banks and bids by states*

Table 1B gives the distribution of target banks and bids classified by state over the period 1971–1986. Florida had the largest number of target banks (21 cases or 17 percent of the total number of target banks) followed by New Jersey (13 cases) and Pennsylvania (12 cases). The largest number of bids (17 cases or 13 percent of the total

Table 1B
Distribution of target banks and bids by state (from 1971 to 1986).

| State [a] | Targets [b] | Bids [c] | State [a] | Targets [b] | Bids [c] |
|---|---|---|---|---|---|
| Alabama | 1 | 1 | Missouri | 3 | 3 |
| Alaska | 2 | 0 | North Carolina | 1 | 12 |
| Arizona | 1 | 0 | New Jersey | 13 | 11 |
| California | 3 | 6 | New York | 8 | 17 |
| Colorado | 2 | 2 | Ohio | 3 | 7 |
| Connecticut | 7 | 5 | Oklahoma | 1 | 0 |
| D.C. | 1 | 0 | Oregon | 1 | 0 |
| Florida | 21 | 13 | Pennsylvania | 12 | 15 |
| Georgia | 3 | 5 | Rhode Island | 1 | 3 |
| Indiana | 3 | 0 | South Carolina | 4 | 1 |
| Kentucky | 1 | 0 | Tennessee | 3 | 2 |
| Louisiana | 1 | 1 | Texas | 9 | 8 |
| Maine | 3 | 0 | Virginia | 3 | 5 |
| Maryland | 2 | 1 | Washington | 1 | 0 |
| Massachusetts | 3 | 6 | Wisconsin | 1 | 1 |
| Michigan | 5 | 5 | Total | 123 [d] | 130 [e] |

[a] States not on the list did not have banks involved in mergers.
[b] Number of target banks in the corresponding state.
[c] Number of bids made by banks located in the corresponding state.
[d] Of the 123 target banks, 118 were the subject of a single bid, 3 were the subject of a double bid and 2 were the subject of a triple bid. To be included in the sample, a second bid must be made no earlier than 6 weeks after a first bid.
[e] The total number of bids is equal to 118 single bids + 3 double bids + 2 triple bids = 130 bids. These 130 bids were made by 78 different bidding banks.

number of bids) were made by banks located in New York, followed by Pennsylvania (15 cases) and Florida (13 cases). A total of 123 banks, located in 30 states and the District of Columbia, were the subject of a merger or takeover during the $16\frac{1}{2}$ year period from 1971 to 1987. These target banks received 130 bids extended by 78 different bidders. Some acquiring banks made a bid for more than one target bank and some targets were the subject of more than one bid. Of the 123 target banks listed in Table 1B, 118 were the subject of a single bid, 3 were the subject of a double bid and 2 were the subject of a triple bid, yielding a total of 130 bids. Note that in the case of multiple bids, a second or third bid has been included in the sample only if it occurred at least 5 weeks after the preceding bid.

### 2.2. *Distribution of bids according to the year made and whether the takeover is interstate or intrastate*

The upper part of Table 1C gives the distribution of bids over the 16-year period beginning in 1971 and ending in 1986. A look at Table 1C indicates a significantly larger number of bids in the 1980s than in the 1970s. Over the 10-year period from 1971 to 1980, 23 bids were made (18 percent of the total), whereas 107 bids were made between 1981 and 1986 (82 percent of the total). Note that no multiple bids occurred in the 1970s.

The bottom part of Table 1C gives the geographical distribution of bids. Close to two-thirds of all bids (81 cases out of a total of 130 bids) were made for targets located in the same state as the bidder (intrastate mergers). Twenty-six percent were made for targets located in the same region as the bidder (the states making up the 6 different regions are listed in Table 1C). The remaining 15 bids involved interstate mergers other than regional banking mergers.

### 2.3. *Size and capitalization ratio for the sample of target and bidding banks*

The top of Table 1D reports the book value of total assets of both target and bidding banks at the end of the calendar year preceding the takeover announcement week. The average size of a bidding bank total assets is $9 billion, almost 4 times larger than the average size of a target bank total assets ($2.3 billion). This result confirms what most previous research in mergers and acquisitions has shown: bidders, on average, are much larger than their targets.

The results in the bottom of Table 1D indicate, however, that there is no significant difference, on average, between the capitalization ratio (book value of equity divided by book value of total assets) of bidding banks and target banks. The average ratio is approximately 6 percent for both bidders and targets, ranging from a minimum of 3.56 percent to a maximum of 10.71 percent for bidders and a minimum of 1.64 percent to a maximum of 11.25 percent for targets.

Table 1C
Distribution of bids according to year made and whether the takeover is intrastate or interstate.

| Year | First bid | Second bid | Third bid | Total |
|---|---|---|---|---|
| 1971 | 2 | 0 | 0 | 2 |
| 1972 | 12 | 0 | 0 | 2 |
| 1973 | 3 | 0 | 0 | 3 |
| 1974 | 1 | 0 | 0 | 1 |
| 1975 | 6 | 0 | 0 | 6 |
| 1976 | 2 | 0 | 0 | 2 |
| 1977 | 0 | 0 | 0 | 0 |
| 1978 | 1 | 0 | 0 | 1 |
| 1979 | 3 | 0 | 0 | 3 |
| 1980 | 3 | 0 | 0 | 3 |
| 1981 | 7 | 2 | 2 | 11 |
| 1982 | 15 | 1 | 0 | 16 |
| 1983 | 26 | 0 | 0 | 26 |
| 1984 | 12 | 0 | 0 | 12 |
| 1985 | 23 | 1 | 0 | 24 |
| 1986 | 17 | 1 | 0 | 18 |
| Total | 123 | 5 | 2 | 130 |
| Intrastate | 76 | 4 | 1 | 81 |
| Regional [a] | 33 | 1 | 0 | 34 |
| Other [b] | 14 | 0 | | 115 |
| Total | 123 | 5 | 2 | 130 |

[a] There are 6 regions. Region 1 has 6 states (MA, ME, RI, CT, NH and VT). Region 2 has 4 states (PA, NJ, NY and DE). Region 3 has 11 states (OH, KY, MI, WI,IL, IN, MN, MO, IA, NE and KS). Region 4 has 10 states (GA, FL, SC, NC, VA, TN, DC, AL, MS and WV). Region 5 has 4 states (TX, LA, AR and OK). Region 6 has 13 states (UT, ID, AZ, WA, NV, CA, OR, AK, HI, MT, CO, NM and WY).

[b] Involve cases of interstate mergers other than regional banking mergers.

## 3. Methodology

In the following chapters we perform several tests of the hypotheses described in Chapter II using a variety of methodologies and statistical techniques. As mentioned earlier, most of our empirical

Table 1D
Size and capitalization ratio of the sample of target and bidding banks.

| Characteristics | Target banks | Bidding banks |
|---|---|---|
| Number | 123 | 78 |
| *Total assets* ($thousands) [a] | | |
| Mean | 2,328,569 | 9,018,602 |
| Standard deviation | 3,409,488 | 12,641,773 |
| Minimum | 141,000 | 256,000 |
| Maximum | 22,071,000 | 102,479,000 |
| *Equity / total assets* [b] | | |
| Mean | 0.0624 | 0.0609 |
| Standard deviation | 0.0133 | 0.0126 |
| Minimum | 0.0164 | 0.0356 |
| Maximum | 0.1125 | 0.1071 |

[a] Book value of total assets at the end of the calendar year preceding the takeover announcement week.
[b] Ratio of book value of equity to book value of total assets at the end of the calendar year preceding the takeover announcement week.

tests attempt to measure the reaction of bank stock prices to three different public announcements:

(1) The announcement of a bank (the bidder) that it intends to acquire another bank (the target) by offering to purchase the target's common stocks at a given price. In Chapter V we measure the reaction of both the bidder's and the target's stock prices the week the announcement is made. In Chapter VI we measure the stock price reaction of other banks to the proposed merger. The other banks are either rival banks (banks operating in the same geographical area as the bidder and of similar size) or potential targets (banks operating in the same geographical area as the target and of similar size).
(2) The announcement of the Federal Reserve's decision regarding the pending merger. The announcement date of the regulatory

decision has been obtained for a subsample of 75 cases. The Federal Reserve, as we have seen, can either approve or deny the proposed merger. In Chapter V we measure the reaction of both the bidder's and the target's stock prices the week the announcement is made. We also measure the stock price reaction of other banks to the release of the Federal Reserve's decision.

(3) Various announcements related to interstate banking legislation in Texas, Arizona and Virginia. These include press reports that legislation will be introduced to allow interstate banking, that a bill in favor of interstate banking has been approved and, finally, that the bill has been signed into law. In Chapter VII we measure the market reaction of banks located in the state affected by the legislation as well as banks outside that state.

In what follows we explain how one can measure and analyze the reaction of stock prices to public announcements. This research methodology is then applied to the three different announcements listed above and the empirical results are reported in the subsequent chapters. In addition to the research methodology described below, we use in Chapter VI various statistical tests to explain cross-sectional differences in the reaction of bank stock prices to the announcement of merger proposals. These tests are described in Chapter VI.

### *3.1. Measuring the reaction of stock prices to new information*

The observed change in the stock price of a bank during the week a merger proposal is announced cannot be attributed exclusively to that announcement because stock prices during that week are affected by a multitude of factors other than the announcement of the merger proposal. If we just want to measure the effect of the announced merger on the stock price of a bank, we must first neutralize the movements in prices that result from factors other than the specific announcement under investigation.

Define $R_{it}$ as the realized (observed) return of stock i during week t and $E(R_{it})$ as the expected return of stock i during week t, that is, the return we anticipated to achieve on that stock *if the merger proposal was not announced.* The movement in prices that can be attributed to the announcement is the difference between $R_{it}$ and $E(R_{it})$. We can call this difference the unexpected return ($e_{it}$) of stock i during week t and write:

$$e_{it} = R_{it} - E(R_{it}). \tag{1}$$

To calculate $e_{it}$ we must estimate $E(R_{it})$, the unobservable, expected return on stock i during week t. Several statistical techniques have been suggested to estimate $E(R_{it})$. Most popular among them are the market model (Fama et al. (1969) and Fama (1976)) and the mean-adjusted return approach (Brown and Warner (1980) and (1985)). These methods are briefly described below.

### *3.1.1. The market model*

This model assumes that security returns are distributed according to a multivariate normal distribution. In this case, it can be shown that security returns are generated by the following stochastic process:

$$R_{it} = \alpha_i + \beta_i R_{mt} + e_{it}, \tag{2}$$

where
$i$ $= 1, \ldots, n$,
$t$ $= 1, \ldots, w$,
$R_{it}$ = rate of return on stock i over week t,
$R_{mt}$ = rate of return on the CRSP value-weighted index over week t,
$\beta_i$ $= \mathrm{cov}(R_{it}, R_{mt})/\mathrm{var}(R_{mt})$,
$\alpha_i$ $= E(R_{it}) - \beta_i E(R_{mt})$,
$e_{it}$ = the stochastic disturbance term of stock i in week t which is normally distributed with a zero mean, and serially and contemporaneously uncorrelated with constant variance ($\sigma^2$).

$$\mathrm{cov}(e_{it}, e_{js}) = 0, \quad \text{for all } i \neq j \text{ and } t \neq s,$$

$$\mathrm{cov}(e_{it}, R_{mt}) = 0, \quad \text{for all } t.$$

The market portfolio is a portfolio that contains all risky assets in proportion to their market value. In practice, we use a stock market index that is a value-weighted index of all stocks in the CRSP tape. The beta coefficient of stock i is a measure of the sensitivity of that stock to the general market movements. It is defined as the ratio of the covariance of stock i's returns with those of the market divided by the variance of the market returns.

Running an OLS regression of $R_{it}$ on $R_{mt}$ (with 52 weekly rates of returns ending 6 weeks *before* the announcement of the proposed merger and hence outside the event period), we can estimate the parameters $\hat{\alpha}_i$ and $\hat{\beta}_i$ for each stock in the sample. Using these estimated parameters ($\hat{\alpha}_i$ and $\hat{\beta}_i$) we can rewrite equation (2) as follows:

$$\hat{e}_{it} = R_{it} - \left[\hat{\alpha}_i + \hat{\beta} R_{mt}\right]. \tag{3}$$

Comparing equation (1) with equation (3) indicates that, according to the market model, expected returns can be estimated by taking the sum of the two (observable) terms within brackets in equation (3). Deducting expected returns from observed returns yields an estimate of unexpected returns $\hat{e}_{it}$ which are also referred to as "abnormal" returns. In other words, $[\hat{\alpha}_i + \hat{\beta}_i R_{mt}]$ is the "normal" return of stock i during week t, and the abnormal return of stock i during week t is simply equal to $\hat{e}_{it}$.

Note that the market model given in equation (2) breaks down the total return on stock i into two components: a market component and a firm-specific component. That is, factors affecting stock prices are of two broad types: the general market movements and firm-specific price variations caused by firm-specific events. Deducting $[\hat{\alpha}_i + \hat{\beta}_i R_{it}]$ from $R_{it}$ neutralizes the effect of the general market movements but does not neutralize firm-specific price variations caused by events *other than the announcement of the merger proposal.*

To neutralize firm-specific price variations caused by events other than the particular announcement being investigated (merger proposal or regulator's decision), we can take the cross-sectional average of the unexpected returns (abnormal returns) for the stocks in our sample during each of the 11 weeks that make up the event period centered on the announcement week. We have:

$$AR_t = \bar{e}_t = \frac{1}{n} \sum_{i=1}^{n} e_{it}, \tag{4}$$

$$t = -5, -4, \ldots, 0, \ldots, +4, +5,$$

where $AR_t$ is the sample average abnormal return (same as the sample average unexpected return) during week t and n is the number of stocks in the sample. The cross-sectional average neutralizes firm-specific price variations unrelated to the event of interest because that event did not occur at the same point in time for the n stocks in the sample.

The last step in the analysis of abnormal returns is to calculate cumulative average abnormal returns (CAR's) from week $t_1$ to week $t_2$ within the event period ($t = -5, -4, \ldots, 0, \ldots, +4, +5$). The week the announcement is made is week 0, the pre-announcement period covers the 5 weeks preceding the announcement and the post-announcement period covers the 5 weeks following the announcement. The cumulative average abnormal returns for the n stocks in the sample from week $t_1$ to week $t_2$ is computed as

$$CAR[t_1, t_2] = \sum_{t=t_1}^{t_2} AR_t. \tag{5}$$

### 3.1.2. *The mean-adjusted-return approach*

In this approach, the historical mean return of stock i over the 52 weeks ending 6 weeks before the announcement is used as an estimate of stock i's expected return. In this case the unexpected return of stock i during week t is calculated as

$$\hat{e}_{it} = R_{it} - \overline{R}_i, \tag{6}$$

where $\overline{R}_i$ is equal to

$$\overline{R}_i = \sum_{-57}^{-6} R_{it} \Big/ 52.$$

The unexpected returns $e_{it}$ are then used to estimate average abnormal returns ($AR_t$) and cumulative average abnormal returns $CAR[t_1, t_2]$ for the sample of n stocks according to equations (4) and (5). In chapter V we compare these $AR_t$ and $CAR[t_1, t_2]$ to those obtained with the market model approach in order to examine the sensitivity of our results to the choice of methodology.

### *3.2. Testing for the statistical significance of abnormal returns*

Estimated mean returns may be different from zero although true, unobservable, mean returns are in fact zero. Estimated mean returns must be subjected to a statistical test to find out whether they are significantly different from zero for a given level of significance. Below we describe the significance tests used to accept or reject the hypothesis that mean returns are different from zero. We also present a set of significance tests to determine whether two mean returns are different from each other.

#### *3.2.1. Significance tests for mean returns*

To test whether the sample estimated average abnormal weekly rates of returns and cumulative average abnormal returns are significantly different from zero, we first calculate, for each stock and for each week, a standardized abnormal return ($SR_{it}$) as follows:

$$SR_{it} = \frac{e_{it}}{\sigma_i} \approx t(51), \tag{7}$$

where $\sigma_i$ is the estimated standard deviation of the returns of stock i calculated over the 52-week estimation period. It is assumed that $SR_{it}$ are identically distributed independent random variables, each having a t-distribution with 51 degrees of freedom. Given a sample of n stocks we can now compute a cross-sectional average standardized abnormal return ($ASR_t$) for each one of the 11 weeks that make up the event period:

$$ASR_t = \frac{1}{n} \sum_{i=1}^{n} SR_{it}, \qquad (8)$$

$$t = -5, -4, \ldots, 0, \ldots, +4, +5.$$

Since $e_{it}$ is assumed to be independent across time t and normally distributed, $AST_t$ follows a t-distribution and the t-statistic is:

$$\text{t-stat.} = \sqrt{n} \cdot ASR_t \approx t(51), \qquad (9)$$

which is used to test the hypothesis whether the average abnormal returns ($AR_t$) are significantly different from zero at various levels of significance.

A similar procedure is employed to test the hypothesis whether the cumulative average abnormal returns are significantly different from zero. The relevant t-statistic in this case is:

$$\text{t-stat.} = \left( \frac{n}{t_2 - t_1 + 1} \right)^{1/2} \cdot \sum_{t_1}^{t_2} ASR_t, \qquad (10)$$

where $t_1$ is the first week and $t_2$ is the last week of the period over which returns are cumulated.

In addition to the statistical tests described above, we also use a t-statistic adjusted for the cross-sectional variation of abnormal returns during week t. This modified t-statistic can be expressed as follows:

$$\text{t-stat.}^* = \frac{\text{t-stat.}}{\sigma_t}, \qquad (11)$$

where t-stat. is the t-statistic defined in equations (9) and (10) and $\sigma_t$ is the cross-sectional standard deviation of the n stocks in the sample during week t ($\sigma_t$ is not necessarily equal to one).

### *3.2.2. Significance tests for the difference between two mean returns*

Finally, to test whether the abnormal returns of two different samples of stocks are statistically different from each other, we define the following t-statistic:

$$\text{t-stat.} = \left(ASR_t^1 - ASR_t^2\right)/SD, \tag{12}$$

where $ASR_t^1$ and $ASR_t^2$ are the average standardized abnormal returns of the two different samples and SD the standard deviation of the difference between $ASR_t^1$ and $ASR_t^2$ calculated over the 52 weeks where:

$$SD^2 = \frac{1}{t-2} \cdot \sum_{t=1}^{52} (Z_t - Z)^2,$$

with

$$Z_t = ASR_t^1 - ASR_t^2,$$

$$Z = \frac{1}{T} \sum_{t=1}^{52} Z_t,$$

and T = the number of observations in the estimation period (52 weeks).

### *3.3. Defining potential competitors*

In examining the impact of merger activities on the structure of the industry and on potential rivals, we classified the banking system according to the type of business. The most common classification is between wholesale and retail banking. Different types of banks differ significantly with respect to the nature of their customer, sources of funds, asset allocation, margins, expenses, etc. Also banks offer different products and satisfy the demand of different sectors in the economy. Therefore, banks should be grouped separately according to type of business when defining competition, concentration, and economies of scale.

In practice, however, the classification of banks is not an easy task for the simple reason that there is no pure "retail" or "wholesale" bank. Usually banks deal in both areas and any distinction is based solely on the proportion of these two activities in each bank. As an example, even a large wholesale bank like Citicorp has a certain proportion of its activities in retail banking. For the purpose of this study, we use the size of the bank, defined by total assets, as a proxy for the type of market in which a bank is involved. We define three groups of banks on the basis of size. The small-bank group has total assets of 1 billion or less in 1983. Banks in this group have an average ratio of equity capital to total assets of about 6.8 percent. Therefore, they are allowed to extend loans to a single borrower of up to \$6–7 million (up to 10 percent of their equity capital). In general this group of banks will include all the small community banks which mostly provide consumer loans. The second group, mid-size banks, includes the superregional banks that are involved in both wholesale and retail banking. Finally, the group of large banks, with total assets exceeding \$15 billion, includes banks that are involved mostly in wholesale banking.

In sum, it seems that the size of a bank can serve as a good proxy for the type of banking product offered.

CHAPTER IV

# BANK FAILURES, DIVERSIFICATION AND THE PROHIBITION OF INTERSTATE BANKING

The fear that the failure of one bank might cause a collapse of confidence in the banking system as a whole has always been one of the main reasons for bank regulation (see, for example, Diamond and Dybvig (1983), Swary (1986) and Jacklin and Bhattacharya (1988)). Such a contagion effect would cause losses to banks and their stockholders, disrupt the monetary system and destabilize the economy (see Bernanka (1983) who provides evidence of the real costs of bank runs during the Great Depression). This fear has led to the creation of the Federal Deposit Insurance Corporation (FDIC). It is also frequently voiced by regulators as the reason for their actions (for example, the Continental Illinois crisis of 1984). However, regulatory action which prohibits interstate banking constrains portfolio diversification, thus increasing the probability of bank failures. The recent accelerating growth in bank failures and problem banks has reemphasized the importance of this issue to bank regulators.

This chapter documents the historical distribution of bank failures in the United States during the period 1982–1986. It examines the link that may exist between bank failure and the inability of banks to diversify their loan portfolios because of the prohibition on interstate banking. A review of the literature on bank safety and the gains from diversification has been covered in Chapter I, Section 2.4

## 1. Why do banks fail?

A look at Table 2A shows that the number of failed banks in the United States has been rising steadily, from 10 banks in 1981 up to 200 banks in 1988 (and 21 assistance transactions). And because the

Table 2A
Bank failures as a percentage of insured banks. [a]

| Year | Number of failed banks [b] | Number of insured banks as of January 1st | Percentage of insured bank failures [c] |
|---|---|---|---|
| 1981 | 10 | 14,758 | 0.07% |
| 1982 | 42 | 14,746 | 0.28% |
| 1983 | 48 | 14,766 | 0.33% |
| 1984 | 79 | 14,763 | 0.54% |
| 1985 | 120 | 14,785 | 0.81% |
| 1986 | 138 | 14,779 | 0.93% |
| 1987 | 184 | 14,672 | 1.25% |
| 1988 | 200 | 14,289 | 1.40% |

[a] Source: FDIC.
[b] Includes banks in the 50 states, the District of Columbia and Puerto Rico.
[c] Ratio of the number of failed banks (column 2) to the number of insured banks (column 3).

number of insured banks has remained more or less the same (about 14,700 banks) over that 8-year period, bank failures as a percentage of insured banks has also risen steadily, from 0.07 percent of all insured banks in 1981 up to 1.40 percent of all insured banks in 1988. In 1988, the FDIC reported the *first operating loss* in its history, and a reduction of approximately 23 percent in the FDIC fund (the 1987 balance amounted to $18.3 billions).

The reasons for bank failure are varied, and are usually the outcome of both internal factors (poor and inefficient management of banks) and external factors (adverse economic conditions and structural rigidities in the banking industry). Poor management alone cannot explain the steady rise in bank failures. Instead, bank failures are most likely the result of a combination of factors: adverse economic conditions (such as unexpected changes in inflation and interest rates coupled with mismatched balance-sheets), poor judgement, bad luck and a rigid banking structure.

Structural rigidities in the banking industry result from those laws and regulations that prevent banks from diversifying both geographically (prohibition against interstate banking) and across products (prohibition against investment banking activities, insurance business, etc.). Because these limitations reduce the ability of banks to diversify, they increase the exposure of banks to risk (both interest-rate risk and credit risk) and hence their probability of failing. In particular, the prohibition against interstate banking may prevent banks from diversifying efficiently their credit risk. This statement, however, requires some qualifications. If a bank operates in a state that has a well-diversified economy, then the bank's loan portfolio can be easily diversified by extending loans to businesses in different sectors of the economy. But if the bank operates in a state with an economy built around one or two strong sectors that are sensitive to shifting economic conditions (such as energy, agriculture and real estate), then diversification cannot be efficiently achieved within the state borders. In such a case, the prohibition against interstate banking may be a contributing factor in bank failure.

However, this argument does not imply that if interstate banking were allowed, bank failures would not occur. Since the reasons for bank failures are many, certain banks will fail regardless of interstate banking legislation. In fact, poor management may be a strong factor behind bank failures in states with well-diversified economies. But in those states with economies built around a few cyclical sectors such as energy, real estate, and to some extent, agriculture, both poor management and the lack of diversification opportunities (resulting from the prohibition of interstate banking) may explain bank failures.

How can we test this proposition? By looking at two sets of empirical evidence. First we examine the historical distribution of bank failures *across states*. If poor management *alone* was the reason for bank failures, we should not observe any significant differences in the rate of bank failures across states. Therefore, if a given state has a rate of bank failure that is significantly higher than the national average, and if that state is characterized by an economy that is *not* well-diversified, then this would suggest that the inability of banks to diversify their loan portfolios is partly responsible for the reported higher than average rate of bank failures in that state.

The second set of empirical evidence is based on the examination of the structure of correlation coefficients between bank common stock returns. As pointed out in Chapter II, the gains from diversifying between two assets are inversely related to the magnitude of the correlation coefficient between the returns on these two assets: the lower the correlation coefficient, the higher the risk reduction via diversification. This implies that a bank can reduce the credit risk of its loan portfolio by holding loans whose cash flows are minimally correlated. We therefore want to know whether the correlation coefficients between loans extended within a state are significantly different from the correlation coefficients between intrastate loans and out-of-state loans. If out-of-state loans have significantly *lower* correlation coefficients than intrastate loans, then banks should be able to reduce their overall credit risk and diminish their potential rate of failure via interstate diversification of their loan portfolio. This diversification can be achieved in several ways, for example, by purchasing loans made to out-of-state entities, by extending loans to out-of-state entities via the establishment of an out-of-state branch/subsidiary, or by acquiring an out-of-state bank. Obviously, the prohibition against interstate banking restricts the ability of banks to take advantage of the risk-reduction potential offered by interstate diversification. In section 4 we present various empirical tests that measure and compare intrastate correlation coefficients with interstate correlation coefficients.

## 2. Bank failures: The record by states from 1982 to 1986

Table 2B gives the number of bank failures, their corresponding deposits in millions of dollars from 1982 to 1986, and cumulative 5-year data. Over this period, 423 banks failed (this number is smaller than that reported in Table 2A because Puerto Rico is included in Table 2A but not in Table 2B) with total deposits valued at $32,431.7 millions. The states with the largest number of failed banks are Texas (54 banks), Oklahoma (39 banks) and Kansas (35 banks). In the case of Texas, this number represents almost 13 percent of all bank failures. However, when examining bank failures by size of deposits, New York tops the list with $12,178.7 million (for 10 bank failures). This represents almost 38 percent of all failed bank deposits, followed by Oklahoma ($3,381.3 million or 10.43 percent of all deposits) and Texas ($2,487.1 million or 7.67 percent of all deposits). New York has the highest failure rate by deposits simply because it has, on average, larger banks than other states. Finally, note that 15 states did not experience any bank failures during the 5-year period from 1982 to 1986. These are states located mostly in New England (CO, ME, NH, RI, VT) and the Southeast (DC, DE, GA, MA, NC, SC).

## 3. Percentage of bank and deposit failures across states: Differences among states

The data reported in Table 2B are not very useful for the purpose of cross-state comparisons. Texas had the largest number of failed banks over the period 1982–1986 but it also had the largest number of banks in operation in 1981 (1,529 banks or 10.35 percent of all banks in the United States). Instead, the relevant data is the number of failed banks in a state as a percentage of the number of banks operating in that state, as shown in Table 2C. In the case of Texas, 54 banks failed in that state during 1982–1986, representing 3.53 percent of the 1529 banks in operation in Texas in 1981. This compares with a national average of 2.86 percent, with 16 states above that figure (see Table 2C). The highest percentages of bank failures are in Oregon (13.68 percent), Tennessee (9.32 percent) and California (8.46 percent). Again, because of the size effect we should look at the percentage of deposit failure rather than the percentage of bank failures. In this case the national average is 2.56 percent (see the bottom of Table 2C), and the highest percentages of deposit failures are in Oklahoma (14.37 percent), Tennessee (9.12 percent) and New York (7.46 percent).

Are these percentages significantly different from one another? That is, do failure rates differ significantly among states? We can

Table 2B
Number of bank failures and corresponding deposits [a] per state from 1982 to 1986.

| | 1982 | | 1983 | | 1984 | | 1985 | | 1986 | | 5-year total | |
|---|---|---|---|---|---|---|---|---|---|---|---|---|
| | Number | Deposits | Number | Deposits | Number | Deposits | Number | Deposits | Number | Deposits | Number | Deposits |
| 1. Alabama | 1 | (13.1) | 1 | (6.8) | 1 | (36.8) | 2 | (144.4) | 1 | (15.6) | 6 | (186.7) |
| 2. Alaska | 0 | – | 0 | – | 0 | – | 0 | – | 1 | (38.8) | 1 | (38.8) |
| 3. Arizona | 0 | – | 0 | – | 0 | – | 0 | – | 0 | – | 0 | – |
| 4. Arkansas | 3 | (35.0) | 1 | (15.5) | 2 | (44.2) | 1 | (23.2) | 0 | – | 7 | (117.9) |
| 5. California | 2 | (30.8) | 5 | (339.7) | 6 | (463.6) | 7 | (229.2) | 8 | (267.6) | 28 | (1330.9) |
| 6. Colorado | 0 | – | 1 | (11.9) | 2 | (5.9) | 6 | (84.1) | 7 | (91.0) | 16 | (192.9) |
| 7. Connecticut | 0 | – | 0 | – | 0 | – | 0 | – | 0 | – | 0 | – |
| 8. Delaware | 0 | – | 0 | – | 0 | – | 0 | – | 0 | – | 0 | – |
| 9. D.C. | 0 | – | 0 | – | 0 | – | 0 | – | 0 | – | 0 | – |
| 10. Florida | 1 | (171.7) | 0 | – | 2 | (26.3) | 2 | (49.9) | 3 | (710.3) | 8 | (958.2) |
| 11. Georgia | 0 | – | 0 | – | 0 | – | 0 | – | 0 | – | 0 | – |
| 12. Hawaii | 0 | – | 0 | – | 0 | – | 0 | – | 0 | – | 0 | – |
| 13. Idaho | 0 | – | 0 | – | 0 | – | 0 | – | 1 | (54.7) | 1 | (54.7) |
| 14. Illinois | 5 | (88.1) | 6 | (202.0) | 5 | (75.2) | 2 | (15.3) | 1 | (18.8) | 19 | (399.4) |
| 15. Indiana | 0 | – | 0 | – | 2 | (73.2) | 1 | (11.0) | 1 | (8.0) | 4 | (92.2) |
| 16. Iowa | 2 | (74.5) | 0 | – | 3 | (55.8) | 11 | (152.1) | 10 | (259.3) | 26 | (541.7) |
| 17. Kansas | 0 | – | 1 | (26.5) | 7 | (71.0) | 13 | (242.2) | 14 | (254.4) | 35 | (594.1) |
| 18. Kentucky | 0 | – | 1 | (18.3) | 1 | (21.7) | 0 | – | 2 | (16.2) | 4 | (56.2) |
| 19. Louisiana | 0 | – | 0 | – | 1 | (56.2) | 0 | – | 8 | (627.8) | 9 | (684.0) |
| 20. Maine | 0 | – | 0 | – | 0 | – | 0 | – | 0 | – | 0 | – |
| 21. Maryland | 0 | – | 0 | – | 0 | – | 0 | – | 0 | – | 0 | – |
| 22. Massachusetts | 1 | (10.5) | 0 | – | 0 | – | 0 | – | 0 | – | 1 | (10.5) |
| 23. Michigan | 1 | (16.8) | 0 | – | 1 | (68.2) | 0 | – | 0 | – | 2 | (85.0) |
| 24. Minnesota | 1 | (789.4) | 1 | (12.6) | 4 | (64.4) | 6 | (123.6) | 5 | (106.5) | 17 | (1096.5) |

| | | | | | | | | | | | | |
|---|---|---|---|---|---|---|---|---|---|---|---|---|
| 25. Mississippi | 0 | – | 0 | – | 1 | (153.0) | 0 | – | 2 | (15.2) | 3 | (168.2) |
| 26. Missouri | 2 | (18.4) | 1 | (6.6) | 2 | (44.1) | 9 | (271.5) | 7 | (147.4) | 21 | (488.0) |
| 27. Montana | 0 | – | 1 | (11.6) | 0 | – | 0 | – | 1 | (40.5) | 2 | (52.1) |
| 28. Nebraska | 0 | – | 1 | (6.2) | 5 | (48.6) | 13 | (87.0) | 6 | (145.7) | 25 | (287.5) |
| 29. Nevada | 0 | – | 1 | (10.5) | 0 | – | 0 | – | 0 | – | 1 | (10.5) |
| 30. New Hamsphire | 0 | – | 0 | – | 0 | – | 0 | – | 0 | – | 0 | – |
| 31. New Jersey | 1 | (578.4) | 1 | (31.3) | 1 | (494.6) | 0 | – | 0 | – | 3 | (1,104.3) |
| 32. New Mexico | 0 | – | 0 | – | 0 | – | 3 | (164.4) | 2 | (169.4) | 5 | (334.8) |
| 33. New York | 4 | (4498.4) | 2 | (2169.4) | 0 | – | 4 | (5510.9) | 0 | – | 10 | (12178.7) |
| 34. North Carolina | 0 | – | 0 | – | 0 | – | 0 | – | 0 | – | 0 | – |
| 35. North Dakota | 0 | – | 0 | – | 0 | – | 0 | – | 0 | – | 0 | – |
| 36. Ohio | 0 | – | 0 | – | 0 | – | 0 | – | 0 | – | 0 | – |
| 37. Oklahoma | 3 | (613.9) | 1 | (10.4) | 5 | (204.6) | 13 | (280.5) | 17 | (2271.9) | 39 | (3381.3) |
| 38. Oregon | 0 | – | 0 | – | 5 | (68.7) | 3 | (116.9) | 0 | – | 13 | (503.2) |
| 39. Pennsylvania | 1 | (1956.8) | 5 | (317.6) | 0 | – | 0 | – | 0 | – | 1 | (1956.8) |
| 40. Rhode Island | 0 | – | 0 | – | 0 | – | 0 | – | 0 | – | 0 | – |
| 41. South Carolina | 0 | – | 0 | – | 0 | – | 0 | – | 0 | – | 0 | – |
| 42. South Dakota | 0 | – | 1 | (39.3) | 1 | (2.8) | 0 | – | 1 | (6.3) | 3 | (48.4) |
| 43. Tennessee | 3 | (41.6) | 12 | (1485.8) | 11 | (256.8) | 5 | (96.6) | 2 | (48.6) | 33 | (1929.4) |
| 44. Texas | 7 | (361.9) | 3 | (679.2) | 6 | (233.5) | 12 | (285.4) | 26 | (927.1) | 54 | (2487.1) |
| 45. Utah | 0 | – | 0 | – | 1 | (6.7) | 1 | (79.9) | 3 | (61.8) | 5 | (148.4) |
| 46. Vermont | 0 | – | 0 | – | 0 | – | 0 | – | 0 | – | 0 | – |
| 47. Virginia | 1 | (12.7) | 0 | – | 0 | – | 0 | – | 0 | – | 1 | (12.7) |
| 48. Washington | 1 | (550.5) | 0 | – | 0 | – | 0 | – | 0 | – | 1 | (550.5) |
| 49. West Virginia | 1 | (26.9) | 0 | – | 1 | (15.5) | 0 | – | 0 | – | 2 | (42.4) |
| 50. Wisconsin | 0 | – | 0 | – | 0 | – | 1 | (30.4) | 1 | (34.8) | 2 | (65.2) |
| 51. Wyoming | 0 | – | 1 | (17.4) | 2 | (28.7) | 5 | (91.2) | 7 | (105.2) | 15 | (242.5) |
| Total | 41 | (9889.4) | 47 | (5418.6) | 78 | (2620.1) | 120 | (8059.7) | 137 | (6442.9) | 423 | 32431.7 |

[a] Total deposits in dollars.

Table 2C
Percentage of bank and deposit failures by state.

| State | Number of banks on 12/31/81 | Number of failed banks 1982–1986 | Percentage of bank failures [a] | Total deposits on 12/31/81 [b] | Deposits of failed banks 1982–1986 | Percentage of deposit failure [c] |
|---|---|---|---|---|---|---|
| 1. Alabama | 308 | 6 | 1.95% | 15521 | 186.7 | 1.20% |
| 2. Alaska | 12 | 1 | 8.33% | 1924 | 38.8 | 2.02% |
| 3. Arizona | 37 | 0 | 0.00% | 12124 | 0.0 | 0.00% |
| 4. Arkansas | 264 | 7 | 2.65% | 10319 | 117.9 | 1.14% |
| 5. California | 331 | 28 | 8.46% | 152308 | 1330.9 | 0.87% |
| 6. Colorado | 483 | 16 | 3.31% | 14719 | 192.9 | 1.31% |
| 7. Connecticut | 57 | 0 | 0.00% | 11628 | 0.0 | 0.00% |
| 8. Delaware | 21 | 0 | 0.00% | 3031 | 0.0 | 0.00% |
| 9. D.C. | 19 | 0 | 0.00% | 6049 | 0.0 | 0.00% |
| 10. Florida | 505 | 8 | 1.58% | 42713 | 958.2 | 1.24% |
| 11. Georgia | 427 | 0 | 0.00% | 19899 | 0.0 | 0.00% |
| 12. Hawaii | 12 | 0 | 0.00% | 5060 | 0.0 | 0.00% |
| 13. Idaho | 27 | 1 | 3.70% | 4394 | 54.7 | 2.24% |
| 14. Illinois | 1295 | 19 | 1.47% | 88816 | 399.4 | 0.45% |
| 15. Indiana | 407 | 4 | 0.98% | 28016 | 92.2 | 0.33% |
| 16. Iowa | 655 | 26 | 3.97% | 19755 | 541.7 | 2.74% |
| 17. Kansas | 619 | 35 | 5.65% | 15183 | 594.1 | 3.91% |
| 18. Kentucky | 344 | 4 | 1.16% | 17672 | 56.2 | 0.32% |
| 19. Louisiana | 273 | 9 | 3.30% | 23739 | 684.0 | 2.88% |
| 20. Maine | 37 | 0 | 0.00% | 3000 | 0.0 | 0.00% |
| 21. Maryland | 94 | 0 | 0.00% | 13620 | 0.0 | 0.00% |
| 22. Massachusetts | 45 | 1 | 2.22% | 22867 | 10.5 | 0.04% |
| 23. Michigan | 377 | 2 | 0.53% | 43865 | 85.0 | 0.19% |
| 24. Minnesota | 763 | 17 | 2.23% | 25281 | 1096.5 | 4.34% |
| 25. Mississippi | 171 | 3 | 1.75% | 10779 | 168.2 | 1.56% |
| 26. Missouri | 734 | 21 | 2.86% | 29219 | 488.0 | 1.67% |
| 27. Montana | 167 | 2 | 1.20% | 4923 | 52.1 | 1.06% |

| | | | | | | |
|---|---|---|---|---|---|---|
| 28. Nebraska | 466 | 25 | 5.36% | 10491 | 287.5 | 2.74% |
| 29. Nevada | 14 | 1 | 7.14% | 3440 | 10.5 | 0.31% |
| 30. New Hampshire | 72 | 0 | 0.00% | 3113 | 0.0 | 0.00% |
| 31. New Jersey | 161 | 3 | 1.86% | 31363 | 1104.3 | 3.52% |
| 32. New Mexico | 89 | 5 | 5.62% | 5764 | 334.8 | 5.81% |
| 33. New York | 334 | 10 | 2.99% | 163288 | 12178.7 | 7.46% |
| 34. North Carolina | 73 | 0 | 0.00% | 19326 | 0.0 | 0.00% |
| 35. North Dakota | 179 | 0 | 0.00% | 5167 | 0.0 | 0.00% |
| 36. Ohio | 380 | 0 | 0.00% | 44303 | 0.0 | 0.00% |
| 37. Oklahoma | 508 | 39 | 7.68% | 23530 | 3381.3 | 14.37% |
| 38. Oregon | 95 | 13 | 13.68% | 10946 | 503.2 | 4.60% |
| 39. Pennsylvania | 363 | 1 | 0.27% | 67759 | 1956.8 | 2.89% |
| 40. Rhode Island | 17 | 0 | 0.00% | 5536 | 0.0 | 0.00% |
| 41. South Carolina | 83 | 0 | 0.00% | 7001 | 0.0 | 0.00% |
| 42. South Dakota | 154 | 3 | 1.95% | 6539 | 48.4 | 0.74% |
| 43. Tennessee | 354 | 33 | 9.32% | 21156 | 1929.4 | 9.12% |
| 44. Texas | 1529 | 54 | 3.53% | 105372 | 2487.1 | 2.36% |
| 45. Utah | 68 | 5 | 7.35% | 6109 | 148.4 | 2.43% |
| 46. Vermont | 28 | 0 | 0.00% | 2235 | 0.0 | 0.00% |
| 47. Virginia | 224 | 1 | 0.45% | 21704 | 12.7 | 0.06% |
| 48. Washington | 110 | 1 | 0.91% | 19056 | 550.5 | 2.89% |
| 49. West Virginia | 243 | 2 | 0.82% | 9284 | 42.4 | 0.46% |
| 50. Wisconsin | 643 | 2 | 0.31% | 22632 | 65.2 | 0.29% |
| 51. Wyoming | 109 | 15 | 13.76% | 3278 | 242.5 | 7.40% |
| Total (average) | 14.780 | 423 | 2.86% | 1.264.816 | 32431.7 | 2.56% |

[a] Ratio of 5-year cumulative bank failures (1982–1986) in column 3 to the total number of banks in the corresponding state at the end of 1981 (column 2).

[b] In millions of dollars.

[c] Ratio of 5-year cumulative deposit failures (1982–1986) in column 6 to total deposits in the corresponding state at the end of 1981 (column 5).

*Source:* The FDIC Annual Report.

answer this question by performing a simple statistical test. Our null hypothesis is that the failure rates are the same in all states. Can we reject this hypothesis? We show below that we can reject it at a 1 percent significance level. Hence, failure rates do differ across states. And since a majority of states with failure rates above the national average are characterized by economies that are generally not well diversified (such as Oklahoma, Tennessee, and Texas), we conclude that there is some evidence consistent with the proposition stated earlier: the rate of bank failures differs across state and is associated with economic conditions in that state during the period examined. Thus, the inability of banks to diversify their loan portfolios is *partly* responsible for the reported higher than average rate of bank failures in some states. As pointed out above, this proposition and the evidence supporting it, should not be interpreted to mean that if interstate banking were allowed, there would be no bank failures.

The following statistical test allows us to reject the null hypothesis that banks have the same failure rate. Define $X_i$ as the total number of failed banks in state i ($1 \leq i \leq 51$) over the 5-year period from 1982 to 1986. And define $N_i$ as the total number of banks in state i on December 31, 1981 (the beginning of the 5-year period). The probability of failure in state i is given by:

$$p_i = \frac{X_i}{N_i}, \quad i = 1, \ldots, 51,$$

and the probability of failure at the national level is given by:

$$P^* = \sum_{i}^{51} X_i \Big/ \sum_{i} N_i,$$

which is equal to 2.86 percent (see Table 2C). In the case of *deposit* failures, $P^*$ is equal to 2.56 percent (again see Table 2C). The null hypothesis can now be formally stated as follows:

$$H_0 : p_1 = \cdots = p_i = \cdots = p_{51} = P^*.$$

The appropriate statistic to test this hypothesis is the following chi square test on $X_i$:

$$\xi^2 = \sum_{i=1}^{51} \frac{(X_i - N_i \cdot P^*)^2}{N_i \cdot P^*} \approx \chi^2\ (50).$$

The chi square determines whether there is a significant difference between the expected failure frequency $N_i \cdot P^*$ and the observed frequency $X_i$. The sample statistic is $\chi^2 = 364.71$ in the case where $X_i$ is the number of bank failures, and $\chi^2 = 44508.99$ in the case where $X_i$ is the value of failed deposits. Since these sample statistics are larger than the critical value for $\chi^2$ at the 1 percent level of significance (76.15), we can reject the null hypothesis: failure rates are not the same among the states.

In order to further examine the cause of differences in bank failures among states, the Sperman rank correlation statistic is used to measure the association between bank failure and economic condition from state to state. The following two variables are used to measure the magnitude of bank failures:

Variable a: Percentage of bank failures in the state (see Table 2C)
Variable b: Percentage of deposit failures in the state (see Table 2C).

Economic condition in each state is represented by the following two variables:

Variable c: The rate of unemployment in the state (annual average 1982–1986) (from the Survey of Current Business (May 1988) Vol. 68)
Variable d: The rate of growth in Gross State Product (from the Statistical Abstract of the United States (1988)).

The estimated correlation coefficients and their corresponding t-statistics are given below:

| Pairs of variables | Correlation coefficient | t-value |
|---|---|---|
| Variable a with variable c | 0.221 | 1.59 |
| Variable a with variable d | −0.245 | 1.77 * |
| Variable b with variable c | 0.271 | 1.97 * |
| Variable b with variable d | −0.320 | 2.36 ** |

A single asterisk indicates statistical significance at the 10 percent level and double asterisks indicate statistical significance at the 2.5 percent level. These empirical results provide statistical evidence of a negative relationship between the number of bank failures in a state and economic condition in that state.

## 4. An examination of the cross correlation structure of banks' common stock returns

At the beginning of this chapter, we stated that banks can reduce the credit risk of their loan portfolios and diminish their potential rate of failure via interstate diversification of their loan portfolios. This diversification effect will be beneficial to banks if the correlation coefficients between intrastate and out-of-state loan cash flows are significantly lower than the correlation coefficients between the cash flows of loans extended within a state.

Unfortunately, we cannot calculate correlation coefficients between loan cash flows because these cash flows are not available to us. But we can use an indirect measurement method. A bank's loan cash flows should be highly positively correlated to that bank's total net cash flows (aggregate cash inflows minus aggregate cash outflows). Further, the total net cash flows should be highly positively correlated to that bank's common stock returns. Hence we can use cross correlation coefficients between banks' common stock returns as proxies for cross correlation coefficients between banks' cash flows from loans. Actually, we used two proxies: cross correlation coefficients between banks' common stock returns and cross correlation coefficients between banks' residual returns. Residual returns are mean-adjusted returns as defined in Chapter III. Results for total returns do not differ significantly from those for residual returns. Below we present and discuss the results based on residual returns only.

### *4.1. The structure of intrastate correlations*

Table 3A presents a summary of the correlation coefficients between the residual returns of all pairs of banks within 9 states. These are the states for which we had weekly residual returns between January 1980 and June 1982 for at least 8 banks. The period used for this test is the one prior to the beginning of the interstate banking movement. Money center banks were excluded from their respective states (CA, IL, PA, MA and NY) and put together as a separate group (15 banks). The second column of Table 3A gives the number of banks in each state. Correlation coefficients were calculated between residual returns: the first half of the data is used to estimate mean returns and the second half to generate mean-adjusted returns (residual returns), which are then used to estimate correlation coefficients. Table 3A shows the number of distinct correlation coefficients between all possible pairs of bank residual returns within each state, the percentage of significant coefficients (at a 5 percent level) that are positive and negative, and the average, maximum, and minimum values of these correlation coefficients.

The appropriate test statistic to determine the statistical significance of a cross correlation coefficient (COR) is the following t-test on COR:

$$t = \sqrt{n-2} \cdot \frac{\mathrm{COR}}{\sqrt{1-(\mathrm{COR})^2}} \approx t(63),$$

where n is the number of weekly residual returns (n = 65). If the absolute value of that sample statistic exceeds the critical value of the t-statistic at the 5 percent level, we reject the hypothesis that the cross-correlation coefficient is equal to zero (that is, the cross-coefficient is different from zero at the 5 percent significance level). The results reported in Table 3A indicate that most coefficients are either

Table 3A
Correlation coefficients between the residual returns of all pairs of banks within a state. [a]

| State | Number of banks | Correlation coefficients | | | | | |
|---|---|---|---|---|---|---|---|
| | | Number [b] | % significant [c] | | Average | Maximum | Minimum |
| | | | Positive | Negative | | | |
| California | 9 | 36 | 5.56% | 0.00% | 0.1008 | 0.3509 | −0.0747 |
| Florida | 15 | 105 | 40.95% | 0.00% | 0.2265 | 0.5168 | −0.0716 |
| Michigan | 8 | 28 | 28.57% | 0.00% | 0.1356 | 0.4334 | −0.1006 |
| New Jersey | 14 | 91 | 26.48% | 0.00% | 0.1315 | 0.5383 | −0.1195 |
| New York | 9 | 36 | 27.78% | 2.78% | 0.1973 | 0.4654 | −0.2722 |
| Ohio | 10 | 45 | 20.00% | 2.22% | 0.1094 | 0.4169 | −0.3360 |
| Pennsylvania | 14 | 91 | 42.86% | 0.00% | 0.2133 | 0.6434 | −0.1897 |
| Texas | 11 | 55 | 66.92% | 0.00% | 0.3937 | 0.5985 | 0.1684 |
| Virginia | 8 | 28 | 14.29% | 4.17% | 0.1276 | 0.4601 | −0.2655 |
| Money center banks | 15 | 105 | 95.15% | 0.00% | 0.4393 | 0.6841 | 0.1285 |

[a] Based on weekly residual returns. Data begins on 1/4/1980 and ends on 6/26/1982. The first half of the data is used to estimate mean returns and the second half to generate mean-adjusted returns (residual returns) which are then used to estimate correlation coefficients.

[b] Number of distinct correlation coefficients. If N is the number of banks in the state, then there are $N(N-1)/2$ distinct pairs of banks or correlation coefficients.

[c] Percentage of correlation coefficients that are significantly different from zero at the 0.05 level.

significantly positive or insignificantly different from zero. There are only three coefficients that are significantly negative: one in New York (−0.2722), one in Ohio (−0.3360) and one in Virginia (−0.2655). The percentage of significantly positive correlation coefficients varies from a minimum of 5.56 percent in California (2 out of 36 coefficients) to a maximum of 66.92 percent in Texas (37 out of 55 coefficients). These numbers reveal a clear picture: the residual returns of California banks are essentially independent of one another, whereas those of Texas banks are mostly positively correlated (note that Texas is the only state in the sample without a negative correlation coefficient). This phenomenon may reflect the fact that, in comparison to California, Texas does not have a well-diversified economy. Banks in Texas lend to a limited number of sectors. Since the performances of these sectors are positively related (for example energy and real estate), banks in Texas, in contrast to banks in California, have highly correlated residual returns. Clearly, the benefits of interstate banking are greater for banks in Texas than for those in California. Finally, note the strength of the correlation coefficients within the 15 money center banks. Over 95 percent of all correlation coefficients are significantly positive and none are negative. Money center banks constitute a very homogeneous group. If a money center bank wishes to reduce its credit risk via diversification, a merger with another money center bank would obviously be a poor choice. As we will see in Section 4.3, money center banks would greatly benefit from diversifying with non-money-center banks.

### *4.2. The structure of intra-regional correlations*

Many states have reciprocal agreements with other states allowing their respective banks to merge across state borders. Using our sample of banks we formed 6 broad geographical regions. The states in each of these regions and the corresponding number of banks are given in Table 3B. Table 3B provides the same information for regions as provided by Table 3A for states. As with intrastate correlations, intra-regional correlations are mostly positive. There are only 6 significantly negative correlation coefficients: one in regions 1, 2 and 3 and three in region 4. But the percentage of

Table 3B
Correlation coefficients between the residual returns of all pairs of banks within a region. [a]

| Region | States in the region | Number of banks | Correlation coefficients | | | | | |
|---|---|---|---|---|---|---|---|---|
| | | | Number [b] | % significant [c] | | Average | Maximum | Minimum |
| | | | | Positive | Negative | | | |
| 1 | MA, ME, RI, CT, NH, VT | 16 | 120 | 19.17% | 0.83% | 0.1286 | 0.4829 | −0.4240 |
| 2 | PA, NJ, NY, DE | 42 | 861 | 27.64% | 0.12% | 0.1655 | 0.6434 | −0.2600 |
| 3 | OH, KY, MI, WI, IL, IN, MN, MO, IA, NE, KS | 38 | 703 | 28.59% | 0.14% | 0.1667 | 0.6401 | −0.3360 |
| 4 | GA, FL, SC, NC, VA, TN, DC, AL, MS, WV | 49 | 1176 | 19.22% | 0.26% | 0.1630 | 0.5293 | −0.3271 |
| 5 | TX, LA, AR, OK | 17 | 136 | 47.06% | 0.00% | 0.2066 | 0.5785 | −0.1932 |
| 6 | UT, ID, AZ, WA, NV, CA, OR, AK, HI, MT, CO, NM, WY | 31 | 465 | 29.89% | 0.00% | 0.1753 | 0.5714 | −0.1695 |
| Money center banks | NY, CA, IL, PA, MA | 15 | 105 | 95.15% | 0.00% | 0.4393 | 0.6841 | 0.1285 |

[a] Based on weekly residual returns. Data begins on 1/4/1980 and ends on 6/26/1982. The first half of the data is used to estimate mean returns and the second half to generate mean-adjusted returns (residual returns) which are then used to estimate correlation coefficients.
[b] Number of distinct correlation coefficients. If $N$ is the number of banks in the state, then there are $N(N-1)/2$ distinct pairs of banks or correlation coefficients.
[c] Percentage of correlation coefficients that are significantly different from zero at the 0.05 level.

significantly positive intra-regional coefficients is smaller, on average, than in the case of intrastate coefficients. If we consider the 9 states in Table 3A as one group, 34.17 percent of all correlation coefficients are positive (176 out of 515 coefficients). If we consider the 6 regions in Table 3B as one group, 25.74 percent of all correlation coefficients are positive (891 out of 3461 coefficients). There are, on average, more diversification opportunities within a region than within a state. Note that this is true only on average. Some states may have lower correlations within their borders than within the region in which they belong. Nevertheless, the results reported in Table 3B provide some evidence in favor of regional banking agreements.

### *4.3. The structure of interstate correlations*

We have seen in Section 4.1 and Table 3A that California is the state in our sample that has the lowest percentage of banks with significantly positive intrastate correlations (5.56 percent). And Texas is the state with the highest percentage of banks with significantly positive *intrastate* correlations (67.27 percent). We can therefore conclude that the benefit from interstate diversification should be substantially larger for Texas banks than for California banks. However, this conclusion calls for some qualifications. Banks in California and Texas would benefit, on average, from *interstate* diversification only if interstate correlation coefficients are, on average, *lower* than intrastate correlation. Although this may be the case for Texas banks, it may not be the case for California banks. Thus we need to compare directly intrastate correlations to interstate correlations.

Table 3C reports the interstate correlations between California banks and banks in the other 8 states in the sample, as well as between California banks and money center banks. Most correlation coefficients are statistically equal to zero and the percentage of significantly positive correlations varies from a low of 2.78 percent (for banks in Michigan) to a high of 17.78 percent (for banks in Ohio), with an average of 8.86 percent if we consider all 801 interstate correlations. Clearly, these numbers are of the same order

Table 3C

Correlation coefficients between the residual returns of each bank in California and each bank in another state. [a,b]

| State pairs [c] | Correlation coefficients | | | | | |
|---|---|---|---|---|---|---|
| | Number [d] | % significant [e] | | Average | Maximum | Minimum |
| | | Positive | Negative | | | |
| [California (9), California (9)] | 35 | 5.56% | 0.00% | 0.1008 | 0.3509 | −0.0747 |
| [California (9), Florida (15)] | 135 | 7.41% | 0.74% | 0.0528 | 0.5085 | −0.2942 |
| [California (9), Michigan (8)] | 72 | 2.78% | 0.00% | 0.0588 | 0.4563 | −0.2215 |
| [California (9), New Jersey (14)] | 126 | 7.14% | 0.79% | 0.0570 | 0.4095 | −0.3155 |
| [California (9), New York (9)] | 81 | 7.41% | 0.00% | 0.0588 | 0.6690 | −0.2317 |
| [California (9), Ohio (10)] | 90 | 17.78% | 1.11% | 0.0883 | 0.4830 | −0.3350 |
| [California (9), Pennsylvania (14)] | 126 | 11.11% | 0.79% | 0.0917 | 0.5975 | −0.2611 |
| [California (9), Texas (11)] | 99 | 6.06% | 2.02% | 0.0579 | 0.5422 | −0.3744 |
| [California (9), Virginia (8)] | 72 | 11.11% | 0.00% | 0.0743 | 0.5359 | −0.2143 |
| [California (9), Money center (15)] | 135 | 6.67% | 0.74% | 0.5600 | 0.5225 | −0.2618 |

[a] Based on weekly residual returns. Data begins on 1/4/1980 and ends on 6/26/1982. The first half of the data is used to estimate mean returns and the second half to generate mean-adjusted returns (residual returns) which are then used to estimate correlation coefficients.

[b] The first line gives the intrastate correlations for California (see Table 3A). The last line gives the correlations between California banks and the money center banks.

[c] The number in parentheses following the state's name indicates the number of banks in that state (see Table 3A).

[d] If N1 is the number of banks in state 1 and N2 the number of banks in state 2 then the total number of correlation coefficients between each bank in state 1 and the N2 banks in state 2 is equal to N1 times N2.

[e] Percentage of correlation coefficients that are significantly different from zero at the 0.05 level.

Table 3D

Correlation coefficients between the residual returns of each bank in Texas and each bank in another state. [a,b]

| State pairs [c] | Correlation coefficients | | | | | |
|---|---|---|---|---|---|---|
| | Number [d] | % significant [e] | | Average | Maximum | Minimum |
| | | Positive | Negative | | | |
| [Texas (11), Texas (11)] | 55 | 66.92% | 0.00% | 0.3937 | 0.5985 | 0.1684 |
| [Texas (11), California (9)] | 99 | 6.06% | 2.02% | 0.0579 | 0.5422 | −0.3744 |
| [Texas (11), Florida (15)] | 165 | 7.27% | 1.82% | 0.0308 | 0.7845 | −0.3793 |
| [Texas (11), Michigan (8)] | 88 | 10.23% | 2.27% | 0.0622 | 0.5540 | −0.2784 |
| [Texas (11), New Jersey (14)] | 154 | 9.09% | 1.95% | 0.0377 | 0.8839 | −0.5511 |
| [Texas (11), New York (9)] | 99 | 10.10% | 2.02% | 0.0530 | 0.6518 | −0.3432 |
| [Texas (11), Ohio (10)] | 110 | 15.45% | 0.00% | 0.0847 | 0.5803 | −0.2305 |
| [Texas (11), Pennsylvania (14)] | 154 | 15.58% | 1.95% | 0.0728 | 0.6034 | −0.3253 |
| [Texas (11), Virginia (8)] | 88 | 7.95% | 1.14% | 0.0580 | 0.6417 | −0.2741 |
| [Texas (11), Money center (15)] | 165 | 9.70% | 0.61% | 0.0588 | 0.7790 | −0.3285 |

[a] Based on weekly residual returns. Data begins on 1/4/1980 and ends on 6/26/1982. The first half of the data is used to estimate mean returns and the second half to generate mean-adjusted returns (residual returns) which are then used to estimate correlation coefficients.

[b] The first line gives the intrastate correlations for Texas (see Table 3A). The last line gives the correlations between Texas banks and the money center banks.

[c] The number in parentheses following the state's name indicates the number of banks in that state (see Table 3A).

[d] If N1 is the number of banks in state 1 and N2 the number of banks in state 2 then the total number of correlation coefficients between each bank in state 1 and the N2 banks in state 2 is equal to N1 times N2.

[e] Percentage of correlation coefficients that are significantly different from zero at the 0.05 level.

of magnitude as in the case of intrastate correlations. The implication is that, on average, California banks will not be able to reduce significantly the credit risk of their loan portfolios via interstate diversification. Again, this finding is true only on average. There are banks located in California that have significantly negative correlation coefficients with out-of-state banks. But their number is limited. Actually, there are only 6 such cases out of 801 possible interstate correlations.

Table 3D reports the interstate correlations between Texas banks and banks in the other 8 states in the sample, as well as between Texas banks and the money center banks. As in the case of California (see Table 3C), most correlation coefficients between banks in Texas and out-of-state banks are statistically equal to zero. The percentage of significantly positive correlations varies from a low of 6.06 percent (for banks in California) to a high of 15.58 percent (for banks in Pennsylvania), with an average of 10.34 percent if we consider all 957 interstate correlations. But contrary to the case of California banks, interstate correlation coefficients are, on average, significantly *lower* than intrastate correlation coefficients in the case of Texas. Obviously, banks in Texas have the potential to reduce significantly the credit risk of their loan portfolios via interstate diversification. The reason this option is not available to California banks is that intrastate correlations are mostly zero in that state. In order to gain from interstate diversification, interstate correlations should be lower than zero, that is, they should be negative. In any case, we have seen that significant *negative* correlations between bank residual returns are rarely observed.

Finally, note that the correlation coefficients of money center banks with California and Texas banks are mostly statistically equal to zero. In other words, the residual returns of money center banks are mostly independent of the residual returns of banks in California and Texas. Evidence (not reported here) shows that this phenomenon is also true for the other 7 states in the sample. This implies that money center banks will greatly benefit from diversification with non-money center banks, since 95.15 percent of all correlation coefficients *between* money center banks are significantly positive with an average value of 0.4393 (see Table 3A).

## 5. Summary and concluding remarks

This chapter examined the historical distribution of bank failures in the United States. The number of failed banks has risen steadily in the last decade, going from 10 banks in 1981 (0.07 percent of all insured banks) to 200 banks in 1988 (1.40 percent of all insured banks).

We have argued that bank failures are the outcome of a combination of factors not easily isolated. Some of these factors are internal (poor management, etc.), or external (adverse economic conditions, a rigid banking structure, etc.). We have shown that the rate of bank failures differs significantly among states and that the percentage of bank failures is negatively correlated with economic conditions in each state. This result can be interpreted to mean that poor management, *per se*, cannot fully explain why banks fail (unless we are ready to assume that the quality of bank management varies across states, an unlikely phenomenon). External factors are also likely to influence the probability that a bank will fail. These external factors are essentially adverse economic conditions coupled with a rigid banking structure. Two extreme cases should be considered. First is the case of a bank that operates in a state with a well-diversified economy (an economy with many different sectors whose performance are not highly correlated). This bank will be able to diversify the credit risk of its loan portfolio, minimize its exposure to credit risk, and hence reduce its probability of failure. The second case is that of a bank that operates in a state with an economy that is *not* well diversified (an economy with a few sectors whose performance are highly positively correlated). This bank will be unable to take advantage of the risk-reduction benefits of diversification and its loan portfolio will be strongly exposed to credit risk, hence raising its probability of failure.

We have presented some evidence consistent with this proposition. Using a sample of 113 banks operating in one of 9 states (CA, FL, MI, NJ, NY, OH, PA, TX, and VA), we found that California is a good example of the first case and Texas a good example of the second. Banks operating in California are found to have residual stock returns that are essentially independent of one another. In contrast banks operating in Texas are found to have residual stock returns that are significantly positively related to one another. We have also found that both California and Texas banks have residual stock returns that are, on average, unrelated to the residual stock returns of out-of-state banks. This implies that, on average, banks in California will not benefit from interstate diversification since average intrastate correlations are about the same as average interstate correlations. The opposite is true for banks located in Texas. They should benefit from interstate diversification because average interstate correlations are significantly *lower* than average intrastate correlations.

What can we conclude? Clearly, the benefits of interstate banking are mixed. It has been argued that the potential gains from diversification *alone* justify a position in favor of interstate banking legislation. But as evidence presented here suggests, although interstate banking may be good for states such as Texas, it is less so for states such as California. In other words, interstate banking may be good for some states but of little consequence for others (as far as the diversification motive is concerned). This may explain why the issue of interstate banking is dealt with at the state level rather than at the federal level. And it is not surprising that Texas, since September 1986, allows any out-of-state banks to operate in Texas, whereas California will permit interstate banking only after January 1991.

Two qualifications are in order. First, interstate banking can be justified for reasons other than diversification. For example, some have argued that because U.S. banks are much smaller than some of their Japanese and European counterparts, they are at a competitive disadvantage vis-à-vis foreign banks on the worldwide banking market. Bank mergers across state borders can produce a number of large U.S. banks that may be able to compete with foreign banks on a worldwide basis. Second, although the prohibition against interstate banking may be a contributing factor behind the recent rise in the rate of bank failures, this proposition does not imply that when nationwide interstate banking becomes a reality, banks will no longer fail. Some will avoid failure via interstate diversification. Others will fail regardless of interstate banking legislation. As pointed out earlier, this is where the quality of management makes a difference.

CHAPTER V

# CAPITAL MARKET REACTION TO THE ANNOUNCEMENTS OF BANK MERGERS AND THE SUBSEQUENT RELEASE OF FEDERAL RESERVE DECISIONS

This chapter examines the behavior of the common stock prices of banks involved in a merger proposal and tests some of the hypotheses discussed in Chapter II: the manager-utility-maximization hypothesis and the hubris hypothesis, the diversification hypothesis and the information hypothesis. The other hypotheses are tested in Chapter VI. A review of the literature on capital market reaction to the announcement of bank mergers and the subsequent release of Federal Reserve decisions was covered in Chapter I, Section 3.3.

## 1. Bank mergers and common stock prices

In the following pages we present and discuss the empirical results related to the reaction of bank common stock prices to two types of announcements: the announcement of an acquisition proposal and the announcement of the regulator's decision regarding the proposed merger (approval or denial). In both cases we examine the stock price behavior of target banks separately from the stock price behavior of bidding banks.

The sample properties and the source of data are presented in Chapter III. The sample is made up of weekly common stock returns for 123 target banks, 118 of which were the subject of a single bid, 3 the subject of a double bid and 2 the subject of a triple bid. We will examine the 118 single bid cases separately from the 5 multiple bid cases in order to capture any differences that may exist between single bid and multiple bid cases.

The reaction of bank common stock prices to the announcement of an acquisition is examined separately from the announcement of the regulator's decision. In each case we take an 11-week period that is divided into three subperiods: (1) a 5-week pre-announcement period (from week −5 to week −1); (2) the announcement or event week (week 0); and a 5-week post-announcement period (from week +1 to week +5). This sequence is illustrated in Figure 1.

The reaction of bank common stock prices to acquisition proposals and the subsequent regulator's decision is best captured by average abnormal common stock returns. Abnormal returns are calculated by deducting expected return from actual return. Expected returns are estimated with two models: the market model and the mean-adjusted-return model. The models' parameters are estimated with data outside the 11-week test period. Specifically, they are estimated using a 52-week period beginning in week −57 and ending in week −6, as shown in Figure 1. We report the results for both models. This will tell us if the choice of methodology to estimate abnormal returns has any effect on the results of our empirical tests.

The rest of this chapter is organized as follows. In Section 2, we examine the behavior of the abnormal returns of target banks during the 11 weeks surrounding the announcement of the acquisition proposal (target banks subject of only one bid). In Section 3, we examine the behavior of the abnormal returns of bidding bank during the same 11-week period. The results of Section 3 will provide a test of both the manager-utility-maximization hypothesis and the hubris hypothesis. As discussed in Chapter II, a bidder should acquire another bank because the acquisition is a wealth-creating investment to the bidding bank's shareholders. But acquisitions may also be motivated by non-wealth creating behavior. For example, acquisitions may be motivated by the desire to increase the acquiring bank's size (manager-utility-maximization hypothesis) or because the manager of the acquiring bank *wrongly* believes that the target bank is undervalued (the hubris hypothesis). In the latter case a bidding bank may engage in an acquisition even though it may be a negative net present value proposition. This could lead the shareholders of the

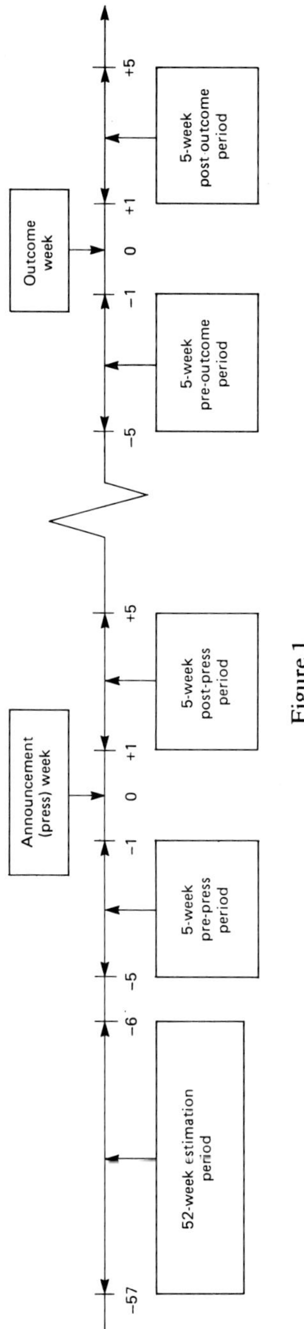

52-week estimation period
5-week pre-press period
Announcement (press) week
5-week post-press period
5-week pre-outcome period
Outcome week
5-week post outcome period
−57
−6
−5
−1
0
+1
+5
−5
−1
0
+1
+5


Figure 1

bidding bank to oppose the acquisition. As a result we should observe a drop in the bidding bank's common stock price during the week the acquisition proposal is announced.

Both the manager-utility-maximization hypothesis and the hubris hypothesis predict a drop in the bidding bank's common stock price when the merger proposal is announced. We have also seen in Chapter II that according to these two hypotheses, mergers should not create any net aggregate wealth to shareholders. We should only observe a wealth transfer from the bidding bank's shareholders to the target bank's shareholders. The dollar losses incurred by the bidding bank's shareholders should be equal to the dollar gains realized by the target bank's shareholders. The validity of this wealth-transfer phenomenon is tested in section 4, for the case of banking firms.

In Section 5, we report the results of the behavior of both target and bidding banks' abnormal returns during the 11-weeks surrounding the announcement of the Federal Reserve decision (approval or denial). This review will provide us with an indirect test of the information hypothesis discussed in Chapter II. If the increase in the price of a target bank is due to the revelation that the target bank is undervalued, then a denial of the acquisition should *not* result in a drop of the target bank's price back to its original level. In other words, the fact that the merger will not occur does not affect the fact that the undervaluation was revealed at the time of the acquisition announcement. In Section 6, we investigate whether the *risks* of the target and bidding banks were affected by the merger. This will provide an indirect test of the diversification hypothesis. Finally, in Section 7 we examine three special cases: the case of acquisition proposals that were subsequently cancelled; the case of multiple bids; and the case of acquisition proposals in which the target bank was insolvent (technically bankrupt) at the time the merger proposal was announced. Note that the case of cancelled acquisition will also provide an indirect test of the information hypothesis since a cancelled acquisition proposal should have no effect on the fact that undervaluation was revealed at the time of the acquisition announcement. Section 8 contains a summary of our results and some concluding remarks.

## 2. Behavior of the average abnormal returns of target banks during the weeks surrounding the announcement of a merger proposal

The behavior of the abnormal returns of the sample of target banks during the 11-week period surrounding the announcement of a merger proposal is summarized in Table 4A for those target banks (numbering 118) that were the subject of only one bid. The case of multiple bids is examined separately in Section 7.

The sample weekly average abnormal returns (AR) have been estimated using two methodologies: the market model (shown in the upper left-hand side of Table 4A) and the mean-adjusted-return model (shown in the upper right-hand side of Table 4A). The two approaches are described in detail in Chapter III. Two t-statistics are reported for each average abnormal return: the upper value is the standard t-statistic and the lower value is a t-statistic that has been adjusted for the cross-sectional dispersion of abnormal returns (see Chapter III for an explanation). All average abnormal returns that are significantly different from zero at the 0.05 level according to *both* t-statistics are framed. Finally, Table 4A gives the distribution of the t-statistics of the 118 individual abnormal returns that make up the sample (one for each bank in the sample). The table shows the number of target banks whose abnormal returns are significantly positive at the 0.05 level ($t(AR) \geq 2$); the number of target banks whose abnormal returns are significantly negative at the 0.05 level ($t(AR) \leq 2$); and the number of target banks whose abnormal returns are statistically equal to zero ($-2 < t(AR) < 2$). The lower part of Table 4A reports the cumulative average abnormal returns for the sample of 118 banks over the 5-week pre-announcement period (CAR $[-5, -1]$), the 5-week post-announcement period (CAR $[+1, +5]$), and the entire 11-week period surrounding the announcement of the merger proposal (CAR $[-5, +5]$).

The results in Table 4A indicate that the price of a target bank's shares increases, on average, by about 11.50 percent during the week the announcement of the acquisition proposal is made. The result is unaffected by the methodology employed to estimate abnormal returns. Further, both methodologies adjust for the effect of market-

Table 4A

Target-banks abnormal returns during weeks surrounding the announcement of a merger (118 cases). [a] Sample period: January 1968 to June 1987. Abnormal returns are measured using two methodologies.

| Event chronology | Market model methodology [b] | | | | | Mean-adjusted return methodology [c] | | | | |
|---|---|---|---|---|---|---|---|---|---|---|
| | AR [d] | t(AR) [e] | t(AR) ≥ 2 [f] | t(AR) ≤ −2 [g] | −2 < t(AR) < 2 [h] | AR [d] | t(AR) [e] | t(AR) ≥ 2 [f] | t(AR) ≤ −2 [g] | −2 < t(AR) < 2 [h] |
| Week −5 | 1.14% | 3.56<br>2.89 | 8 | 0 | 110 | 1.41% | 6.86<br>2.91 | 22 | 6 | 90 |
| Week −4 | 0.54% | 1.79<br>1.45 | 8 | 3 | 107 | 0.86% | 4.41<br>1.87 | 20 | 17 | 81 |
| Week −3 | 0.35% | 0.68<br>0.55 | 8 | 2 | 108 | 0.52% | 3.45<br>1.47 | 19 | 12 | 87 |
| Week −2 | 0.04% | 0.51<br>0.41 | 7 | 3 | 108 | 0.34% | 2.43<br>1.03 | 19 | 11 | 88 |
| Week −1 | 3.99% | 14.13<br>11.49 | 35 | 2 | 81 | 4.27% | 23.54<br>10.00 | 49 | 10 | 59 |
| Week 0 | 11.54% | 41.12<br>33.44 | 68 | 4 | 46 | 11.72% | 67.41<br>28.62 | 88 | 4 | 26 |
| Week +1 | −0.98% | −0.93<br>−0.76 | 5 | 8 | 105 | −0.71% | −3.60<br>−1.51 | 11 | 16 | 91 |

| | | | | | | | | | | |
|---|---|---|---|---|---|---|---|---|---|---|
| Week +2 | −0.[illegible]7% | −0.98<br>−0.80 | 2 | 5 | 111 | 0.01% | −1.00<br>−0.42 | 10 | 12 | 96 |
| Week +3 | −0.15% | −0.20<br>−0.16 | 5 | 3 | 109 | 0.35% | 2.72<br>1.15 | 15 | 5 | 97 |
| Week +4 | −0.44% | −1.63<br>−1.33 | 2 | 2 | 114 | −0.15% | −0.91<br>−0.39 | 9 | 7 | 102 |
| Week +5 | −0.51% | −1.80<br>−1.47 | 4 | 3 | 111 | −0.32% | −1.61<br>−0.69 | 8 | 7 | 103 |
| CAR[−5, −1] [i] | 6.07% | 9.24 | 50 | 13 | 55 | 7.48% | 10.22 | 63 | 19 | 36 |
| CAR[+1, +5] [j] | −2.24% | −2.30 | 16 | 22 | 80 | −0.82% | −1.96 | 23 | 35 | 60 |
| CAR[−5, +5] [k] | 15.37% | 17.07 | 77 | 9 | 32 | 18.30% | 31.27 | 92 | 14 | 12 |

[a] Of the 123 target banks in our sample, 118 were subject to a single bid over our sample period (see Table 1B). Only these banks were examined. The subsample of target banks that were the subject of multiple bids is examined separately in Section 7.2.

[b] The market model methodology is described in Chapter III, Section 3.1.1.

[c] The mean-adjusted return methodology is described in Chapter III, Section 3.1.2.

[d] AR = Average abnormal return over week t for the sample of 118 announcements. See Chapter III for a definition. Framed returns are significant at the 0.05 level.

[e] t(AR) = t-statistic for the AR. Significant returns at the 5 percent level are framed. The upper value is the standard t-statistic described in Chapter III, Section 3.2.1. The lower value is a t-statistic that is adjusted for the cross-sectional dispersion of abnormal returns. It is described in Chapter III, Section 3.2.1.

[f] Number of t(AR) that are equal or larger than 2.

[g] Number of t(AR) that are equal or smaller than 2.

[h] Number of t(AR) that are larger than −2 and smaller than 2.

[i] CAR = Cumulative average abnormal returns over the period indicated in brackets. CAR and their corresponding t-statistics are described in Chapter III, Section 3.1. Framed returns are significant at the 0.05 level. CAR[−5, −1] are cumulative average abnormal returns over the 5-week pre-announcement period.

[j] Cumulative average abnormal returns over the 5-week post-announcement period. Framed coefficients are significant at the 0.05 level.

[k] Cumulative average abnormal returns over the entire 11-week period surrounding the announcement week. Framed coefficients are significant at the 0.05 level.

related price movements as well as price movements related to events other than the acquisition proposal. Therefore, the reported increase in price can be safely attributed to the announcement of the acquisition proposal. Note that only 4 banks out of the 118 banks in the sample reacted negatively to the merger announcement (the 4 cases for which $t(AR) \leq -2$). The majority experienced a significant increase in price (68 according to the market model methodology and 88 according to the mean-adjusted-return methodology), with the rest not displaying any significant price change.

The reaction of a target bank's stock prices to the acquisition announcement is as expected. Prices increased, on average, by 4 percent during the week immediately preceding the announcement week (week $-1$). Another indication of pre-announcement reaction is given by CAR $[-5,-1]$. Over the 5-week pre-announcement period, prices went up by 6 to 7.50 percent, depending on the methodology used to estimate abnormal return.

There should be no post-announcement reaction in an efficient market. The behavior of weekly average abnormal returns indicates that this is indeed the case, although CAR $[+1,+5]$ (the 5-week post-announcement period) has a significantly negative value of 2.24 percent when estimated with the market model methodology. But it is doubtful that this cumulative decline in price could have been taken advantage of in order to earn abnormal returns via short sales of target bank shares following the announcement of a merger proposal. Note that only 16 out of 118 banks had a significant drop in price over the 5-week post-announcement period.

In summary, based on the results of the sample, we can reject the hypothesis that abnormal returns of target banks are equal to zero during the announcement week of an acquisition proposal. The price of target bank shares increase, on average, by 15 percent during the *two* weeks immediately preceding the merger announcement.

## 3. Behavior of the average abnormal returns of bidding banks during the weeks surrounding the announcement of a merger proposal: A test of the manager-utility-maximization and hubris hypotheses

Table 4B provides the same information as Table 4A, but for the sample of bidding banks. These banks made a total of 130 bids over our sample period (see Table 1B). However, the sample size in Table 4B is 126 since the 4 bids that were made on the 4 insolvent target banks were excluded. These bids are examined separately in Section 7.3.

As in Table 4A, abnormal returns that are significantly different from zero at the 0.05 level according to both t-statistics are framed. A look at the pattern of weekly average abnormal returns indicates that the price of bidding bank shares decreased, on average, during the week of the announcement of the acquisition proposal. The average decline in price is 1.68 percent when measured with the market model methodology, and 1.37 percent when measured with the mean-adjusted-return methodology. This price decline is small compared to the rise in price experienced by target banks. But it is significant at the 0.01 level. Note, however, that the majority of bidding banks do not display a significant change in price and that a few actually exhibit a significant increase in price. The pattern of weekly average abnormal returns indicates that the announcement of an acquisition proposal is an unexpected event and that the adjustment of bidding bank stock prices to the information revealed by the merger announcement is completed during the announcement week. What is the information revealed by the merger announcement that can explain the reported average decline in the share price of bidding banks? One hypothesis consistent with this share price decline is that the bidding bank's shareholders perceive bank acquisition to be, on average, negative net-present-value investments to the acquiring banks. Under this hypothesis, banks may engage in activities that have negative net present values. This is because either the objective of the bank's managers is not to maximize shareholders wealth, but rather to maximize bank size (manager-utility-maximization hypothesis) or because the manager of the bidding bank *wrongly* believes that the target bank is undervalued (the hubris hypothesis).

Table 4B

Bidding banks abnormal returns during weeks surrounding their announcement of a merger (126 cases). [a] Sample period: January 5, 1968 to June 26, 1987. Abnormal returns are measured using two methodologies.

| Event chronology | Market model methodology [b] | | | | | Mean-adjusted return methodology [c] | | | | |
|---|---|---|---|---|---|---|---|---|---|---|
| | AR [d] | t(AR) [e] | $t(AR) \geq 2$ [f] | $t(AR) \leq -2$ [g] | $-2 < t(AR) < 2$ [h] | AR [d] | t(AR) [e] | $t(AR) \geq 2$ [f] | $t(AR) \leq -2$ [g] | $-2 < t(AR) < 2$ [h] |
| Week −5 | 0.39% | 1.11<br>0.99 | 6 | 2 | 118 | 0.62% | 3.08<br>1.70 | 18 | 10 | 98 |
| Week −4 | −0.44% | −1.64<br>−1.47 | 3 | 2 | 121 | −0.09% | −0.58<br>−0.32 | 15 | 12 | 99 |
| Week −3 | −0.63% | −2.32<br>−2.08 | 2 | 5 | 119 | −0.39% | −1.96<br>−1.08 | 10 | 16 | 100 |
| Week −2 | −0.35% | −1.38<br>−1.23 | 2 | 3 | 121 | −0.21% | −2.34<br>−1.29 | 11 | 15 | 100 |
| Week −1 | −0.03% | −0.28<br>−0.25 | 9 | 3 | 114 | 0.19% | 0.08<br>0.05 | 17 | 14 | 95 |
| Week 0 | −1.68% | −5.60<br>−5.00 | 5 | 24 | 97 | −1.37% | −9.15<br>−5.06 | 11 | 38 | 77 |
| Week +1 | −0.25% | −0.79<br>−0.71 | 5 | 6 | 115 | −0.17% | −0.79<br>−0.43 | 14 | 18 | 94 |
| Week +2 | −0.11% | 0.37<br>0.33 | 5 | 3 | 118 | 0.07% | 0.81<br>0.45 | 17 | 12 | 97 |

| | | | | | | | | | | |
|---|---|---|---|---|---|---|---|---|---|---|
| Week +3 | −0.28% | −1.63<br>−1.46 | 2 | 6 | 118 | 0.03% | 0.10<br>0.05 | 14 | 16 | 96 |
| Week +4 | 0.02% | −0.83<br>−0.74 | 8 | 7 | 111 | 0.16% | 0.21<br>0.11 | 14 | 13 | 99 |
| Week +5 | [−0.59%] | −2.17<br>−1.94 | 2 | 3 | 121 | −0.46% | −3.04<br>−1.68 | 8 | 19 | 99 |
| CAR[−5, −1] [i] | [−1.06%] | −2.02 | 18 | 28 | 80 | 0.12% | 0.98 | 16 | 14 | 96 |
| CAR[+1, +5] [j] | [−1.21%] | −2.26 | 18 | 32 | 76 | −0.36% | −1.21 | 38 | 41 | 47 |
| CAR[−5, +5] [k] | [−3.96%] | −4.58 | 24 | 56 | 56 | [−1.62%] | −4.10 | 38 | 56 | 32 |

[a] Bidding banks made 130 bids over our sample period (see Table 1B). Four bids were excluded from the sample because the target banks were insolvent, thus yielding a sample size of 126 bids. The 4 cases of insolvent target banks are examined separately in Section 7.3.
[b] The market model methodology is described in Chapter III, Section 3.1.1.
[c] The mean-adjusted return methodology is described in Chapter III, Section 3.1.2.
[d] AR = Average abnormal return over week t for the sample of 118 announcements. See Chapter III for a definition. Framed returns are significant at the 0.05 level.
[e] t(AR) = t-statistic for the AR. Significant returns at the 5 percent level are framed. The upper value is the standard t-statistic described in Chapter III, Section 3.2.1. The lower value is a t-statistic that is adjusted for the cross-sectional dispersion of abnormal returns. It is described in Chapter III, Section 3.2.1.
[f] Number of t(AR) that are equal or larger than 2.
[g] Number of t(AR) that are equal or smaller than 2.
[h] Number of t(AR) that are larger than −2 and smaller than 2.
[i] CAR = Cumulative average abnormal returns over the period indicated in brackets. CAR and their corresponding t-statistics are described in Chapter III, Section 3.1. Framed returns are significant at the 0.05 level. CAR[−5, −1] are cumulative average abnormal returns over the 5-week pre-announcement period.
[j] Cumulative average abnormal returns over the 5-week post-announcement period. Framed coefficients are significant at the 0.05 level.
[k] Cumulative average abnormal returns over the entire 11-week period surrounding the anouncement week. Framed coefficients are significant at the 0.05 level.

If most acquirers behave as size-maximizers, or if they are infected by hubris, the price of *target* bank shares will be bid up to the point where acquisition proposals become negative net-present-value investments for the acquiring bank. This may trigger some selling pressure and a downward adjustment of bidding banks share prices to reflect the loss of wealth resulting from what bidding bank shareholders perceive as an unprofitable investment. We can conclude that the results reported in Table 4A and Table 4B are consistent both with the manager-utility-maximization hypothesis and the hubris hypothesis. The finding that there are no significant benefits to acquiring firm shareholders is consistent with previous studies in both financial and non-financial mergers. In this respect, see for example, Sushka and Bendeck (1988), and Born, Eisenbeis and Harris (1988) for a sample of bank mergers, and Jensen and Ruback (1983), and Jarrell, Brickley and Netter (1988) for a sample of mergers involving non-financial firms. In a recent study Cornett and De (1989) document significant positive abnormal returns for bidding banks involved in interstate mergers.

## 4. Do mergers create net aggregate wealth for bank shareholders? Another look at the manager-utility-maximization and hubris hypotheses

We have seen in the previous two sections that the shareholders of target banks realized, on average, a capital gain of 11.54 percent during the week of the announcement of the merger proposal. In contrast, the shareholders of the bidding banks realized, on average, a capital loss of 1.68 percent. If we consider the entire 11-week period, the gain to target shareholders is 15.37 percent and the loss to bidding shareholders 3.96 percent. All these returns are measured using the market model methodology and can be found in Tables 4A and 4B.

The drop in the price of bidding bank shares and the rise in the price of target bank shares are consistent with both the manager-utility-maximization and the hubris hypotheses. We have seen in Chapter II that, according to these two hypotheses of mergers, there should not be any creation of net aggregate wealth to shareholders. If these two hypotheses are correct, we should observe a straightforward wealth transfer from bidding bank shareholders to target bank shareholders. In this case, target shareholder dollar gains should indeed equal bidding shareholder dollar losses.

What is the evidence from our sample of bank merger announcements? To answer this question we must first convert the percentage gains and losses into dollar gains and losses. Suppose that p is the price of a bank stock at the beginning of the week, p′ is its price at the end of that week and n the (fixed) number of shares outstanding. Then, V, the dollar market value of the bank, is equal to $n \cdot p$ and we can express the weekly price return as:

$$R_T = \frac{p'_T - p_T}{p_T} = \frac{n_T p'_T - n_T p_T}{n_T p_T} = \frac{V'_T - V_T}{V_T} = \frac{\Delta V_T}{V_T},$$

where the subscript T indicates the target bank and $\Delta V_T$ the change in the market value of the target bank. The same would apply for the bidding bank for which we have:

$$R_B = \frac{\Delta V_B}{V_B},$$

where subscript B indicates the bidding bank and $\Delta V_B$ the change in the market value of the bidding bank.

There is net aggregate value creation if:

$$\Delta V_T + \Delta V_B > 0,$$

and since $\Delta V_T = R_T \cdot V_T$ and $\Delta V_B = R_B \cdot V_B$, we can rewrite the above condition as:

$$R_T V_T + R_B V_B > 0$$

or

$$R_T \left( \frac{V_T}{V_B} \right) + R_B > 0.$$

This equation indicates that there is net aggregate value creation as a result of a merger announcement, if the rate of return to target shareholders ($R_T$) multiplied by the relative market value of the target and bidding banks ($V_T/V_B$) plus the rate of return to bidding shareholders ($R_B$) is positive.

To verify whether that condition is satisfied on average, we need to calculate $R_T(V_T/V_B) + R_B$ for *each merger announcement* and then compute an average value (Bradley, Desai and Kim (1988)). We did not proceed in this fashion. Instead we multiplied average $R_T$ by average $V_T/V_B$ and added average $R_B$, where the ratio of average owners' equity of target bank to that of bidding bank serves as a proxy for the relative market value of the two groups of banks. Because this approach is an approximation, we should interpret our results with caution. The average relative stockholders' equity *book* value, $V_T/V_B$, is equal to 0.408 for our sample. Hence, in the case of returns measured during the announcement week, we have:

$$(11.54\%)(0.408) + (-1.68\%) = 3.03\%.$$

In the case of cumulative returns over the entire 11-week period surrounding the announcement of the merger proposal, we have:

$$(15.37\%)(0.408) + (-3.96\%) = 2.31\%.$$

Both values are positive, indicating some net aggregate wealth creation for shareholders. This result is inconsistent with both the manager-utility-maximization and the hubris hypotheses. But we cannot draw any definitive conclusion because the net aggregate wealth condition was not properly estimated. Furthermore, relative value must be measured in market value terms and not in book (or accounting) value terms. Note, however, that the study by Bradley et al. (1988) measures the net aggregate wealth condition correctly and rejects the hubris hypothesis. Using a cross-sectional sample of industries, Bradley et al. report that "a successful tender offer increases the combined value of the target and acquiring firms by an average of 7.40 percent", a conclusion that is not consistent with the manager-utility-maximization and hubris hypotheses of firm mergers.

## 5. Market reaction to the Federal Reserve decision regarding the merger proposal

### *5.1. Price behavior of bidder shares*

According to the Bank Merger Act and the Bank Holding Company Act, the Federal Reserve must approve an acquisition proposal before the merger between two banks can take place. Most bank mergers are approved by the Federal Reserve, though a few are denied. Denial is usually made either because the financial condition of the applicant (the bidding bank) is deemed inadequate to justify a successful takeover or because the proposed merger is considered anti-competitive. Therefore, the denial order may contain new information on the applicant that was not known to the market at the time the acquisition was announced. When the regulator's denial order is made because of the inadequate financial condition of the applicant, negative information regarding the applicant is now revealed to the market. If this information was known to the market at the time of the merger announcement, we should not observe any change in the price of the applicant's shares the week the denial order is issued. If this information was not known to the market at the time of the merger announcement, then we should observe a drop in the price of the applicant's shares the week the denial order is issued.

When the regulator's denial order is made for anti-competitive reasons, the effect on the applicant's share price is less obvious. Suppose that the price of the applicant's shares increased when the acquisition proposal was first announced because the market anticipated that some real benefits would accrue to the applicant if the acquisition is completed. In this case, the denial order should trigger a decrease in price back to its original level since the merger will not take place. But we have seen that, on average, applicant share prices drop the week of the acquisition announcement. In this case, a denial order should trigger a rise in the applicant's share price to its pre-merger announcement level since the applicant has been prevented from making an acquisition that was perceived by the market to be a negative net present value investment.

Table 5

Regulatory effect: Market reaction to merger announcements and to the subsequent federal reserve decision.

| Federal Reserve decision (sample size) | Announcement period [a] | | | | Outcome period [b] | | | |
|---|---|---|---|---|---|---|---|---|
| | CAR[−5, −1] [c] | AR[0] [d] | CAR[+1, +5] [e] | CAR[−5, +5] [f] | CAR[−5, −1] [c] | AR[0] [d] | CAR[+1, +5] [e] | CAR[−5, +5] [f] |
| I. *Approved mergers* | | | | | | | | |
| Target banks (65) | 5.17%* | 13.85%* | 14.38%* | 16.24%* | −1.55% | 1.69%* | −2.11% | −3.51% |
| | (6.40) | (37.89) | (18.44) | (14.24) | (1.29) | (3.41) | (0.97) | (1.67) |
| Bidding banks (67) | 0.46% | −1.69%* | −2.47%* | −2.31%* | −0.18% | 0.03% | −0.20% | −0.02% |
| | (0.38) | (4.58) | (3.22) | (2.11) | (0.58) | (0.04) | (0.04) | (0.50) |
| II. *Denied mergers* | | | | | | | | |
| Target banks (8) | 8.37% | 16.00%* | −1.64% | 22.73%* | −8.23%* | −7.29%* | −3.83% | −19.35%* |
| | (3.02) | (14.60) | (0.49) | (6.11) | (2.46) | (6.30) | (1.07) | (4.28) |
| Bidding banks (8) | 0.34% | 0.42% | −3.86% | −3.11% | 0.58 | −0.54% | −3.77% | −3.73% |
| | (0.50) | (0.00) | (1.29) | (0.53) | (0.19) | (0.67) | (1.66) | (1.45) |

[a] Average abnormal returns (measured using the market model methodology) for target and bidding banks during the period surrounding the merger announcement. At that time the Federal Reserve decision is, of course, not yet known. We report these returns to find out whether the market can distinguish between those mergers which will be subsequently approved by the Federal Reserve and those which will be denied. Sample size in parentheses.

[b] Average abnormal returns for target and bidding banks during the period surrounding the outcome week, that is, the week the Federal Reserve announces whether it has approved or denied the merger. Sample size in parentheses.

[c] Cumulative average abnormal returns over the 5-week period preceding the event week (week zero). Absolute values of t-statistics are in parentheses below the corresponding returns. Asterisks indicate significance at the 0.05 level.

[d] Average abnormal return over the event week. Absolute values of t-statistics are in parentheses below the corresponding returns. Asterisks indicate significance at the 0.05 level.

[e] Cumulative average abnormal returns over the 5-week period following the event week (week zero). Absolute values of t-statistics are in parentheses below the corresponding returns. Asterisks indicate significance at the 0.05 level.

[f] Cumulative average abnormal returns over the 11-week period centered on the event week. Absolute values of t-statistics are in parentheses below the corresponding returns. Asterisks indicate significance at the 0.05 level.

The preceding discussion implies that the net effect of a denial order on the applicant's share price is not clear. What about the effect of an approval order? The reaction of the applicant's share price on the announcement of the acquisition proposal reflects the market probability that the acquisition will take place. The approval is a highly probable event but since it is not a certain event we should observe some positive market reaction at the time the approval order is issued.

In summary, the reaction of bidder share prices (the applicants) to the announcement of the Federal Reserve's decision is ambiguous in the case of a denial order. In the case of an approval order, we should observe a relatively small positive market reaction which reflects the resolution of uncertainty. The empirical evidence is presented in Table 5. We have a subsample of 67 approved mergers and 8 denied mergers. Abnormal returns are estimated using the market model. The left-hand side of Table 5 gives the reaction of bank share prices during the 11-week period surrounding the announcement of the acquisition proposal. At that time, the Federal Reserve decision was not yet known. The reason we report these results is to see if there are differences between the price behavior of the entire sample (see Tables 4A and 4B) of banks and the subsample of banks for which we had data on the regulator's decision.

The reaction of bank share prices during the 11-week period surrounding the announcement of the Federal Reserve decision (the outcome period) is reported on the right-hand side of Table 5. A look at that table indicates that the behavior of the applicants' share prices around the announcement of the acquisition proposal is not significantly different from that reported in Table 4B for the entire sample: bidders experience a significant drop in the price of their shares during the week the merger is announced as well as a cumulative drop over the 5-week post-announcement period. Note that the returns of bidders whose acquisition proposal was later denied by the Federal Reserve are insignificantly different from zero. Statistical insignificance may be due to the small sample size. It can also be interpreted to mean that the market anticipates those mergers that will later be denied by the Federal Reserve and hence stock prices are not affected by the announcement of the merger proposal. Turning to the right-hand side of Table 5, we see that bidder share prices are not significantly affected by the Federal Reserve decision, be it an approval or a denial order. This is consistent with an earlier discussion regarding the market reaction to denial orders. As for approval orders, we expected to observe a small positive market reaction but the evidence indicates that this is not the case. The regulator's approval order does not seem to have any information content for bidding banks. Note that the regulator's denial order may have some information content for bidding banks but, because we have seen that the price reaction can be either positive or negative, we do not observe, on average, any change in price.

### *5.2. Price behavior of target shares: A test of the information hypothesis*

How does the Federal Reserve decision affect the share price of target banks? First let's examine the case of approvals. We have seen that any perceived benefits from a merger accrue to the shareholders of the target bank: target bank share prices rise by an average of 11.50 percent during the week of the merger announcement (see Table 4A), whereas bidding bank share prices fall by an average of 1.50 percent during that week. To the extent that the approval is not fully anticipated the week of the merger announcement, we should observe a rise in the price of target bank share prices during the week the approval order is issued. A look at Table 5 indicates that this is indeed the case: the share prices of target banks whose merger has been approved by the Federal Reserve increase, on average, by 1.69 percent during the week the approval order is issued. Although it declined by 3.51 percent over the entire 11-week period surrounding the announcement of the regulator's decision, this drop in price is not significantly different from zero. Note that there is a significant difference during the 5-week *post*-merger-announcement period between the price behavior of target bank shares whose mergers were subsequently approved and those banks whose mergers were denied: target banks whose mergers were subsequently approved saw their share prices rise by 14.38 percent, whereas target banks whose mergers were subsequently denied saw their share prices decline by

1.64 percent (the decline is equal to 2.30 percent for the whole sample, as shown in Table 4A). There is no obvious explanation for this phenomenon. Given its magnitude ((14.38 percent) minus (−1.64 percent) equals 16.02 percent), we may be tempted to refer to it as evidence of market inefficiency. But to profit from this phenomenon one must be able to identify the two portfolios *before* the Federal Reserve decision.

We now turn to the case of target banks that were involved in denied applications for mergers. This is a case of particular interest because it provides an indirect test of the information hypothesis. We have seen in Chapter II that this hypothesis attempts to explain the rise in the price of target bank shares when a merger proposal is announced. According to the information hypothesis, the price of target bank shares rises because the merger proposal reveals that these banks are undervalued. If this were the case, then the fact that the merger is denied should not affect the share price of target banks. The denial order does not take away the fact that the target bank is undervalued. But if the share price of target banks drops when the denial order is issued, then the original price increase must be attributed to factors other than undervaluation. Specifically, the original price increase must be attributed to factors that require the completion of the merger (such as synergies, removal of poor managers, etc.). A look at Table 5 indicates that the share price of target banks that were subsequently denied to merge increased, on average, by 16 percent the week the merger proposal was announced and by 22.73 percent during the 11-week period surrounding the merger announcement. But their share declined by 7.29 percent the week the denial order was issued and by 19.35 percent during the 11-week period surrounding the denial announcement. Obviously, any gains realized by the shareholders of target banks during the 11-week announcement period were wiped out during the subsequent 11-week outcome period. Also, note that the denial order was somewhat anticipated. The share price of target banks that were the subject of a denial order declined by 8.23 percent over the 5-week pre-outcome period whereas the share price of target banks that were the subject of an approval order did not change significantly over the same 5-week pre-outcome period. In summary, the evidence reported in Table 5 indicates that the regulator's decision affects the wealth of target bank shareholders and that the information hypothesis can be rejected.

## 6. Analysis of risk shifts due to mergers: A test of the diversification hypothesis

The preceding analysis examined the stock price behavior of target and bidding banks around both the announcement of an acquisition proposal and the announcement of the regulator's decision (approval or denial). We now turn to the examination of risk shifts due to mergers. The question we wish to answer is whether the variance of the stock returns of target and bidding banks have changed as a result of the merger. According to the diversification hypothesis, the merger should reduce the risk, and hence the return variability, of the merged banks. If this were the case, the risk of the merging banks following the regulator's approval of the proposed merger should be lower than their separate risks prior to the announcement of the proposed merger.

### *6.1. Measuring the risk of bank stock prices*

The total risk of a bank can be measured by the variance of its common stock returns. If the market model expressed in equation (2), Chapter III, holds, then the variance of returns can be written as:

$$\text{var}(R_{it}) = \beta_i^2 \text{ var}(R_{mt}) + \text{var}(e_{it}),$$

given that $\text{cov}(R_{mt}, e_{it})$ is equal to zero for all t. $\text{Var}(R_{it})$ denotes the variance of bank i's rate of returns, $\text{var}(R_{mt})$ the variance of the market index's rate of returns and $\text{var}(e_{it})$ the variance of bank i's abnormal returns (residual variance). The first component of total variance ($\beta_i^2 \text{var}(R_{mt})$) is referred to as systematic risk and the second component ($\text{var}(e_{it})$) as unsystematic risk. Unsystematic risk can be diversified away by security holders but systematic risk cannot since most securities have positive beta coefficients. As the number of securities held in a portfolio increases, systematic risk approaches var($R_{mt}$), the market variance, and unsystematic risk approaches zero.

Mergers, if they have any risk-reduction effect, should lower systematic risk (by lowering beta), unsystematic risk, or both. To test for possible changes in the estimated variance of return, we compare the estimated variance of bank common stock returns prior to the announcement of the merger proposal (from week −53 to week −1 *before* the week the proposed merger is announced) with the estimated variance of bank common stock returns following the regulator's *approval* of the merger (from week +1 to week +53 *after* the week the merger's approval is announced). If a change in the variance does occur, we then determine whether this change is caused by a shift in systematic risk (beta), unsystematic risk, or both. Note that any risk-reduction effect, if present, should be in principle reflected in both systematic risk (beta) and unsystematic risk.

### *6.2. Empirical results*

The empirical results are summarized in Tables 6A and 6B. The first table presents the results for target banks and the second for bidding banks. At the bottom of the tables we have the data for all banks. Above, we have the data for 3 subgroups of banks: large banks, medium-size banks and small banks. Large banks have at least $10 billion of assets before 1983 and at least $15 billion of assets after 1983; medium-size banks have assets between $1 and $10 billion before 1983 and between $1.5 and $15 billion after 1983; and small banks have at most $1 billion of assets before 1983 and at most $1.5 billion of assets after 1983. The reason we divided the sample into 3 size-related groups is to find out if risk shifts due to mergers differ according to bank size. Finally, recall that pre-announcement risk is measured prior to the announcement of the merger proposal (from week −53 to week −1 before the week the proposed merger is announced) and post-approval risk is following the regulator's approval of the merger (from week +1 to week +53 after the week the merger's approval is announced).

Total variance, beta coefficient, market variance and residual variance (unsystematic risk) are estimated for each bank in the sample and their *average* values reported in Tables 6A and 6B. We then compare the pre-announcement average risk to the post-ap-

Table 6A
Analysis of risk shift due to bank mergers: Decomposition of target banks' variance of returns according to the market model [a] for three size categories.

| *Size of target* [b] / Estimation period | Number of announcements | Average variance return | Average beta | Average variance market | Average variance residual |
|---|---|---|---|---|---|
| *Small banks* | | | | | |
| Pre-announcement [c] | 34 | 0.3151 | 0.3591 | 0.0605 | 0.2959 |
| Post-approval [d] | 6 | 0.1621 | 0.4313 | 0.0337 | 0.1496 |
| T-stat. for difference [e] | | 0.97 | −0.39 | 1.55 | 0.99 |
| *Medium banks* | | | | | |
| Pre-announcement | 31 | 0.1703 | 0.4033 | 0.0467 | 0.1591 |
| Post-approval | 7 | 0.0871 | 0.3277 | 0.0395 | 0.0785 |
| T-stat. for difference | | 2.28 | 0.68 | 1.05 | 2.44 |
| *Large banks* | | | | | |
| Pre-announcement | 2 | 0.4591 | 1.4217 | 0.0434 | 0.3613 |
| Post-approval | 1 | 0.0420 | 0.3710 | 0.0227 | 0.0389 |
| T-stat. for difference | | – | – | – | – |
| *All banks* | | | | | |
| Pre-announcement | 67 | 0.2524 | 0.4113 | 0.0536 | 0.2346 |
| Post-approval | 14 | 0.1160 | 0.3752 | 0.0358 | 0.1061 |
| T-stat. for difference | | 1.75 | 0.32 | 2.02 | 1.77 |

[a] Variance of returns = $(\text{beta})^2$ (variance of the market) + residual variance. See Chapter III for a description of the market model.

[b] Large banks have at least \$10 billion of assets before 1983 and at least \$15 billion of assets after 1983; medium banks have assets between \$1 and \$10 billion before 1983 and between \$1.5 and \$15 billion after 1983; small banks have at most \$1 billion of assets before 1983 and at most \$1.5 billion of assets after 1983.

[c] From week −53 to week −1 before the week the merger is announced.

[d] From week 1 to week 53 after the week the merger's approval is announced.

[e] T-statistics for the differences between pre-announcement and post-approval estimates of risk.

Table 6B
Analysis of risk shift due to bank mergers: Decomposition of bidding banks' variance of returns according to the market model [a] for three size categories.

| *Size of bidder* [b]<br>Estimation period | Number of announcements | Average variance return | Average beta | Average variance market | Average variance residual |
|---|---|---|---|---|---|
| *Small banks* | | | | | |
| Pre-announcement [c] | 7 | 0.2290 | 0.4760 | 0.0856 | 0.2105 |
| Post-approval [d] | 7 | 0.1385 | 0.3360 | 0.0348 | 0.1305 |
| T-stat. for difference [e] | | 1.17 | 1.30 | 2.18 | 1.10 |
| *Medium banks* | | | | | |
| Pre-announcement | 48 | 0.1360 | 0.5732 | 0.0517 | 0.1129 |
| Post-approval | 47 | 0.1501 | 0.6259 | 0.0418 | 0.1319 |
| T-stat. for difference | | −0.37 | −0.78 | 1.77 | −0.50 |
| *Large banks* | | | | | |
| Pre-announcement | 13 | 0.1602 | 0.9738 | 0.0409 | 0.1217 |
| Post-approval | 12 | 0.1544 | 1.1365 | 0.0464 | 0.0956 |
| T-stat. for difference | | 0.25 | −1.27 | −0.69 | 1.30 |
| *All banks* | | | | | |
| Pre-announcement | 68 | 0.1502 | 0.6398 | 0.0531 | 0.1246 |
| Post-approval | 66 | 0.1497 | 0.6880 | 0.0419 | 0.1251 |
| T-stat. for difference | | 0.02 | −0.75 | 2.27 | −0.02 |

[a] Variance of returns = $(\text{beta})^2$ (variance of the market) + residual variance. See Chapter III for a description of the market model.
[b] Large banks have at least $10 billion of assets before 1983 and at least $15 billion after 1983; medium banks have assets between $1 and $10 billion before 1983 and between $1.5 and $15 billion after 1983; small banks have at most $1 billion of assets before 1983 and at most $1.5 billion of assets after 1983.
[c] From week −53 to week −1 before the week the merger is announced.
[d] From week 1 to week 53 after the week the merger's approval is announced.
[e] T-statistics for the differences between pre-announcement and post approval estimates of risk.

proval average risk. A t-test for the difference in means allows us to determine whether the difference in average risk is statistically significant. Sample sizes are indicated in Tables 6A and 6B. Note that in the case of target banks (Table 6A), the post-approval sample size is significantly smaller than the pre-announcement sample size because the shares of most target banks cease trading soon after the regulator approves the merger. In the case of bidding banks (Table 6B), pre-announcement sample size and post-approval sample size are almost the same because the shares of most bidding banks keep trading after the merger is approved.

Turning first to the results for target banks, note that a significant drop in total variance is observed for the sample of all banks and that the source of this risk-reduction is a drop in *unsystematic risk* rather than a drop in the beta coefficient. We also note a size effect. Although risk-reduction is observed in all 3 size categories, it is only significant in the case of medium-size banks. The sample size is too small in the case of large banks to allow us to draw any meaningful conclusions.

A look at Table 6B indicates that bidding banks do not display any significant shift in risk. This result is inconsistent with the diversification hypothesis. But it may be partly due to the difference in size between target and bidding banks. We have seen in Chapter III (Table 1D) that target banks are, on average, 4 times smaller than bidding banks. If we assume that the correlation between the returns of target and bidding banks are the same for all pairs of merging banks, then the smaller the target relative to the bidder, the greater is the potential for risk reduction for the target bank. Note, however, that the assumption of same correlation between all pairs of merging banks is in general not valid, as we have seen in Chapter IV.

## 7. Some special cases: Cancelled mergers, multiple bids and insolvent target banks

Some special cases were excluded from our earlier analysis. These are banks that were involved in a merger proposal that was later cancelled (4 cases), target banks that were the subject of multiple bids (3 double bids and 2 triple bids), and target banks that were insolvent (technically bankrupt) at the time of the announcement of the merger proposal.

### *7.1. The case of cancelled mergers: Another test of the information hypothesis*

Merger proposals that were subsequently cancelled are of interest because they provide a further test of the information hypothesis. A cancelled merger is similar to a denied merger. If the information hypothesis is correct, then the share price of the target bank should rise when the merger is announced and remain the same when the merger is cancelled (see Section 5.2). The results are summarized in Table 7. The market model is used to estimate abnormal returns. The week the merger is announced, the share price of target banks rises on average by 11.20 percent and that of the bidding banks rises on

Table 7
Cancellation effect: Market reaction to merger announcements and the subsequent cancellation of the merger.

| | Target banks (4 cases) | Bidding banks (4 cases) |
|---|---|---|
| *Announcement of merger* | | |
| CAR[−5, −1] [a] | 8.08% (0.81) [e] | −2.15% (1.19) [e] |
| AR[0] [b] | 11.20%* (4.80) | 3.46%* (6.20) |
| CAR[+1, +5] [c] | −9.53% (1.35) | 0.60% (0.49) |
| CAR[−5, +5] [d] | 9.74% (1.08) | 1.91% (0.73) |
| *Announcement of cancellation* | | |
| CAR[−5, −1] [a] | −7.48%* (2.14) | 3.40% (0.11) |
| AR[0] [b] | −12.05%* (4.42) | −1.59% (1.27) |
| CAR[+1, +5] [c] | −4.63% (0.86) | −3.05% (0.61) |
| CAR[−5, +5] [d] | −24.16%* (3.36) | −1.24% (0.84) |

[a] Cumulative average abnormal returns over the 5-week pre-announcement period.
[b] Average abnormal returns over announcement week.
[c] Cumulative average abnormal returns over the 5-week post-announcement period.
[d] Cumulative average abnormal returns over the entire 11-week period surrounding the announcement week.
[e] Absolute value of t-statistics. Asterisks indicate significance at the 0.05 level.

average by 3.46 percent. The price reaction of target banks is the same as that reported for the full sample (see Table 4A) despite their very small sample size (only 4 cases). But the price reaction of bidding banks is the opposite of that reported for the full sample (see Table 4B): in the full sample the share price of bidding banks declined by about 1.50 percent. This result does not have an obvious explanation. It is not clear why merger proposals that are subsequently cancelled are perceived as wealth-creating investments by bidding bank shareholders, whereas merger proposals that are subsequently completed are perceived as wealth-destroying investments.

What happens when the merger proposal is cancelled? The share price of the target bank drops, on average, by 12.05 percent, eliminating the original rise in price that occurred during the week that the merger proposal was announced. As in the case of the regulator's denial order, the price behavior of target banks involved in mergers that were subsequently cancelled is inconsistent with the information hypothesis. Finally, note that the share price of bidding banks is not significantly affected by the announcement of the merger cancellation.

### *7.2. The case of multiple bids*

We have 3 cases of double bids and 2 cases of triple bids on the same target bank, thus our sample of multiple bids includes 5 target banks. These 5 banks were the subject of 5 first and second multiple bids and 2 banks were the subject of a third multiple bid. The reaction of both target and bidding bank share prices are reported in Table 8. Abnormal returns are estimated using the market model.

The price of target bank shares increased by about 25 percent during the 11-week period surrounding each one of the multiple bids. Note that the 5-week period following the first and second multiple bids does not overlap the 5-week period preceding the second and third multiple bids. We have eliminated from our sample all cases where two bids occurred less than 6 weeks apart. The principal difference between the price behavior of target bank shares involved in a single bid and those involved in multiple bids is that in

Table 8
Multiple bids effect: Market reaction to a series of bids on the same target bank.

| | CAR[−5, −1] [b] | AR[0] [c] | CAR[+1, +5] [d] | CAR[−5, +5] [e] |
|---|---|---|---|---|
| *Target banks* [a] | | | | |
| First multiple bid (5) | 7.89%* (2.78) | 14.54%* (10.99) | 26.15%* (9.19) | 24.77%* (5.80) |
| Second multiple bid (5) | 15.96%* (6.36) | 7.68%* (3.80) | 9.10%* (2.45) | 24.21%* (6.01) |
| Third multiple bid (2) | 14.29%* (4.22) | 14.57%* (7.24) | 11.24%* (2.33) | 25.72%* (4.48) |
| *Bidding banks* | | | | |
| First multiple bid (5) | 4.52% (1.34) | −2.13%* (2.08) | −7.87%* (2.49) | −5.22% (1.19) |
| Second multiple bid (5) | −10.74%* (3.49) | −1.25% (0.40) | −6.55% (1.24) | −14.01%* (2.25) |
| Third multiple bid (2) | −7.37% (1.23) | 0.38% (0.17) | −6.51% (1.17) | −13.89% (1.63) |

[a] There are 2 triple bids, and 3 double bids. Hence we have 5 cases of a first bid, 5 cases of a second bid and 2 cases of third bid.

[b] Cumulative average abnormal returns over the 5-week pre-announcement period. Absolute value of t-statistic in parentheses. Asterisks indicate significance at the 0.05 level.

[c] Average abnormal returns over the announcement week.

[d] Cumulative average abnormal returns over the 5-week post-announcement period week.

[e] Cumulative average abnormal returns over the entire 11-week period surrounding the announcement.

the former case we observed a relatively small but significant average *decline* in price during the 5-week post-announcement period (−2.24 percent; see Table 4A), whereas in the multiple-bid cases we have a relatively large and significant rise in price during the 5-week post-bid period: 26.15 percent after the first bid, 9.10 percent after the second and 11.24 percent after the third. Also, the second and third bids are not unexpected: prices rise by 15.96 percent during the 5-week period preceding the second bid and by 14.29 percent during the

5-week period preceding the third bid. Obviously, multiple bids create significantly greater wealth to target bank shareholders than do single bids. This result is consistent with previous studies (Bradley, Desai and Kim (1988) and James and Wier (1987a, 1987b)) which found that the number of (potential) bidders appears to be an important explanatory variable of market reaction.

Turning to the price behavior of bidding bank shares, we note that their price declines the week the first and second bids are made. Prices also decline during the 5-week period following a bid as well as the 5-week period preceding the second and third bids. Overall, bidding banks involved in multiple bids lose more of their shareholders' wealth than bidding banks involved in a single bid.

### *7.3. The case of insolvent target banks*

Four target banks were insolvent (technically bankrupt) at the time of the announcement of an acquisition proposal. The price behavior of the banks involved in the acquisition is reported in Table 9. The market model is used to estimate abnormal returns. Since the shares of 2 of the 4 target banks stopped trading the week following the merger announcement, the post- announcement price behavior should be interpreted with caution.

The striking result in Table 9 is the drop in the share price of target banks (11.91 percent) and the rise in the share price of bidding banks (3.32 percent). This is exactly the opposite of what we reported in all previous tests. The reason for this decline in share prices is unclear. A bankrupt bank can merge with a healthier bank. Alternatively, the Federal Deposit Insurance Corporation (FDIC) can either rescue the bank or liquidate it.

The FDIC has two methods to handle insolvent banks. In the deposit pay-off approach, the FDIC liquidates the failed bank's assets and pays off the insured depositors. In the purchase and assumption transaction (P&A) approach, the FDIC auctions the failed bank's assets, except for non-performing loans and all external liabilities. The four cases in our sample were treated by the FDIC as

Table 9
Market reaction to the announcement of a merger with a target bank that has filed for bankruptcy.

| | Target banks [a] (4 cases) | Bidding banks (4 cases) |
|---|---|---|
| *Pre-announcement period* | | |
| CAR[−5, −1] [b] | −1.16% | 5.58% |
| t(CAR) [c] | (1.07) | (0.97) |
| *Announcement week* | | |
| AR[0] [d] | −11.91%* | 3.32%* |
| t(AR) [c] | (2.14) | (2.37) |
| *Post-announcement period* | | |
| CAR[+1, +5] [e] | 40.71%* | −2.66% |
| t(CAR) [c] | (2.95) | (0.44) |
| *Entire period* | | |
| CAR[−5, +5] [f] | 28.85% | 6.24% |
| t(CAR) [c] | (0.83) | (0.98) |

[a] Trading in the shares of 2 of the 4 target banks stopped the week following the merger announcement.
[b] Cumulative average abnormal returns over the 5-week pre-announcement period.
[c] Absolute value of t-statistics. Asterisks indicate significance at the 0.05 level.
[d] Average abnormal returns over the announcement week. Three out of 4 cases have significant abnormal returns.
[e] Cumulative average abnormal returns over the 5-week post-announcement period.
[f] Cumulative average abnormal returns over the entire 11-week period surrounding the announcement week.

P&A transactions. The acquirer is determined by a first price sealed bid auction. Bidders participate with no fees, however, and are given a very short period of time (one to two days) to submit their bid. A limited number of banks and bank holding companies are invited to participate in an auction (those which meet certain criteria on size, financial health, location, etc.). Before October 1982, only in-state banks could be invited to bid for a failed bank's assets in P&A auctions. The Garn-St Germain Depository Institution Act now grants out-of-state banking organizations the opportunity to bid for large banks with total assets of $500 million or more.

Therefore, legal restrictions on out-of-state banks have limited the number of potential bidders and helped raise the bidder's returns. The effect of this auction process on the wealth of bidding banks that acquire a failed bank through an auction under P&A policy of the FDIC has been examined in several studies, which have reached contradictory conclusions. On the one hand, Sushka and Bendeck (1988) and James and Wier (1987b) find positive returns. As James and Wier conclude: "Thus, sales of failed bank assets differ in several aspects from ordinary bank acquisition. They offer an opportunity to study whether the mechanism used to sell an asset affects its price. In this paper we present evidence supporting the hypothesis that the FDIC's procedures result in wealth transfer to winning bidders". On the other hand, Pettway and Trifts (1985) and Giliberto and Varaiya (1989) report negative returns to bidding banks. Pettway and Trifts examined the market reaction to 11 winning bidders in P&A transactions over the period 1972–81 and conclude that the winning bidders overbid for failed banks. In a recent comprehensive study, Giliberto and Varaiya looked at a sample of 219 P&A transactions over the period 1965–1985 and conclude that the winning bidders indeed overpayed. Finally, Cornett and De (1989), using a sample of 10 acquisition proposals that involved failed banks, report that the *out-of-state* bidding banks experience negative abnormal return insignificantly different from zero.

The sample in this study includes three in-state and one out-of-state acquisitions. The findings for this small sample of failed bank acquisitions are consistent with the result of James and Wier, namely, positive abnormal returns to winning bidders representing a wealth transfer from the FDIC to acquiring banks.

## 8. Summary and concluding remarks

This chapter examined the stock market reaction to the announcement of bank mergers and the subsequent release of Federal Reserve decisions regarding approval or denial of the proposed merger. We have also examined three special cases of merger announcements. The case of merger proposals that were subsequently cancelled; the case of mergers involving multiple bids; and the case of merger proposals in which the target bank was insolvent (technically bankrupt) at the time the merger proposal was announced. The examination of the stock market reaction to these announcements has shed some light on the issue of why banks (and other firms) merge.

Below we present a summary of our results and their interpretation:

(1) The price of a sample of 118 target bank shares that were the subject of a single bid increased, on average, by about 11.50 percent during the week the announcement of the intended acquisition is made. Bidding banks share prices, however, decreased on average by about 1.50 percent for a sample of 126 bids. These results are unaffected by the methodology employed to estimate the stock price reaction to the proposed mergers. They are consistent with both the manager-utility-maximization hypothesis and the hubris hypothesis of mergers. Under these hypotheses, banks may engage in activities that have negative net present values because the objective of bank managers is not consistent with the principle of shareholder wealth maximization. If most acquirers behave as size-maximizers, or are infected by hubris, the price of *target* bank shares will be bid up to the point where acquisition proposals become negative net-present-value investments for acquiring banks.

(2) The reaction of target bank stock prices to the acquisition announcement is anticipated by the market. Prices increase, on average, by 4 percent during the week immediately preceding the announcement week. For bidding banks, however, no abnormal price movements are observed in the sample of bids prior to the announcement week.

(3) The market for bank mergers is efficient. No abnormal price movements are observed in the sample of target banks and the sample of bids after the announcement week. The price adjustment

of target and bidding banks to the information revealed by the merger announcement is completed by the time the merger proposal is announced.

(4) There is some tentative evidence that bank mergers create net aggregate wealth to shareholders. The dollar gains realized by the shareholders of target banks exceed, on average, the dollar losses incurred by the shareholders of bidding banks. This result is inconsistent with the manager-utility-maximization and the hubris hypotheses of mergers, which predicts that mergers do not create net aggregate wealth to shareholders. These hypotheses state that mergers should only induce a straightforward wealth transfer from bidding bank shareholders to target bank shareholders.

(5) Bidder share prices are not significantly affected by the Federal Reserve decision to either approve or deny the proposed merger. The subsample of bidders whose acquisition proposal was later approved by the regulator experienced an average drop in price of 1.70 percent during the week the merger proposal was announced. But, interestingly, the subsample of bidders whose acquisition proposal was later denied by the regulator experienced no significant change in price during the week the merger proposal was announced. This result is consistent with the hypothesis that the market has the ability to predict a denial order and hence bidder stock prices are not affected by the announcement of the merger proposal.

(6) The share prices of target banks whose merger has been approved by the Federal Reserve increase, on average, by 1.69 percent during the week the approval order is issued, but the share prices of target banks whose merger has been denied by the Federal Reserve declined, on average, by 7.29 percent during the week the denial order is issued. Any gains realized by the shareholders of target banks during the merger proposal period were wiped out during the subsequent period surrounding the denial announcement. These results are not consistent with the information hypothesis. According to this hypothesis, the price of target bank shares rises because the merger proposal reveals that these banks are undervalued. If this were the case, then the fact that the merger is denied

should not affect the share price of target banks. The denial order by itself does not take away the fact that the target bank is undervalued.

(7) The risk of bidding banks does not seem to be affected by mergers. The variability of stock returns before the announcement of the merger proposal is not significantly different from the variability of stock returns after the Federal Reserve has issued its approval order. The risk of target banks, however, seems to be affected by mergers. Both total variability and unsystematic variability in the stock returns of target banks *decreases* after the merger is approved. It seems then that the shareholders of target banks benefit doubly from the merger: their wealth increases and their risk is reduced. This result is consistent with the diversification hypothesis according to which a merger should reduce the risk, and hence the return variability of the merged banks. But it is not clear why the gains from risk-reduction accrue to the shareholders of target banks. This phenomenon can be related to the fact that the average size of target banks is significantly smaller than that of bidding banks.

(8) We have shown that the share price of target banks drops, on average, 12.05 percent during the week a proposed merger is cancelled. This drop eliminates the original rise in price that occurred during the week the merger proposal was announced and is inconsistent with the information hypothesis.

(9) Multiple bids create significantly greater wealth to target bank shareholders than do single bids. Bidding banks involved in multiple bids lose more of their shareholders' wealth than bidding banks involved in a single bid.

(10) Finally, we found that during the week bidding banks announce their intention to merge with a target bank that is insolvent, the price of the *target* bank declines and that of the *bidding* bank rises, on average. This is exactly the opposite of what we reported in all the previous tests. These findings can be explained by the sale mechanism used by the FDIC in failed bank auctions. This mechanism limits the number of bidders and results in wealth transfer from the FDIC to the acquiring banks.

CHAPTER VI

# EXPLAINING CAPITAL MARKET REACTION TO MERGER ANNOUNCEMENTS

## 1. Introduction

The empirical evidence on bank mergers reported in the previous chapter indicates that, during the week a merger proposal is announced, the stock price of target banks increases, on average, by 11.50 percent and that of bidding banks decreases, on average, by 1.50 percent. Note, however, that target bank stock prices do not all rise by the same magnitude. Actually, some stock prices do not change while others even drop (see Table 4A). Likewise, bidding bank stock prices do not all fall by the same magnitude. Some stock prices do not change while others rise (see Table 4B).

How can these differences in market reaction across our sample of target and bidding banks be explained? The objective of this chapter is to examine this question by identifying a number of exogenous variables which can explain the observed cross-sectional differences in market reaction during the announcement week of a merger proposal. These variables are described in Section 2 below. They include: (1) whether the merger is intrastate or interstate, (2) whether the target bank is acquired for cash or securities, (3) whether the relative size of the target and bidding banks is large or small, and (4) whether the target bank performed well or poorly prior to the announcement of the merger proposal.

Several methodologies are used to explain the cross-sectional differences in the stock price reactions of target and bidding banks when merger proposals are announced. First, a dichotomization analysis is carried out. Second, a multiple-variable cross-sectional regression analysis is performed. The first method consists in separating our sample into two non-overlapping subsamples according to an exogenous variable (such as cash versus securities, intrastate versus interstate, etc.) and comparing the market reaction of the two subsamples. One weakness of this approach is that it analyzes one variable at a time and does not account for the effect of the other exogenous variables. This weakness is corrected by employing a multiple-variable cross-sectional regression analysis with dummy variables, as shown in Sections 8 and 9. But this approach has its own limitations. It imposes a linear relationship between the cross sectional variations in stock price reactions and the exogenous variables, a condition that may not be satisfied in reality. In addition, the confounding effect of several variables (multicollinearity) makes it harder to analyze the effect of different variables. Nevertheless, the use of both approaches should allow us to shed some light on the factors that cause the stock price of target and bidding banks to change in response to the announcement of a merger proposal. This, in turn, will permit us to test some of the alternative merger hypotheses expounded in Chapter II.

## 2. Alternative explanatory variables

The list of explanatory, or independent, variables is given in Table 10A. Note that it does not include one of the binary variables mentioned above: whether the merger is intrastate or interstate. The minimum, average, and maximum values of these variables as well as their standard deviations are found in Table 10B for a sample of 126 observations representing either single banks (V2, V6, V7, V9, V10 and V11) or pairs of banks (V1, V4, V5 and V8).

*Relative size*. The ratio of the target bank's total assets to the bidding bank's total assets at the end of the calendar year preceding the takeover announcement week. Its average value is 0.3784, meaning that bidding banks are, on average, 2.64 larger than their targets. But not all bidders are larger than their target since relative size is sometimes greater than one (the maximum relative size is 2.6250, meaning that in this case the bidder's size is only 38.10 percent that of the target). The absolute size of the bidder's assets varies from a low of $256 million to a high of $102,478 million (note that the absolute size in Table 10B is stated in logarithms of thousand

Table 10A
List of independent variables used in the cross sectional analysis of the abnormal returns of target and bidding banks during the takeover announcement week.

| | | |
|---|---|---|
| V1 | = | *Relative size* at the end of the calendar year preceding the takeover announcement week. |
| | = | Total assets of target bank divided by the total assets of bidding bank. |
| V2 | = | *Absolute size of bidding bank* at the end of the calendar year preceding the takeover announcement week. |
| | = | Logarithm of the total assets of bidding bank. |
| V3 | = | *Means of takeover payment.* |
| | = | Dummy variable equal to −1 if payment is for cash and 0 if payment is for combination of cash and securities. |
| V4 | = | *Relative capitalization* at the end of the calendar year preceding the takeover announcement week. |
| | = | Total equity of target bank as a percentage of target bank total assets divided by total equity of bidding bank as a percentage of bidding bank total assets. |
| V5 | = | *Relative profitability* over the two calendar years preceding the takeover announcement week. |
| | = | Average return on equity (ROE) of target bank divided by average return on equity of bidding bank (ROE is the ratio of year-end after-tax earnings to the average of beginning and ending total equity position; average ROE is average of ROE one calendar years before the merger announcement and two calendar year before the merger announcement). |

dollars). Relative size may be a significant variable in the creation of monopoly power and for the examination of potential economies of scale.

*Relative capitalization.* The ratio of the target's equity (as a percentage of total assets) to that of the bidder's equity. It is on average equal to one, meaning that target and bidding banks have, on average, the same equity-to-total-assets ratio. But here again we have wide differences around the mean value (see minimum and maximum values in Tables 10B). A bank's equity position (its capital adequacy position) is an issue of special importance in banking due to the fact that regulators use this measure frequently to assess the stability of banking organizations.

Table 10A (continued)

| | | |
|---|---|---|
| V6 | = | *Relative profitability of target bank* over the two calendar years preceding the takeover announcement week. |
| | = | Average return on equity of target bank divided by average return on equity of banks in the state or the region where the target bank is located (see V5 for definition of average ROE). |
| V7 | = | *Stock market performance of target bank* over a period of 52 weeks preceding the takeover announcement week. |
| | = | Cumulative abnormal return (using the market model) of target bank common stock from week 58 to week 6 preceding the takeover announcement week. |
| V8 | = | *Degree of diversification* between target and bidding banks over a period of 52 weeks preceding the takeover announcement week. |
| | = | Correlation coefficient between the stock market returns of target and bidding banks from week 58 to week 6 preceding the takeover announcement week. |
| V9 | = | *Number of potential target banks.* Number of banks in the same size group as the target bank (banks are assigned to one of three size groups). |
| V10 | = | *Number of potential bidding banks.* Number of banks in the size groups that are larger than the size group in which the target bank belongs (banks are assigned to one of three size groups). |
| V11 | = | *Concentration ratio in state of target bank.* Total deposits of the 3 largest banks in the state divided by the total deposits of all banks in the state. For mergers that took place before 1983, the concentration ratio is calculated at the end of 1978. For mergers that took place in 1983 and beyond, the concentration ratio is calculated at the end of 1983. |

In August 1988, following the Basle Convergence Agreement (see Appendix I), the Federal Reserve Board implemented a new risk-based capital standard (see Appendix II) along an international agreement to adopt uniform capital adequacy standards. These new standards will have a major impact on how banks manage their assets, price their products and services, and structure their capital. Moreover, because the rules will change the treatment of goodwill, the regulation will have a significant effect on bank expansion strategies and will alter the structure of most bank combinations.

Table 10B
Average values of independent variables (each variable has 126 observations).

| Variable [a] | Symbol | Mean value | Standard deviation | Minimum value | Maximum value |
|---|---|---|---|---|---|
| Relative size | V1 | 0.3784 | 0.3857 | 0.0361 | 2.6250 |
| Absolute size of bidder | V2 | 8.5287 | 1.1016 | 5.5452 | 11.5374 |
| Relative capitalization | V4 | 1.0789 | 0.3166 | 0.3007 | 2.3967 |
| Relative profitability | V5 | 0.7613 | 0.4485 | −1.1491 | 1.7088 |
| Relative profitability of target | V6 | 0.9047 | 0.5070 | −1.0806 | 1.6816 |
| Market performance of target | V7 | 0.1359 | 0.3966 | −0.8900 | 1.0819 |
| Degree of diversification | V8 | 0.1538 | 0.1640 | −0.3084 | 0.6130 |
| Number of potential targets | V9 | 26.04 | 37.95 | 2.00 | 200.00 |
| Number of potential bidders | V10 | 13.79 | 35.44 | 0 | 190.00 |
| Concentration ratio | V11 | 0.3631 | 0.1340 | 0.1500 | 0.8870 |

[a] See Table 10A for the definitions of the independent variables.

The new risk-adjusted capital adequacy standard has profound and immediate implications for the management of all bank holding companies and the banks under their control. For those bank holding companies that do not presently meet the final 8 percent total capital and 4 percent core capital ratios, the impact is relatively straightforward. Despite the fact that the new standards do not officially become effective until the end of 1992, banks whose risk-weighted capital ratios fall below the 1992 requirements will be under a great deal of pressure to bring their ratios up to the 8 percent minimum as soon as possible. Even if the stock market were not penalizing capital-short banks (see below), the incentive to raise ratios would be strong because satisfaction of the final 8 percent requirement will be a prerequisite for regulatory approval of proposed mergers and acquisitions even before the 1992 deadline. Capital-short bank holding companies will adjust their asset mixes by shifting into low risk-weight investments to raise their risk-weighted capital ratios as quickly and as inexpensively as possible. If adjustments on the asset side are insufficient, these bank holding companies will seek to raise the least-expensive forms of capital that will enable them to conform to the new guidelines. An alternative strategy for a bank to improve its capital asset ratio would be to merge with a high capital ratio institution (in this respect, see for example, Dahl and Shrieves (1989)).

*Relative profitability*. The ratio of the target's return-on-equity (ROE) to that of the bidder's ROE. Its mean value is 0.7613, that is, target banks are, on average, less profitable than their bidders. But some target banks are more profitable than their bidders (note that the maximum value is higher than one in Table 10B). The relative profitability of a target bank (variable V6) is the ratio of the target's ROE to that of the average ROE of banks in the state or the region where the target bank is located. Target banks are, on average, less profitable than the other banks operating in the same geographical area.

*The stock market performance of target banks*. Measured by estimating the bank's cumulative abnormal stock returns (using the market model described in Chapter III) from week 58 to week 6 preceding the merger announcement week. The average cumulative abnormal returns (CAR) is 13.59 percent with a standard deviation of 39.66 percent. Some target banks outperformed the market (the maximum CAR is 108.19 percent) while others underperformed it (the minimum CAR is −89.00 percent).

*The correlation between a target bank stock returns and those of its bidder*. Measured by the correlation coefficient between the stock returns of the target and those of the bidder from week 58 to week 6 preceding the merger announcement week. Recall that the lower the value of that correlation coefficient, the higher the potential diversification gains that can be achieved via a merger. The average value of the correlation coefficient is 0.1538 with a minimum value of −0.3084 and a maximum value of 0.6130. There is a wide spread in correlation coefficients, that is, the potential for risk reduction via diversification through merger exhibits significant cross-sectional variation in our sample.

The last three independent variables listed in Table 10A are the *number of alternative target banks, the number of potential bidding banks* and the *concentration ratio* in the state in which the target bank is located. The first variable measures the number of banks in the same size group as the target bank (banks are assigned to one of three size groups as discussed in Chapter V, Section 6.2). The average number of alternative target banks is 26 with a minimum value of 2 and a maximum of 200. The second variable, the number of potential bidding banks, measures the number of banks that are larger than the size group in which the target bank belongs. The average number of potential bidding banks is 14 with a minimum value of zero and a maximum of 190. Previous studies by James and Wier (1987a, 1987b), and Cornett and De (1989) found that gains to acquirers are negatively related to the number of potential bidders. Moreover, this variable was found to be one of the significant variables in explaining the magnitude of market reaction. Finally, the third variable, the concentration ratio, measures the ratio of the deposits of the three largest banks in a state to the deposits of all banks in that state. It is a measure of the degree of banking competition in that state. The average value of that ratio is 36.31 percent with a minimum value of 15.00 percent (lowest concentration and highest degree of competition) and a maximum value of 88.70 percent (highest concentration and lowest degree of competition). The concentration ratio is used as a surrogate for potential monopoly power.

## 3. Market reaction to alternative means of payment in bank mergers: Cash offers versus security offers

Some target banks are acquired for cash, some for securities issued by the bidding banks (these could be common or preferred stocks as well as straight or convertible debt) and others for a combination of cash and securities. The question then is whether the means of payment has any significance and, if it has, how can it be explained. Several studies have shown that the abnormal returns of target and bidding firms are significantly higher in the case of cash offers than in the case of security offers (Huang and Walkling (1987); Harris,

Table 11A
A summary of alternative hypotheses regarding the reaction of target and bidding banks' stock prices in response to an acquisition for cash vs. an acquisition for stocks.

| Alternative hypothesis | Impact on target-bank stock | Impact on bidding-bank stock |
|---|---|---|
| 1. *Personal tax effects* | | |
| Hypothesis | A cash offer creates an immediate tax liability to the shareholders of the target bank who are taxed on the difference between what they initially paid for their shares and the cash they receive when they sell these shares to the bidding bank. In the case of a stock offer, the tax liability is deferred until the stock is sold. Hence, target-bank shareholders should prefer stock offers to cash offers and higher bids should be made in cash offers in order to compensate target-bank shareholders for the incremental tax-liability they create. | Cash acquisitions are an alternative to cash dividends. The former may create future capital gains whereas the latter creates immediate income. Capital gains, however, are taxed at a lower rate than dividend income. Hence, bidding-bank shareholders should prefer cash acquisitions (and no incremental dividend payments) to stock acquisitions (and possible incremental dividend payments) because the former reduces the present value of their personal tax liability. |
| Implication for abnormal returns | Target-bank abnormal returns should be higher when the announced takeover will be paid with cash rather than stocks. | Bidding-bank abnormal returns should be higher when the announced takeover will be paid with cash rather than stocks. |

Franks and Mayer (1987); Wansley, Lane and Yang (1983)). In Section 3.2 we examine if this phenomenon is also observed in a sample of takeovers involving banks. In Section 3.1 we review the

Table 11A (continued)

| Alternative hypotheses | Impact on target-bank stock | Impact on bidding-bank stock |
|---|---|---|
| 2. *Agency effects* | | |
| Hypothesis | | Define free cash flow as cash flow in excess of what is needed to finance all of the bank's profitable investments. According to Jensen (1986), management has a tendency to use free cash flow to make unprofitable investments that expand resources under its control rather than returning the excess cash to shareholders. Hence, bidding-bank shareholders should prefer cash offers because cash offers divert free cash flow away from unprofitable internal investments that benefit management at the expense of shareholders. |
| Implication for abnormal returns | | Bidding-bank abnormal returns should be higher when the announced takeover will be paid with cash rather than stocks. |

various hypotheses that were put forward to explain this phenomenon.

### *3.1. Why should cash offers differ from security offers?*

Higher abnormal returns associated with cash offers compared to security offers have been explained by personal-tax effects, agency

Table 11A (continued)

| Alternative hypotheses | Impact on target-bank stock | Impact on bidding-bank stock |
|---|---|---|
| 3. *Information effects* | | |
| Hypothesis | Target-bank shareholders will prefer stock offers whenever they believe their shares are undervalued because they can retain an equity participation in the merged bank allowing them to capture some of the subsequent gains when the undervaluation is revealed (Hansen (1987)). Since target-bank shareholders prefer stock offers to cash offers, a higher bid must be made in order to induce them to accept a cash offer. | Bidders will make a stock offer whenever they believe their shares are overvalued and cash offers whenever they believe their shares are undervalued (Myers and Majluf (1984)). Hence stock offers indicate that bidding banks believe their shares are overvalued and cash offers indicate that they are undervalued. |
| Implication for abnormal returns | Target-banks abnormal returns should be higher when the announced takeover will be paid in cash rather than stocks. | Bidding-banks abnormal returns should be higher when the announced takeover will be paid with cash rather than stocks because the former reveals that the bidding-bank stock may be undervalued and the latter reveals that it may be overvalued. |

effects and information effects, and capital adequacy position. These alternative explanations and their implications have been summarized in Table 11A.

*Personal tax effects*. A cash offer creates an immediate tax liability to the shareholders of the target bank, who are taxed on their capital gains. That is, they are taxed on the difference between the price they initially paid for their shares and the cash they receive when they sell their shares to the bidding bank. But in the case of a security offer, the tax liability, under certain circumstances, can be deferred until the stock is sold. Although the tax laws usually treat any sale or transfer of stock as a taxable event, Chapter 368 of the Internal Revenue Code lists several types of transactions that may be treated as a tax free exchange of shares in a merger. (For details, see Beatty, Santomero and Smirlock (1987) pp. 18–21.) Also, a cash offer allows an acquiring firm to raise the depreciation basis of the acquired assets to their market value. Hence, target bank shareholders should prefer *security* offers to *cash* offers and *higher* bids should be made in cash offers in order to compensate target bank shareholders for the incremental tax-liability they create. The implication is that target bank abnormal returns should be higher when the announced takeover will be paid with cash rather than securities, to offset the tax burden of the selling stockholders.

What about the reaction of bidding bank stocks? Personal tax effects can also help explain the higher abnormal returns associated with cash offers. The argument rests on the proposition that cash acquisitions are often an alternative to cash dividends. That is, a cash-rich firm can either make a cash acquisition or make a cash dividend. The former may create future capital gains whereas the latter creates immediate income which is taxed at a higher rate than capital gains. Hence, bidding bank shareholders should prefer cash acquisitions (and no incremental dividend payments) to security offers (and possible incremental dividend payments) because the former reduces the present value of their personal tax liability. The implication is that we should observe higher abnormal returns for bidding bank stocks when the announced takeover will be paid with cash rather than securities.

*Agency effects*. Agency effects provide an additional explanation for the higher abnormal returns of bidding banks in the case of cash offers. The argument is based on the notion of free cash flow, which is defined as cash flow in excess of what is needed to finance profitable investments. In principle this free cash flow should be returned to the bank's shareholders either in the form of a cash dividend or via a stock repurchase program. According to Jensen (1986), management has a tendency to use free cash flow to make unprofitable investments that expand the resources under its control rather than returning it to shareholders. Hence, bidding bank shareholders should prefer cash offers because they divert free cash flow away from unprofitable internal investments that benefit management at the expense of shareholders. The implication is that we should observe higher abnormal returns for bidding bank stocks when the announced takeover will be paid with cash rather than securities.

*Information (signalling) effects.* Information (signalling) effects will occur whenever shareholders believe that their shares are not correctly valued by the market. Suppose that target bank shareholders believe their shares are undervalued. In this case they will prefer a stock offer because they can retain an equity participation in the combined banks. This will allow them to capture some of the subsequent gains when the undervaluation is revealed (Hansen (1987)). The problem with this argument, however, is that it should be symmetrical. That is, if target bank shareholders believe their shares are overvalued, they should prefer cash offers. But if their shares are overvalued and *bidders know it*, there will be no takeover attempts. Assuming the argument is valid (asymmetric information), then target bank shareholders prefer stock offers to cash offers and a higher bid must be made in order to induce them to accept cash offers. As a consequence, the abnormal returns of target banks should be higher when the announced takeover will be paid in cash rather than stocks.

Information effects are also at work in a world of asymmetric information in the case of bidding banks. If the bidding bank's managers possess information about the value of their firm, independent of the acquisition, which is not reflected in the pre-acquisition stock price, the bidding bank will finance the acquisition in the most profitable way for the existing stockholders. In this context, suppose that bidders believe their shares are overvalued. In this case they will make a stock offer. But if they believe their shares are undervalued they will make a cash offer (Myers and Majluf (1984)). Accordingly, stock offers signal to the market that bidding banks believe their shares are overvalued and cash offers signal that they are undervalued. Hence, the abnormal returns of bidding banks should be higher when the announced merger will be paid with cash rather than stocks. This is because mergers paid with cash reveal that the bidding bank stock may be undervalued and the mergers paid with stock reveal that bidding bank stock may be overvalued.

*Capital-adequacy effects*. The structure of a business combination may have a dramatic effect on the methods of reporting income and on the measurement of equity capital in the merged organization. Two methods of reporting a business combination are considered by the accounting profession. In Accounting Principal Board Opinion No. 16 the 12 requirements for treating a business combination as a pooling of interests are specified. All other transactions are accounted for by the purchase method.

Essentially, the pooling of interest method is allowed when the nature of the transaction is such that the owners of the separate companies combine efforts in the new merged company. The purchase method involves a group of owners selling its interest to the other group. Consequently, the equity capital of the merged company under the pooling of interest method is the *combined* equity of the previous separate group. The equity capital of the surviving bank under the purchased method is the equity capital of the *acquiring bank* (the same as before the merger). Given the recent emphasis on capital adequacy, such considerations should have an effect on the structuring of bank mergers.

Note that the first three explanations (taxes, agency, and information) make the same prediction for both target and bidding banks. Both should exhibit higher abnormal returns when the announced merger will be paid in cash rather than securities.

On the other hand, capital adequacy considerations imply that a merger announcement involving an exchange of securities will result in a higher capital-to-asset ratio for the merged bank and improve that bank's capital-adequacy position compared to a cash offer. In the current banking regulatory environment this situation should lead to higher abnormal returns.

### *3.2. Empirical evidence*

*Abnormal returns to target bank shareholders.* Our sample of 118 target banks was divided into three subsamples. The first contains the 24 target banks that received a cash offer. The second contains the 39 target banks that received an offer for cash and securities, and the third contains the 55 target banks that received a security offer.

The abnormal returns during the weeks surrounding the merger announcements for each means of payment are reported in the upper left-hand side of Table 11B. The differential returns between the three types of means of payment are reported in the lower left-hand side of Table 11B. Abnormal returns associated with cash offers exceed, on average, those associated with security offers by 5.76 percent during the week the merger proposals are announced. This is the only significant return differential reported in Table 11B. Although cumulative abnormal returns associated with cash offers are higher than those associated with security offers by 3.29 percent during the entire 11-week period surrounding the merger announcement week, these excess returns are not significantly different from zero (their t-statistic equals 0.60). We conclude that there is some evidence that abnormal returns associated with cash offers exceed those associated with security offers, though this phenomenon manifests itself mostly during the week the merger proposal is announced.

*Abnormal returns to bidding bank shareholders.* Our sample of 126 bids was divided into three subsamples. The first contains the 26 bids that were made for cash. The second contains the 42 bids that were made for cash and securities, and the third contains the 58 bids that were made for securities only.

The abnormal returns during the weeks surrounding the merger announcements for each means of payment are reported in the upper

Table 11B

Target and bidding banks' abnormal returns during periods surrounding the announcement of a takeover grouped according to whether the offer is for cash, securities or cash and securities. [a]

| Means of Payment | Target banks | | | | | Bidding banks | | | | |
|---|---|---|---|---|---|---|---|---|---|---|
| | Sample size | CAR[−5, −1] [b] | AR[0] [c] | CAR[+1, +5] [d] | CAR[−5, +5] [e] | Sample size | CAR[−5, −1] [b] | AR[0] [c] | CAR[+1, +5] [d] | CAR[−5, +5] [e] |
| Cash only | 24 | 4.13%* (3.18) | 15.14%* (21.64) | −2.72% (1.13) | 16.54%* (7.91) | 26 | −1.40% (1.07) | −0.29% (0.37) | 0.18% (0.04) | −1.57% (0.87) |
| Cash and securities | 39 | 6.79%* (5.61) | 12.38%* (23.33) | −1.42% (0.58) | 17.75%* (10.42) | 42 | 0.61% (0.22) | −1.75%* (4.85) | 0.93% (0.78) | −0.22% (0.87) |
| Securities only | 55 | 6.40%* (6.70) | 9.38%* (26.28) | −2.53%* (2.13) | 13.25%* (11.01) | 58 | −1.71% (1.75) | −2.26%* (3.88) | −3.33%* (3.93) | −7.30%* (5.00) |
| [cash] − [sec.] [f] | – | −2.27% (0.71) | 5.76%* (1.84) | −0.19% (0.01) | 3.29% (0.60) | – | 0.31% (0.33) | 1.97%* (1.88) | 3.51%* (2.08) | 5.73%* (1.82) |
| [cash] − [cash & sec.] [g] | – | −2.66% (0.79) | 2.76% (0.58) | −1.30% (0.73) | −1.21% (0.23) | – | −2.01% (1.48) | 1.46% (1.45) | −0.71% (0.37) | −1.35% (0.73) |
| [cash & sec.] − [sec.] [h] | – | 0.39% (0.15) | 2.90% (0.92) | 1.11% (0.68) | 4.50% (0.93) | – | 2.32% (1.41) | 0.51% (0.44) | 4.26% (2.72) | 7.08%* (2.57) |

[a] Sample period is from January 1968 to June 1987. Absolute value of t-statistics are in parentheses.
[b] Cumulative average abnormal returns over the 5-week pre-announcement period.
[c] Average abnormal returns over the announcement week.
[d] Cumulative average abnormal returns over the 5-week post-announcement period.
[e] Cumulative average abnormal returns over the entire 11-week period surrounding the announcement week.
[f] Differential returns between cash offers and offers for securities. Asterisks indicate significance at the 0.05 level.
[g] Differential returns between cash offers and offers for cash and securities.
[h] Differential returns between offers for cash and securities and offers for securities.

right-hand side of Table 11B. The differential returns between the three types of means of payment are reported in the lower right-hand side of Table 11B. As predicted, abnormal returns associated with cash offers are significantly higher than those associated with security offers during the announcement week (1.97 percent) as well as during the 5-week post-announcement period (3.51 percent) and the entire 11-week period surrounding the announcement week (5.73 percent). It is also interesting to note that bidding bank abnormal returns are *not* significantly different from zero when the announced mergers will be paid in cash, whereas they are significantly negative when the announced mergers will be paid with securities only. This means that the negative price reaction of bidding bank stocks when these banks announce their intention to merger may be attributed to factors such as personal taxes, agency costs and information asymmetry associated with the offer itself rather than any direct implications of the merger.

These results are consistent with the findings reported in a number of studies that have examined the impact of the medium-of-payment on bidding firm returns. Travlos (1987), who studied a sample of 167 acquisitions, concludes that "the results on pure stock exchange bidding firms show that their stockholders experience significant losses at the announcement of takeover proposal. On the other hand, the results on cash-financing bidding firms show that their stockholders earn 'normal' rates of return on the announcement date". Thus, the unique importance of capital adequacy in banking does not change the importance of the signalling hypothesis. It should be noted, however, that in a recent paper, Cornett and De (1989), reached strikingly different results for a sample of interstate bank mergers. They found that the medium of exchange has no effect on bidder returns in interstate bank mergers.

## 4. Interstate versus intrastate mergers

There is some evidence that the market reaction to the announcement of an interstate merger differs significantly from the market reaction to the announcement of an intrastate merger (de Cossio,

Trifts and Scanlon (1988)). Below we first discuss why this phenomenon should occur and then examine the evidence obtained from our sample of banks.

### *4.1. Why should interstate mergers differ from intrastate mergers?*

The prohibition of interstate mergers has prevented banks from expanding beyond their state borders. We have seen in Chapter I that the use of a number of loopholes and the recent opening by some states of their borders to out-of-state banks have allowed some banks to engage in interstate mergers. What are the incentives for a bank to undertake an interstate merger rather than an intrastate merger? Of all the motives for bank mergers we surveyed in Chapter II, the diversification motive seems to be the most plausible reason for a bank to want to merge with an out-of-state bank. We have also argued in Chapter IV that out-of-state banks generally provide higher opportunities for risk-reduction via diversification than in-state banks.

What about synergies as a motive for merger? Synergies, if they exist, should be easier to achieve when the two merging banks operate in the same geographical area and within the same market rather than in two separate and distant markets. In other words, synergies, if available, are most likely to be exploited in the case of intrastate mergers than in the case of interstate mergers. It can also be argued that interstate mergers, because of the challenge they raise in integrating two banks operating in separate and distant markets, will provide little or no synergetic gains. If this argument is valid then interstate mergers will create, on average, more wealth to shareholders than intrastate mergers, but only if the risk-reduction benefit of diversification via interstate mergers exceeds the incremental synergetic gains that could be achieved via intrastate mergers. However, it is doubtful that the potential gains of interstate diversification will exceed, on average, the potential intrastate synergic gains. We should therefore expect interstate mergers to create less wealth than intrastate mergers. The evidence is reported and discussed in the following sections. In addition, when comparing intrastate bank mergers with interstate bank mergers, we should recall that the number of potential bidders increases when the prohibition on geographical expansion is relaxed. Therefore, it is expected that in interstate banking mergers, multiple bidding would be more likely, and hence bidder returns should be lower.

### *4.2. Geographical effect*

Here we compare the market reaction to the announcement of intrastate mergers to the market reaction to the announcement of interstate mergers by dividing our total sample of merger announcements into two subsamples. One contains all intrastate merger announcements and the other all interstate merger announcements that were made between January 1968 and June 1987.

We have argued in the previous section that intrastate mergers should be more beneficial to shareholders than interstate mergers and, if the market for corporate control is efficient, most of these gains will accrue to the shareholders of target banks.

*Abnormal returns to target bank shareholders.* Of the 118 target banks in our sample, 72 were the subject of an in-state bid and 46 the subject of an out-of-state bid. The abnormal returns associated with each type of bid and the differential returns between the two types of bid are reported in the upper part of Table 12A. As expected, both types of merger announcements produce an increase in the stock price of target banks during the week the merger is announced as well as over the entire 11-week period surrounding the announcement of the merger proposal. But the positive price reaction is higher in the case of intrastate mergers. For example, during the entire 11-week period, the stock price of target banks rises on average by 17.77 percent in the case of an in-state bid and by 11.71 percent in the case of an out-of-state bid. The difference, however, is not statistically significant.

*Abnormal returns to bidding bank shareholders.* Bidding banks made 118 bids, 78 for in-state banks and 48 for out-of-state banks. The abnormal returns associated with each type of bid and the differential returns between the two types of bid are reported in the

Table 12A
Geographical effect. Differential market reaction to takeover announcements: [a]
Intrastate versus interstate.

| | Intrastate | | Interstate | | Differential returns | |
|---|---|---|---|---|---|---|
| | Return | (t-stat.) | Return | (t-stat.) | Return | (t-stat.) |
| *Target banks* | | | | | | |
| Sample size | 72 | | 46 | | – | |
| CAR[−5, −1] [b] | 7.49%* | (8.47) | 3.85%* | (4.20) | 3.64% | (1.50) |
| AR[0] [c] | 12.25%* | (36.05) | 10.44%* | (20.75) | 1.81% | (0.59) |
| CAR[+1, +5] [d] | −1.97% | (1.22) | −2.58%* | (2.13) | 0.61% | (0.44) |
| CAR[−5, +5] [e] | 17.77%* | (15.75) | 11.71%* | (7.65) | 6.06% | (1.35) |
| *Bidding banks* | | | | | | |
| Sample size | 78 | | 48 | | – | |
| CAR[−5, −1] [b] | −0.48% | (1.19) | −2.02%* | (1.86) | 1.54% | (1.22) |
| AR[0] [c] | −0.92%* | (2.17) | −2.93%* | (6.68) | 2.01%* | (2.45) |
| CAR[+1, +5] [d] | −0.14% | (0.64) | −2.65%* | (2.54) | 2.51%* | (1.98) |
| CAR[−5, +5] [e] | −1.54% | (1.66) | −7.60%* | (4.91) | 6.06%* | (2.58) |

[a] Over the period January 1968 to June 1987. Absolute value of t-statistics in parentheses. Asterisks indicate significance at the 0.05 level. See Table 1C for a breakdown of interstate cases.
[b] Cumulative average abnormal returns over the 5-week pre-announcement period.
[c] Average abnormal returns over the announcement week.
[d] Cumulative average abnormal returns over the 5-week post-announcement period.
[e] Cumulative average abnormal returns over the entire 11-week period surrounding the announcement week.

lower part of Table 12A. During the pre-merger announcement period there is a significant negative market reaction in the case of interstate mergers (−2.02 percent) but no significant reaction in the case of intrastate mergers. These findings are consistent with the bidder-competition hypothesis, which predicts a negative relationship between bidders' returns and the number of bidders. These results are in contrast with those reported by Cornett and De (1989), who document significant positive announcement-period abnormal returns for bidding banks in interstate mergers. Note, however, that the differential return (intrastate minus interstate) is not significantly different from zero.

During the announcement week there is a significant negative market reaction in both cases: −0.92 percent for intrastate mergers and −2.93 percent for interstate mergers with a significant differential return. Turning to the post-merger announcement period, there is no significant reaction for intrastate mergers but a significant negative reaction for interstate mergers (−2.65 percent) with a significant differential return. If we look at the entire 11-week period surrounding the merger announcement week we have the same phenomenon: no significant market reaction of intrastate mergers and a significant negative market reaction of −7.60 percent for interstate mergers with intrastate mergers producing excess returns of 6.06 percent.

The evidence, then, indicates that the market reacts to the announcements of *interstate* mergers *less favorably* than to the announcements of *intrastate* mergers and that the differential market reaction is stronger for bidding banks than for target banks.

*Net aggregate wealth creation.* Do interstate mergers create net aggregate wealth to shareholders? We have seen in Chapter V that mergers, on average, create net aggregate wealth over the 11-week period surrounding the announcement week of the merger proposal. How is the wealth created by mergers allocated between interstate and intrastate mergers?

Recall that there is net aggregate wealth creation if the following condition is satisfied (see Chapter V, Section 4):

$$R_T\left(\frac{V_T}{V_B}\right) + R_B > 0.$$

Since $(V_T/V_B)$ is equal to 0.476, we have for *intrastate* mergers, during the entire 11-week period:

$$(17.77\%)(0.476) + (-1.54\%) = 6.92\%,$$

and for interstate banks:

$$(11.71\%)(0.285) + (-7.60\%) = -4.26\%.$$

*There is net aggregate wealth creation in the case of intrastate mergers but none in the case of interstate mergers.* Again, as pointed out in Chapter V, the above numbers should be interpreted with care since the ratio $(V_T/V_B)$ is an average that is measured in book values

Table 12B
Legislative effect. Differential market reaction to takeover announcements: [a] Pre- versus post-interstate legislation.

| | Pre-interstate legislation | | Post-interstate legislation | | Differential returns | |
|---|---|---|---|---|---|---|
| | Returns | (t-stat.) | Returns | (t-stat.) | Returns | (t-stat.) |
| *Target banks* | | | | | | |
| Sample size | 77 | | 41 | | – | |
| CAR[−5, −1] [b] | 7.57%* | (8.81) | 3.26%* | (3.60) | 4.31%* | (1.94) |
| AR[0] [c] | 12.42%* | (36.95) | 9.90% | (19.11) | 2.52% | (1.12) |
| CAR[+1, +5] [d] | −2.05 | (1.34) | −2.55%* | (2.03) | 0.50% | (0.34) |
| CAR[−5, +5] [e] | 17.94%* | (16.18) | 10.61%* | (6.82) | 7.33%* | (1.88) |
| *Bidding banks* | | | | | | |
| Sample size | 84 | | 42 | | – | |
| CAR[−5, −1] [b] | −0.65% | (1.37) | −1.90% | (1.56) | 1.25% | (0.84) |
| AR[0] [c] | −0.78% | (1.64) | −3.50%* | (7.38) | 2.72%* | (2.76) |
| CAR[+1, +5] [d] | −0.69% | (1.31) | −2.27%* | (2.07) | 1.58% | (1.18) |
| CAR[−5, +5] [e] | −2.12%* | (2.30) | −7.68%* | (4.67) | 5.56%* | (2.30) |

[a] Over the period January 1986 to June 1987. Absolute value of t-statistics in parentheses. Asterisks indicate significance at the 0.05 level.
[b] Cumulative average abnormal returns over the 5-week pre-announcement period.
[c] Average abnormal returns over the announcement week.
[d] Cumulative average abnormal returns over the 5-week post-announcement period.
[e] Cumulative average abnormal returns over the entire 11-week period surrounding the announcement week.

rather than market values. It seems then that the net aggregate wealth creation reported in Chapter V for the total sample of mergers is due to *intrastate* mergers. Note that this conclusion is not affected by whether mergers are paid for in cash or securities. We have found similar proportions of cash and security offers in both the subsample of intrastate and interstate mergers.

### *4.3. Legislative effect*

We have mentioned in Chapter I that several loopholes have allowed a number of banks to engage in interstate mergers at a time when the law prohibited interstate banking. Five target banks where the subject of a bid by an out-of-state bank prior to the enactment of legislation allowing interstate banking in their respective states. And six bids were made by out-of-state banks prior to the enactment of interstate banking legislation.

The reactions of target and bidding bank stock prices at the announcement of mergers that occurred before and after the enactment of interstate legislation are reported in Table 12B. A look at the data indicates a similar behavior to that found in Table 12A. Both target and bidding banks reacted to mergers announced *before* the enactment of interstate legislation *more* favorably than to mergers announced after the enactment of interstate legislation. Also, pre-interstate-legislation mergers created net aggregate wealth to shareholders whereas post-interstate-legislation mergers did not. Since most pre-legislation mergers are intrastate mergers, these results are not surprising. They are consistent with those reported in the previous section.

## 5. Bank size and abnormal returns: A test of the synergy hypothesis

The previous analysis of interstate versus intrastate mergers provided an indirect test of the synergy hypothesis. We may attribute the absence of wealth creation in the case of interstate mergers to the market belief that these mergers do not produce any synergetic gains.

Alternative indirect tests of the synergy hypothesis were suggested in Chapter II. There, it was suggested that mergers will produce synergetic gains if economies of scale can be achieved by combining the operations of the merging banks. But as we have seen in Chapter I and II, the evidence indicates that except at relatively low output levels, there does not appear to be economies of scale in banking organizations.

*5.1. Is there an optimal bank size?*

We have already mentioned in Chapter I the conclusion of a review of 13 studies on economies of scale in financial institutions (Clark (1988)): "overall economies of scale appear to exist only at *low* levels of output with *diseconomies* of scale at large output levels". This means that a bank will reach its optimal size rapidly. Actually, the above mentioned survey indicates that the optimal bank size, in terms of deposits, is attained in the neighborhood of $100 million in deposits. Beyond that limit, diseconomies of scale will occur.

But the above results refer to operational efficiency. There may be other reasons why a bank would want to increase its size beyond $100 million in deposits. By increasing its size, the bank may increase its market share and possibly its profitability (see Chapter I, Section 2.2). It may also be able to attract better quality management (see Chapter II, Section 2). Furthermore, the larger the bank the easier its access to the capital markets where it can raise funds rapidly, flexibly and at advantageous terms. Finally, only larger banks can conduct an active asset–liability management policy. For these reasons, we may hypothesize that a bank's optimal size may exceed the $100 million deposit limit found in many studies on economies of scale in banking organizations.

What does this mean? As discussed in Chapter II, Section 6 (the synergy hypothesis) the smaller the bidding bank, the higher the potential for synergetic gains in mergers and the higher the abnormal returns when the merger proposal is announced (the absolute size effect). Also, the smaller the target bank relative to the bidding bank, the higher the potential for synergetic gains and the higher the abnormal returns when the merger proposal is announced. This relative size effect is justified since economies of scale occur at relatively low levels of output. Therefore, the potential for exploiting benefits of scale economies in mergers is greater for a bidding bank that intends to acquire a relatively smaller bank. The evidence is presented and discussed in the following sections.

### *5.2. Absolute size effect*

In our sample, bidding banks were ranked in descending order according to the logarithm of their total assets. The top 30 cases were used to construct a portfolio of large bidding banks and the bottom 30 to construct a portfolio of small bidding banks. The mean value of the large portfolio is $21,195 million and that of the small portfolio is $1,334 million.

The abnormal returns associated with each size portfolio and the differential returns between the large and the small portfolio are reported in the lower part of Table 12C. The information in the upper part of Table 12C pertains to the target banks which were the subject of a bid by the banks in the large and small portfolio of bidders.

A look at the lower part of Table 12C indicates that abnormal returns to small bidders are higher than abnormal returns to large bidders. The empirical evidence is consistent with the absolute size effect. During the 11-week period surrounding the announcement of a merger proposal, small bidding banks outperformed large bidding banks by a significant return of 6.56 percent.

### *5.3. Relative size effect*

For each merger proposal, we calculated the ratio of the target bank's total assets to the bidding bank's total assets. We then ranked these ratios from the highest to the lowest and formed two portfolios, one containing the 30 highest cases and the other containing the 30 lowest cases. The mean value for the highest cases is 0.9103 and that for the lowest cases is 0.0816.

Table 12C
Absolute size effect (logarithm of bidder's total assets). [a] Differential market reaction to takeover announcements: [b] Top 30 versus bottom 30 cases.

| | Top 30 cases | | Bottom 30 cases | | Differential returns | |
|---|---|---|---|---|---|---|
| | Return | (t-stat.) | Return | (t-stat.) | Return | (t-stat.) |
| *Target banks* | | | | | | |
| CAR[−5, −1] [c] | 3.17%* | (2.20) | 4.79%* | (4.06) | −1.62% | (0.54) |
| AR[0] [d] | 14.27%* | (22.74) | 10.12%* | (23.41) | 4.15% | (1.93) |
| CAR[+1, +5] [e] | −1.82% | (1.04) | −2.45% | (0.90) | 0.63% | (0.31) |
| CAR[−5, +5] [f] | 15.62%* | (7.65) | 12.46%* | (9.18) | 3.16% | (0.52) |
| Mean relative size | 9.8799 | | 7.1960 | | | |
| Max. relative size | 11.5374 | | 7.8778 | | | |
| Min. relative size | 9.1727 | | 5.8721 | | | |
| *Bidding banks* | | | | | | |
| CAR[−5, −1] [c] | −2.31% | (1.39) | 0.82% | (0.43) | −3.13% | (1.74) |
| AR[0] [d] | −2.22%* | (3.37) | −0.05% | (1.99) | −2.17% | (1.78) |
| CAR[+1, +5] [e] | −1.06% | (0.61) | 0.19% | (0.28) | −1.25% | (0.67) |
| CAR[−5, +5] [f] | −5.59%* | (2.37) | 0.97% | (0.70) | −6.56%* | (2.05) |
| Mean relative size | 9.9615 | | 7.1960 | | | |
| Max. relative size | 11.5374 | | 7.8778 | | | |
| Min. relative size | 9.2894 | | 5.8721 | | | |

[a] See Table 10A for the definition of this variable which is listed as variable V2.
[b] Over the period January 1968 to June 1987. Absolute value of t-statistics in parentheses. Asterisks indicate significance at the 0.05 level.
[c] Cumulative average abnormal returns over the 5-week pre-announcement period.
[d] Average abnormal returns over the announcement week.
[e] Cumulative average abnormal returns over the 5-week post-announcement period.
[f] Cumulative average abnormal returns over the entire 11-week period surrounding the announcement week.

The abnormal returns associated with each relative size portfolio and the differential returns between the portfolio with the highest relative size and that with the lowest relative size are reported in the lowest part of Table 12D. The information in the upper part of Table 12D pertains to the target banks that were the subject of a bid by the banks in the high and low relative size portfolios.

Table 12D
Relative size effect (total assets (target)/ total assets (bidder)). [a] Differential market reaction to takeover announcements: [b] Top 30 versus bottom 30 cases.

| | Top 30 cases | | Bottom 30 cases | | Differential returns | |
|---|---|---|---|---|---|---|
| | Return | (t-stat.) | Return | (t-stat.) | Return | (t-stat.) |
| *Target banks (30)* | | | | | | |
| CAR[−5, −1] [c] | 3.78%* | (2.58) | 6.85%* | (5.45) | −3.07% | (0.94) |
| AR[0] [d] | 8.32%* | (11.83) | 13.02%* | (20.93) | −4.72% | (1.93) |
| CAR[+1, +5] [e] | −1.73%* | (0.93) | −3.31% | (1.75) | 1.58% | (0.54) |
| CAR[−5, +5] [f] | 10.81%* | (4.81) | 16.93%* | (8.88) | −6.12%* | (0.85) |
| Mean relative size | 0.8877 | | 0.0862 | | | |
| Max. relative size | 2.6250 | | 0.1285 | | | |
| Min. relative size | 0.5287 | | 0.0377 | | | |
| *Bidding banks (30)* | | | | | | |
| CAR[−5, −1] [c] | −1.26% | (1.56) | 0.38% | (0.44) | −1.64% | (0.58) |
| AR[0] [d] | −4.26%* | (4.60) | −0.17% | (0.93) | −4.09%* | (2.54) |
| CAR[+1, +5] [e] | −0.70% | (1.22) | −1.90% | (1.50) | 1.20% | (0.45) |
| CAR[−5, +5] [f] | −6.28%* | (3.27) | −2.25% | (1.68) | −4.03% | (1.22) |
| Mean relative size | 0.9103 | | 0.0816 | | | |
| Max. relative size | 2.6250 | | 0.1208 | | | |
| Min. relative size | 0.532 | | 0.0377 | | | |

[a] See Table 10A for the definition of this variable which is listed as variable V1.
[b] Over the period January 1968 to June 1987. Absolute value of t-statistics in parentheses. Asterisks indicate significance at the 0.05 level.
[c] Cumulative average abnormal returns over the 5-week pre-announcement period.
[d] Average abnormal returns over the announcement week.
[e] Cumulative average abnormal returns over the 5-week post-announcement period.
[f] Cumulative average abnormal returns over the entire 11-week period surrounding the announcement week.

A look at the lower part of Table 12D indicates that the portfolio with the *lowest* relative size (the portfolio containing the cases with the *smallest* target banks relative to their bidders) *outperformed* the portfolio with the *highest* relative size (the portfolio containing the cases with the *largest* target banks relative to their bidders) by 4.09 percent, on average, during the week the merger proposals were announced. Although the same phenomenon manifests itself over the 11-week period surrounding the week the merger proposals are announced, the excess returns earned by the lowest relative size portfolio are not significantly different from zero.

We can conclude that the empirical evidence is consistent with the relative size effect. It was also consistent with the absolute size effect. Hence, the observed stock price reaction of banks when merger proposals are announced lends some support to the synergy hypothesis of mergers. Again, this conclusion is not affected by whether the mergers will be paid for in cash or securities. There are similar proportions of cash and security offers in both the subsamples of large and small-size mergers.

## 6. Bank performance and abnormal returns: A test of the inefficient-management hypothesis

We have argued in Chapter II that a poorly managed bank is a likely candidate for a takeover. We can test this hypothesis by examining the stock price reaction of poorly-managed targets when a merger proposal is announced and compare it to that of well-managed targets. But we must first identify a number of variables that can act as proxies for the quality of a bank management.

### *6.1. Measuring bank performance*

There are several possible measures of bank performance. They fall into two major categories: accounting-based measures and market-based measures. Accounting-based measures are numerous. In this study we selected three: the relative capitalization of the target (with respect to the bidder) and the relative profitability of the target (with respect to either the bidder or other banks in the state). These are, respectively, variables V4, V5 and V6 in Table 10A. The market-based measure of bank performance is its abnormal stock price performance prior to the announcement of the merger proposal. It is listed as variable V7 in Table 10A.

### 6.2. Capitalization effect

We use the same sample dichotomization procedure as that employed to examine the size effects in Sections 5.2 and 5.3. Here one subsample contains the 30 merger cases with the highest relative capitalization ratios and the other subsample contains the 30 merger cases with the lowest relative capitalization ratios. The average value of the 30 highest ratios is 0.9473 and that of the 30 lowest is 0.0837. In the latter case the capitalization ratio of a target is, on average, 12 times smaller than that of its bidder.

Since target banks with lower relative capitalization are assumed to be poorer performers than banks with higher relative capitalization and since, according to the inefficient-management hypothesis, the poorer the target's performance the stronger the stock price reaction, it follows that we should observe higher abnormal returns associated with lower relative capitalization, for both target and bidding banks.

The empirical results are reported in Table 12E. Both target and bidding banks display significantly higher abnormal returns when the target has a lower relative capitalization ratio. During the announcement week, the portfolio of target banks with the lowest relative capitalization ratios earns an average excess return of 7.32 percent and that of bidding banks earns an average excess return of 4.50 percent. Note that the portfolio of bidding banks with the lowest relative capitalization ratios does not exhibit any significant *drop* in price whereas the portfolio with the highest relative capitalization ratios exhibits an average drop in price of 3.89 percent.

The same phenomenon is observed over the 11-week period surrounding the merger announcement week. The portfolio of target banks with the lowest relative capitalization ratio earns an average excess return of 6.14 percent and that of bidding banks earns an average excess return of 4.20 percent.

It seems then that mergers involving a target bank with an equity-to-total assets ratio significantly smaller than that of the

Table 12E
Relative-capitalization effect
$\left(\frac{\text{equity}}{\text{assets}}(\text{target})/\frac{\text{equity}}{\text{assets}}(\text{bidder})\right)$. [a]
Differential market reaction to takeover announcements: [b] Top 30 versus bottom 30 cases.

| | Top 30 cases | | Bottom 30 cases | | Differential returns | |
|---|---|---|---|---|---|---|
| | Return | (t-stat.) | Return | (t-stat.) | Return | (t-stat.) |
| *Target banks* | | | | | | |
| CAR[−5, −1] [c] | 5.21%* | (3.68) | 6.44%* | (4.62) | −1.23% | (0.37) |
| AR[0] [d] | 8.15%* | (12.20) | 15.47%* | (31.35) | −7.32%* | (2.30) |
| CAR[+1, +5] [e] | −0.88% | (0.76) | −3.30% | (1.17) | 2.42% | (1.15) |
| CAR[−5, +5] [f] | 12.48%* | (5.65) | 18.62%* | (11.78) | −6.14% | (1.95) |
| Mean relative cap. | 0.9473 | | 0.0837 | | | |
| Max. relative cap. | 2.6471 | | 0.1219 | | | |
| Min. relative cap. | 0.5370 | | 0.0317 | | | |
| *Bidding banks* | | | | | | |
| CAR[−5, −1] [c] | −1.86% | (1.80) | −0.75% | (0.72) | −1.11% | (0.60) |
| AR[0] [d] | −3.89%* | (4.40) | 0.61% | (0.44) | −4.50%* | (2.42) |
| CAR[+1, +5] [e] | −1.22% | (1.40) | −1.70% | (1.94) | 0.48% | (0.28) |
| CAR[−5, +5] [f] | −6.38%* | (3.49) | −2.18% | (1.66) | −4.20% | (1.80) |
| Mean relative cap. | 0.9473 | | 0.0837 | | | |
| Max. relative cap. | 2.6471 | | 0.1219 | | | |
| Min. relative cap. | 0.5370 | | 0.0317 | | | |

[a] See Table 10A for the definition of this variable which is listed as variable V4.
[b] Over the period January 1968 to June 1987. Absolute value of t-statistics in parentheses. Asterisks indicate significance at the 0.05 level.
[c] Cumulative average abnormal returns over the 5-week pre-announcement period.
[d] Average abnormal returns over the announcement week.
[e] Cumulative average abnormal returns over the 5-week post-announcement period.
[f] Cumulative average abnormal returns over the entire 11-week period surrounding the announcement week.

bidding bank create, on average, significant wealth to target bank shareholders and do not change significantly the wealth of bidding bank shareholders, whereas mergers involving target and bidding banks with similar equity-to-total assets ratios seem to destroy aggregate wealth. Indeed, during the 11-week period surrounding the announcement of the merger proposals, bidders suffered an average of 6.38 percent drop in their stock price (see Table 12E), whereas target bank shareholders realized a size-adjusted gain of only 4.80 percent (see Chapter V, Section 4):

$$R_T \frac{V_T}{V_B} = (12.48\%)(0.385) = 4.80\%,$$

which does not offset the loss incurred by bidders.

The above results provide some support for the inefficient-management hypothesis but they can also be interpreted as consistent with the synergy hypothesis. As pointed out in Chapter II, it is difficult to differentiate empirically between these two hypotheses. Once more, these conclusions are not affected by whether the merger will be paid for in cash or securities. There are similar proportions of cash and security offers in both the subsamples of high and low relative capitalization mergers.

### *6.3. Profitability effects*

Recall that relative profitability is measured with two different ratios. The first is the ratio of the target bank's ROE (return-on-equity) to the bidding bank's ROE. The second is the ratio of the target bank's ROE to the average ROE of those banks in the state or the region where the target bank is located. If these ratios are good proxies for the quality of bank management and if the inefficient-management hypothesis is supported by the data, then higher abnormal returns should be associated with lower ratios, the latter indicating poor performance and hence a higher potential for value creation via merger.

The empirical results, based on the same principle of sample dichotomization as in the previous tests, are reported in Tables 12F and 12G. When relative profitability is measured by the ratio of target's ROE to bidder's ROE, there are no significant market reactions between the portfolios containing the mergers with high

Table 12F
Relative-profitability effect (ROE(target)/ROE(bidder)).[a] Differential market reaction to takeover announcements:[b] Top 30 versus bottom 30 cases.

| | Top 30 cases | | Bottom 30 cases | | Differential returns | |
|---|---|---|---|---|---|---|
| | Return | (t-stat.) | Return | (t-stat.) | Return | (t-stat.) |
| *Target banks* | | | | | | |
| CAR[−5, −1][c] | 3.77%* | (3.72) | 4.90%* | (2.85) | −1.13% | (0.35) |
| AR[0][d] | 10.80%* | (18.76) | 9.80%* | (14.41) | 1.00% | (0.26) |
| CAR[+1, +5][e] | −3.36%* | (2.45) | −2.43% | (0.78) | −0.93% | (0.45) |
| CAR[−5, +5][f] | 11.21%* | (6.51) | 12.27%* | (5.74) | −1.05% | (0.19) |
| Mean relative prof. | 1.1885 | | 0.2272 | | | |
| Max. relative prof. | 1.7083 | | 0.6622 | | | |
| Min. relative prof. | 1.0403 | | −1.1020 | | | |
| *Bidding banks (30)* | | | | | | |
| CAR[−5, −1][c] | −0.40% | (0.16) | 0.87% | (0.14) | −0.33% | (0.20) |
| AR[0][d] | −2.18%* | (4.01) | −2.02%* | (4.48) | −0.16% | (0.12) |
| CAR[+1, +5][e] | 0.33% | (0.02) | −1.12% | (1.27) | 1.45% | (0.71) |
| CAR[−5, +5][f] | −2.24% | (1.30) | −2.27%* | (2.11) | −0.13% | (0.01) |
| Mean relative prof. | 1.1829 | | 0.1902 | | | |
| Max. relative prof. | 1.7083 | | 0.6532 | | | |
| Min. relative prof. | 1.0313 | | −1.1020 | | | |

[a] ROE = Return on equity; see Table 10A for the definition of this variable which is listed as variable V5.
[b] Over the period January 1968 to June 1987. Absolute value of t-statistics in parentheses. Asterisks indicate significance at the 0.05 level.
[c] Cumulative average abnormal returns over the 5-week pre-announcement period.
[d] Average abnormal returns over the announcement week.
[e] Cumulative average abnormal returns over the 5-week post-announcement period
[f] Cumulative average abnormal returns over the entire 11-week period surrounding the announcement week.

and low ratios (see Table 12F). Differences in relative profitability do not seem to matter in that case (at least as far as capital markets are concerned).

Turning to the case were the relative profitability of target banks is measured by the ratio of the target's ROE to the state's average

Table 12G
Relative-profitability effect (ROE(target)/ROE(state)).[a] Differential market reaction to takeover announcements:[b] Top 30 versus bottom 30 cases.

| | Top 30 cases | | Bottom 30 cases | | Differential returns | |
|---|---|---|---|---|---|---|
| | Return | (t-stat.) | Return | (t-stat.) | Return | (t-stat.) |
| *Target banks* | | | | | | |
| CAR[−5, −1][c] | 5.77%* | (4.76) | 7.39%* | (4.06) | −1.62% | (0.54) |
| AR[0][d] | 8.55%* | (15.89) | 12.70%* | (23.41) | −4.15% | (1.98) |
| CAR[+1, +5][e] | −4.35%* | (3.28) | −2.45%* | (1.90) | −1.90% | (0.31) |
| CAR[−5, +5][f] | 9.97%* | (5.79) | 13.13%* | (9.18) | −3.16% | (1.52) |
| Mean relative profit. | 1.3491 | | 0.3034 | | | |
| Max. relative profit. | 1.6812 | | 0.8333 | | | |
| Min. relative profit. | 1.2447 | | −1.0565 | | | |
| *Bidding banks* | | | | | | |
| CAR[−5, −1][c] | −1.32% | (0.99) | 1.04% | (0.26) | −2.36% | (1.18) |
| AR[0][d] | −1.91%* | (2.30) | −1.96%* | (4.33) | −0.05% | (0.03) |
| CAR[+1, +5][e] | −3.39%* | (3.20) | −1.19% | (1.26) | −2.20% | (1.21) |
| CAR[−5, +5][f] | −6.61%* | (3.52) | −2.11% | (1.98) | −4.50% | (1.37) |
| Mean relative profit. | 1.3451 | | 0.2533 | | | |
| Max. relative profit. | 1.6812 | | 0.7500 | | | |
| Min. relative profit. | 1.2366 | | −1.0565 | | | |

[a] ROE = Return on equity; see Table 10A for the definition of this variable which is listed as variable V6.
[b] Over the period January 1968 to June 1987. Absolute value of t-statistics in parentheses. Asterisks indicate significance at the 0.05 level.
[c] Cumulative average abnormal returns over the 5-week pre-announcement period.
[d] Average abnormal returns over the announcement week.
[e] Cumulative average abnormal returns over the 5-week post-announcemet period.
[f] Cumulative average abnormal returns over the entire 11-week period surrounding the announcement week.

ROE (see Table 12G), there is evidence of differential market reaction for target banks and none for bidding banks. During the announcement week, the portfolio containing the target banks with the lowest relative profitability ratios (average value 0.3034) earned an average excess return of 4.15 percent over the portfolio containing the target banks with the highest relative profitability ratios (average value 1.3491). Note that the low-relative-profitability portfolio also outperforms the high-relative-profitability portfolio during the entire 11-week period surrounding the merger proposals but the difference is not significantly different from zero. To conclude, we can say that there is some weak evidence indicating that abnormal returns associated with low relative-profitability target banks are higher than those associated with high relative-profitability target banks when the relative profitability of target banks is measured vis-à-vis the state or the region in which the target bank is located. Again these findings are not affected by whether the merger will be paid for in cash or securities. Both subsamples contain similar proportions of cash and securities offers.

### *6.4. Market performance of target banks*

An alternative, and most likely less biased, way to measure the quality of bank management is to examine a bank's abnormal stock performance over a period of a time. If the bank's stock returns exceed its expected returns (expected returns are given by the market model described in Chapter III, Section 3.1.1), the bank has outperformed the benchmark and we can attribute this measure of market outperformance to good management quality. And if the bank's stock returns are lower than its expected returns, the bank has underperformed the benchmark and we can associate this measure of market underperformance to poor management quality.

The empirical results are reported in Table 12H. The performance of target banks is measured by their cumulative abnormal returns over a period of 52 weeks, commencing 58 weeks before the merger announcement week and ending 6 weeks before that date. A portfolio containing the 20 banks with the highest performance is compared to a portfolio containing the 20 banks with the lowest performance.

During the announcement week low-performance target banks earned, on average, 5.94 percent more than high-performance target banks. And the bidders of low-performance target banks earned, on average, 3.14 percent more than the bidders of high-performance target banks. The same phenomenon occurred during the entire 11-week period surrounding the merger announcement. The low-performance target banks earned, on average, 10.94 percent more than the high-performance target banks. And the bidders of low-performance target banks earned, on average, 9.99 percent more than the bidders of high-performance target banks. All the differential returns are significantly different from zero.

Note the fact that mergers involving low-performance target banks create significant net aggregate wealth (and that bidding bank shareholders earn, in this case, positive returns), whereas mergers

Table 12H
Market-performance-of-target-bank effect (cumulative abnormal return of target bank's stock from week −58 to week −6). [a] Differential market reaction to takeover announcements: [b] Top 20 versus bottom 20 cases.

| | Top 20 cases | | Bottom 20 cases | | Differential returns | |
|---|---|---|---|---|---|---|
| | Return | (t-stat.) | Return | (t-stat.) | Return | (t-stat.) |
| *Target banks* | | | | | | |
| CAR[−5, −1] [c] | 5.85%* | (3.58) | 7.24%* | (4.92) | −1.39% | (0.35) |
| AR[0] [d] | 7.75%* | (8.04) | 13.69%* | (18.38) | −5.94% | (1.88) |
| CAR[+1, +5] [e] | −4.47% | (1.48) | −0.95% | (0.39) | −3.52% | (1.59) |
| CAR[−5, +5] [f] | 8.35%* | (3.71) | 19.29%* | (8.46) | −10.94% | (1.96) |
| *Bidding banks* | | | | | | |
| CAR[−5, −1] [c] | −0.60% | (0.25) | 2.73% | (1.76) | −3.33% | (1.25) |
| AR[0] [d] | −2.29%* | (2.73) | 0.85% | (0.79) | −3.14%* | (2.24) |
| CAR[+1, +5] [e] | −2.43% | (1.61) | 1.33% | (0.84) | −3.76% | (1.67) |
| CAR[−5, +5] [f] | −5.09%* | (2.04) | 4.90% | (1.99) | −9.99%* | (2.98) |

[a] CAR[−58, −6] is used as a proxy for the market performance of the target banks.

[b] Over the period January 1968 to June 1987. Absolute value of t-statistics in parentheses. Asterisks indicate significance at the 0.05 level.

[c] Cumulative average abnormal returns over the 5-week pre-announcement period.

[d] Average abnormal returns over the announcement week.

[e] Cumulative average abnormal returns over the 5-week post-announcement period.

[f] Cumulative average abnormal returns over the entire 11-week period surrounding the announcement week.

involving high-performance target banks do not create any net aggregate wealth (in this case bidding-bank shareholders realize negative returns and there is a wealth transfer from the shareholders of bidding banks to the shareholders of target banks).

The empirical evidence reported in Table 12H provides some support for the inefficient management hypothesis since low-performance target banks are most likely poorly managed and high-performance target banks are most likely well managed. Again, this conclusion is not affected by whether the merger will be paid for in cash or securities.

### *6.5. Market performance of bidding banks*

Does the market performance of *bidders* prior to the merger affect the strength of the stock market reaction of target and bidding banks during the period surrounding the announcement of the merger proposal? The inefficient-management hypothesis is based on the managerial quality of the target bank and *not* that of the bidder. We do not have an *a priori* hypothesis that could predict a differential stock price behavior for bidders with different managerial quality.

What does the empirical evidence indicate? The results are reported in Table 12I. The test procedures are the same as those used in Section 6.4. First, note that the managerial quality of the bidder does not affect the abnormal returns earned by the target shareholders during the period surrounding the announcement of the merger proposals. But the pre-merger market performance of bidders (and hence their managerial quality) does affect the market reaction of bidder shares during the period of time surrounding the announcement of merger proposals. A look at Table 12I shows that high performance bidders suffer an average loss of 3.13 percent during the week the merger proposal is announced, whereas the average stock price of low-performance bidders is unaffected. (The differential return is equal to 3.56 percent and is significantly different from zero). This phenomenon is even stronger during the 11-week period surrounding the announcement of merger proposals. The high-performance bidders lose 11.03 percent and the low-performance bid-

Table 12I
Market-performance-of-bidding-bank-effect (cumulative abnormal returns of bidding bank's stock from week −58 to week −6). [a] Differential market reaction to takeover announcements: [b] Top 20 versus bottom 20 cases.

| | Top 20 cases | | Bottom 20 cases | | Differential returns | |
|---|---|---|---|---|---|---|
| | Return | (t-stat.) | Return | (t-stat.) | Return | (t-stat.) |
| *Target banks* | | | | | | |
| CAR[−5, −1] [c] | 4.56%* | (3.63) | 2.62% | (1.85) | 1.94% | (0.62) |
| AR[0] [d] | 10.59%* | (14.79) | 10.41%* | (13.46) | 0.18% | (0.04) |
| CAR[+1, +5] [e] | −2.70% | (1.32) | −0.60% | (0.19) | −2.10% | (0.03) |
| CAR[−5, +5] [f] | 11.92%* | (5.90) | 12.42%* | (5.17) | −0.50% | (0.07) |
| *Bidding banks* | | | | | | |
| CAR[−5, −1] [c] | −4.45%* | (2.41) | 2.84% | (1.09) | −7.29%* | (3.11) |
| AR[0] [d] | −3.13%* | (3.86) | 0.43% | (1.42) | −3.56% | (1.98) |
| CAR[+1, +5] [e] | −3.60%* | (2.08) | 2.59% | (1.48) | −6.19%* | (3.01) |
| CAR[−5, +5] [f] | −11.03%* | (4.16) | 5.00% | (1.31) | −16.03%* | (4.10) |

[a] CAR[−58, −6] is used as a proxy for the market performance of the bidding banks.
[b] Over the period January 1968 to June 1987. Absolute value of t-statistics in parentheses. Asterisks indicate significance at the 0.05 level.
[c] Cumulative average abnormal returns over the 5-week pre-announcement period.
[d] Average abnormal returns over the announcement week.
[e] Cumulative average abnormal returns over the 5-week post-announcement period.
[f] Cumulative average abnormal returns over the entire 11-week period surrounding the announcement week.

ders earn 5.00 percent (the differential return is equal to 16.03 percent). Finally, note that mergers involving high-performance bidders do not create wealth whereas mergers involving low-performance bidders create a significant amount of net aggregate wealth.

This phenomenon cannot be explained since it is not clear why the bidder's stock price reacts positively to a merger announcement when the bidder has underperformed the market prior to the announcement, and reacts negatively when the bidder has overperformed the market prior to the announcement.

## 7. Target–bidder returns correlation: A test of the diversification hypothesis

One implication of the diversification hypothesis discussed in Chapters I and II is that abnormal returns associated with mergers between two banks with low stock-return correlation should be higher than abnormal returns associated with mergers between two banks with relatively high stock-return correlation. This is so because the lower the correlation coefficient, the larger the potential risk-reduction benefits generated by diversification.

Table 12J
Diversification effect (correlation (residual return of target, residual return of bidder)). [a] Differential market reaction to takeover announcements: [b] Top 20 versus bottom 20 cases.

| | Top 20 cases | | Bottom 20 cases | | Differential returns | |
|---|---|---|---|---|---|---|
| | Return | (t-stat.) | Return | (t-stat.) | Return | (t-stat.) |
| *Target banks* | | | | | | |
| CAR[−5, −1] [c] | 2.31% | (1.90) | 8.71%* | (5.39) | −6.40%* | (2.01) |
| AR[0] [d] | 12.46%* | (16.08) | 16.98%* | (22.37) | −4.52% | (1.79) |
| CAR[+1, +5] [e] | 0.68% | (0.83) | −0.97% | (0.83) | 1.65% | (0.68) |
| CAR[−5, +5] [f] | 14.83%* | (6.57) | 23.88%* | (9.64) | −9.06% | (1.80) |
| *Bidding banks* | | | | | | |
| CAR[−5, −1] [c] | −3.17%* | (2.45) | 1.74% | (0.61) | −4.91%* | (2.05) |
| AR[0] [d] | −3.21%* | (4.03) | −2.11%* | (3.66) | −1.10% | (0.61) |
| CAR[+1, +5] [e] | 1.03% | (0.35) | −1.84% | (1.19) | 2.87% | (1.15) |
| CAR[−5, +5] [f] | −5.19% | (2.59) | −2.11% | (1.45) | −3.08% | (0.74) |

[a] Correlation coefficient of the market model residual returns of target bank and those of bidding bank from week 58 to week 6 preceding the takeover announcement week.

[b] Over the period January 1968 to June 1987. Absolute value of t-statistics in parentheses. Asterisks indicate significance at the 0.05 level.

[c] Cumulative average abnormal returns over the 5-week pre-announcement period.

[d] Average abnormal returns over the announcement week.

[e] Cumulative average abnormal returns over the 5-week post-announcement period.

[f] Cumulative average abnormal returns over the entire 11-week period surrounding the announcement week.

We tested this hypothesis using the dichotomization method. First we estimated the correlation coefficients between the market-model residual returns of each pair of target and bidding banks during the 52 weeks from week 58 to week 6 preceding the merger announcement week and then ranked them from the highest to the lowest. The top 20 cases were used to construct a portfolio containing the lowest correlations. Abnormal returns for the two portfolios are reported in Table 12J.

During the merger announcement week, the lowest-correlation portfolio of target banks earned 4.52 percent more than the highest-correlation portfolio. And over the entire 11-week period surrounding the merger announcement week it earned 9.05 percent more. The lowest-correlation portfolio of bidding banks also earned higher returns than the highest-correlation portfolio during the merger announcement week and the entire 11-week period, but the excess returns are not significantly different from zero. Note that the market anticipates the merger announcements and that low-correlation mergers are associated with significantly higher abnormal returns than high-correlation mergers during the 5-week pre-merger period. These results are consistent with the diversification hypothesis. They are not affected by whether the merger will be paid for in cash or securities. Both subsamples have similar proportions of cash and security offers.

## 8. Cross-sectional regression analysis of target bank abnormal returns

As mentioned earlier in this chapter, the dichotomization analysis used to explain cross-sectional variations in market reactions to the announcements of merger proposals suffers from a major limitation: it does not hold all other factors constant. To remedy this weakness we can use a multiple-variable cross-sectional regression analysis. But this approach suffers from its own inefficiencies since it imposes a linear relationship between the dependent and independent variables, and the priority over variables with confounding effects is, to a large extent, arbitrary.

Table 13A

Cross-sectional regression analysis of target banks' abnormal returns (estimated coefficients for cross-sectional regressions relating target banks' abnormal returns [a] around takeover announcements to the ratio of target's size to bidder's size, the stock market performance of the target bank prior to the takeover announcement and whether the takeover is interstate or intrastate or whether it was announced before or after the entactment of interstate legislation (absolute value of t-statistics in parentheses)).

| | Constant | Independent variables [b] | | | |
|---|---|---|---|---|---|
| | | V1<br>Size target / Size bidder | V7<br>Performance of target bank | D1<br>Inter- vs. intrastate | D2<br>Before vs. after legislation |
| 1. | 0.3269<br>(11.52) | −0.1395<br>(2.65) | | | |
| 2. | 0.2922<br>(8.07) | −0.1525<br>(2.87) | | 0.0643<br>(1.53) | |
| 3. | 0.2784<br>(7.20) | −0.1485<br>(2.82) | | | 0.0780<br>(1.83) |
| 4. | 0.2837<br>(12.93) | | −0.0676<br>(1.29) | | |
| 5. | 0.2583<br>(7.42) | | −0.0633<br>(1.21) | 0.0403<br>(0.94) | |
| 6. | 0.2420<br>(6.51) | | −0.0591<br>(1.13) | | 0.0610<br>(1.39) |
| 7. | 0.3419<br>(11.53) | −0.1490<br>(2.83) | −0.0836<br>(1.69) | | |
| 8. | 0.3088<br>(8.22) | −0.1606<br>(3.02) | −0.0784<br>(1.65) | 0.0598<br>(1.43) | |
| 9. | 0.2960<br>(7.34) | −0.1562<br>(2.98) | −0.0744<br>(1.66) | | 0.0713<br>(1.68) |

[a] Two-week cumulative average abnormal returns prior and up to the announcement week (from week −1 to week 0).

[b] The variables V1 and V7 are defined in Table 10A; D1 = 0 for interstate takeovers, 1 for intrastate takeovers; D2 = 0 for takeover announced after the enactment of interstate legislation, 1 for takeover announced before the enactment of interstate legislation.

### 8.1. Selection of independent variables

A number of cross-sectional regression analyses using the set of independent variables listed in Table 10A were performed and two variables were retained: the ratio of the target size to the bidder size (V1) and the market performance of the target bank (V7). To those we added two dummy variables capturing the difference that exists between intrastate and interstate mergers and mergers that occurred before and after the enactment of interstate banking legislation. The dependent variable is the target bank's two-week cumulative average abnormal returns from week $-1$ to week 0 (the merger announcement week). We then run the following multiple-variable cross-sectional regression:

$$CAR[-1,0] = \delta_0 + \sum_{i} \alpha_i V_i + \sum_{j=1}^{2} \beta_j D_j,$$

where $i = 1$ to 7, $D_1 = 0$ for interstate mergers and $D_1 = 1$ for intrastate mergers, and $D_2 = 0$ for mergers that occurred before the enactment of interstate banking legislation and $D_2 = 1$ for mergers that occurred after.

### 8.2. Empirical results

The estimated coefficients for a number of cross-sectional regressions are reported in Table 13A. There is a significant negative size effect (the smaller the target relative to the bidder, the higher the target bank's abnormal returns associated with the merger announcement). There is also a negative performance effect (the poorer the market performance of the target bank prior to the merger announcement, the higher the target bank's abnormal returns). Finally, there is a difference between mergers that occurred before the enactment of interstate banking legislation and those that occurred after, with higher abnormal returns associated with the former rather than the latter. Note that when we adjust for size, for the target's pre-merger performance, and for the effect of banking legislation, the means of merger payment no longer affects abnormal returns.

## 9. Cross-sectional regression analysis of bidding bank abnormal returns

We now turn to the case of bidding banks and perform a similar test as that described in the previous section.

### 9.1. Selection of independent variables

The independent variables selected to explain the cross-sectional variation of the abnormal returns of bidding banks are: bidder's absolute size (V2), the concentration ratio in the state of the target bank (V11), the profitability of the target bank relative to that of the state in which the bank operates (V6), the number of potential bidders for the target (which is the number of banks in the size groups that are larger than the size group in which the target bank belongs) (V10), a dummy for interstate and intrastate mergers (D1), and a dummy for merger announcements before or after the enactment of interstate banking legislation. Other variables, listed in Table 10A, were tested for inclusion in the regression analysis but did not yield significant results.

### 9.2. Empirical results

The estimated coefficients for a number of cross-sectional regressions are reported in Table 13B. The dependent variable is the abnormal return of the bidding banks. There is neither an absolute nor a relative size effect (both V1 and V2 are insignificant, but the former is not reported in Table 13B). The coefficient for the concentration ratio has the expected sign (higher abnormal returns are associated with lower concentration ratios), but is not significantly different from zero. The same observation can be made about the relative profitability variable: correct sign for the coefficient but statistically insignificant. The only significant coefficients are V10, D1 and D2. *The larger the number of potential bidders, the lower the abnormal returns to bidders*. Potential competition among bidders has the effect of raising the price paid for targets and hence reducing the merger gains that accrue to shareholders of bidding banks. There is a significant difference between intrastate and interstate mergers, the

Table 13B
Cross-sectional regression analysis of bidding banks' abnormal returns
(estimated coefficients for cross-sectional regressions relating bidding banks' abnormal returns[a] around takeover announcements to bidder's size, concentration ratio in target's state, target's relative profitability, the number of potential bidding banks and whether the takeover is interstate or intrastate or whether it was announced before or after the enactment of interstate legislation (absolution value of t-statistics in parentheses).

| | Constant | Independent variables[b] | | | | | |
|---|---|---|---|---|---|---|---|
| | | V2 Bidder's size | V11 Concentration ratio | V6 Relative profitability | V10 Number of potential bidders | D1 Inter- vs. intrastate | D2 Before vs. after legislation |
| 1. | −0.0430<br>(3.86) | $0.0057.10^{-3}$<br>(1.24) | | | | 0.0334<br>(2.78) | |
| 2. | −0.0474<br>(4.44) | $0.0037.10^{-3}$<br>(0.86) | | | | | 0.0402<br>(3.47) |
| 3. | −0.0225<br>(1.06) | | $-0.2867.10^{-3}$<br>(0.64) | | | 0.0254<br>(2.07) | |
| 4. | −0.0390<br>(1.79) | | $-0.0900.10^{-3}$<br>(0.20) | | | | 0.0376<br>(2.98) |
| 5. | −0.0241<br>(1.68) | | | −0.0105<br>(0.94) | | 0.0265<br>(2.30) | |

| | | | | | | | |
|---|---|---|---|---|---|---|---|
| 6. | −0.0344 | | | −0.0082 | | | 0.0370 |
| | (2.34) | | | (0.75) | | | (3.16) |
| 7. | −0.0427 | | | | $-0.3117.10^{-3}$ | 0.0344 | |
| | (4.39) | | | | (1.95) | (2.96) | |
| 8. | −0.0538 | | | | $-0.3770.10^{-3}$ | | 0.0472 |
| | (5.250 | | | | (2.39) | | (4.00) |
| 9. | −0.0557 | $0.7915.10^{-6}$ | | | $-0.3692.10^{-3}$ | 0.0425 | |
| | (4.53) | (1.71) | | | (2.27) | (3.40) | |
| 10. | −0.0612 | $0.5441.10^{-6}$ | | | $-0.4083.10^{-3}$ | | 0.0503 |
| | (5.210 | (1.27) | | | (2.57) | | (4.18) |
| 11. | −0.0236 | $0.7187.10^{-6}$ | $-0.0513.10^{-3}$ | −0.0124 | $-0.4000.10^{-3}$ | 0.0354 | |
| | (0.88) | (1.48) | (1.14) | (0.34) | (2.41) | (2.59) | |
| 12. | −0.0378 | $0.4999.10^{-6}$ | $-0.0322.10^{-3}$ | −0.0102 | $-0.4288.10^{-3}$ | | 0.0449 |
| | (1.43) | (1.10) | (0.71) | (0.28) | (2.62) | | (3.37) |

[a] Two-week cumulative average abnormal returns prior and up to the announcement week (from week −1 to week 0).

[b] The variables V2, V11, V6 and V10 are defined in Table 10A; D1 = 0 for interstate takeovers, 1 for intrastate takeovers; D2 = 0 for takeover announced before the enactment of interstate legislation, 1 for takeover announced after the enactment of interstate legislation.

former being associated with higher abnormal returns. There is also a significant difference between merger announcements made before and after the enactment of interstate banking legislation, the former being associated with higher abnormal returns. These results are consistent with earlier evidence reported in Section 4. They are not affected by whether the merger will be paid for in cash or securities.

## 10. Market reaction of rival banks, potential bidders and alternative targets

Suppose that the banking market is segmented into three size-related segments: a large-bank segment, a medium-bank segment and a small-bank segment. When a merger occurs, the number of banks operating in a given segment may change. For example, if two medium banks merge to create one large bank, the number of medium banks decreases by two and the number of large banks increases by one. This change in the number of banks can produce two effects which we call the "competitive" effect and the "corporate-control" effect.

The first effect refers to the fact that the change in the number of banks operating in a segment may affect competition in that market segment. This may lead to a change in the price charged by banks for their services. To illustrate, consider the above mentioned example. The merger of two medium banks into one large bank has reduced the number of competitors in the medium- bank segment. This may *lessen* competition in that market segment which, in turn, may lead to *higher* "product" prices in that market (the prices charged by medium banks for their services). The merger has also increased the number of competitors in the large-bank segment. This may *strengthen* competition in that market segment which, in turn, may lead to *lower* product prices in the large-segment market. This argument is a generalization of the market-power hypothesis discussed in Chapter II.

The fact that merger activities alter the number of competitors in a banking segment means that the announcement of a merger has implications for merging banks as well as their rivals. To return to our example, a lessening of competitive pressures in the medium-bank segment and the possible accompanying product price increase benefits the merging banks as well as their rivals. Thus, positive abnormal returns should be observed for both the merging banks and their rivals when the merger proposal is announced. Conversely, a strengthening of competitive pressures in the large-bank segment and the possible accompanying product price decrease harms the merging banks as well as their rivals. But the merger announcement should not necessarily generate negative abnormal returns for the merging banks because the negative competitive effect may be offset, for example, by a positive synergetic effect. Indeed, the potential gains from synergy may more than offset the potential losses due to the possible decline in product prices. Note, however, that according to the market-power hypothesis, the merger has negative implications for banks in the large-bank segment since it creates the entry of a new competitor.

We turn now to the second of the two effects mentioned above, the corporate-control effect. Here we refer to the market for corporate control. Merger activities change the number of potential bidders and alternative targets in the market for corporate control. Hence it affects more than just the two merging banks. Our example will again illustrate the point. The merger of the two medium banks has created one large bank. One implication for the market for corporate control is that there are now *less* medium banks for large banks to take over. That is, the supply of medium-size target banks has decreased. This, in turn, means that the merger announcement should have a *positive* impact on medium banks. Specifically, we should observe a rise in the price of their stocks to reflect the reduction in the number of potential target banks.

Another implication of the merger of the two medium banks into one large bank is that there are now *less* medium banks to *bid* for small banks. That is, the demand for small-size target banks has decreased. This, in turn, means that the merger announcement should have a *negative* impact on small banks. Specifically, we should observe a drop in the price of these stocks to reflect the

Table 14A

Market reaction of other banks [a] when bank (A) announces a merger with bank (B).

| Case | Bank (A) + Bank (B) = Bank (AB) | | | Size | | Reaction of other banks [a] according to their size [b] | | | | | |
|---|---|---|---|---|---|---|---|---|---|---|---|
| | Size of A [b] | Size of B | Size of AB | | | N [c] | n [d] | AR[0] [e] | t(AR) [f] | CAR[−1,0] [g] | t(CAR) [h] |
| (1) | Large | Large | Large | (a) | Large | 3 | 48 | −1.78% * | 2.94 | −0.34% | 0.41 |
| | | | | (b) | Medium | 3 | 98 | −0.30% * | 2.73 | 0.44% | 0.06 |
| | | | | (c) | Small | n.a. | 31 | 2.47% * | 2.64 | 1.52% | 1.42 |
| (2) | Large | Medium | Large | (a) | Large | n.a. | 58 | −1.28% * | 3.08 | −0.69% | 1.16 |
| | | | | (b) | Medium | 14 | 383 | −0.36% * | 2.94 | −0.39% * | 2.10 |
| | | | | (c) | Small | n.a. | 297 | 0.49% * | 2.48 | 0.62% * | 2.60 |
| (3) | Large | Small | Large | (a) | Large | n.a. | 1 | −2.33% | 0.52 | 2.04% | 0.32 |
| | | | | (b) | Medium | n.a. | 12 | −1.15% | 0.96 | −1.29% | 0.73 |
| | | | | (c) | Small | 1 | 12 | −0.86% | 0.88 | 0.00 | 0.24 |
| (4) | Medium | Medium | Large | (a) | Large | 3 | 6 | 1.10% | 0.63 | −0.29% | 0.26 |
| | | | | (b) | Medium | 6 | 141 | 1.47% * | 5.06 | 3.73% * | 10.44 |
| | | | | (c) | Small | n.a. | 183 | 1.35% * | 4.61 | 2.42% * | 6.61 |
| (5) | Medium | Medium | Medium | (a) | Large | n.a. | 26 | 1.48% | 1.68 | 1.04% | 1.13 |
| | | | | (b) | Medium | 34 | 573 | 0.86% * | 7.08 | 1.50% | 10.15 |
| | | | | (c) | Small | 33 | 391 | 1.08% * | 8.43 | 1.21% * | 7.45 |

| | | | | | | | | | | | |
|---|---|---|---|---|---|---|---|---|---|---|---|
| (6) | Medium | Small | Medium | (a) | Large | n.a. | 182 | 0.49% * | 2.18 | 0.90% * | 3.08 |
| | | | | (b) | Medium | n.a. | 1185 | 0.09% | 1.03 | −0.03% | 0.62 |
| | | | | (c) | Small | 50 | 1182 | 0.67% * | 10.90 | 0.71% * | 9.08 |
| (7) | Small | Small | Medium | (a) | Large | n.a. | 1 | −4.73% | 1.36 | −5.00% | 1.02 |
| | | | | (b) | Medium | 3 | 25 | 0.90% | 0.51 | 1.72% | 1.46 |
| | | | | (c) | Small | 3 | 42 | 1.19% | 1.78 | 1.00% | 1.56 |
| (8) | Small | Small | Small | (a) | Large | n.a. | 8 | −0.87% | 0.52 | −2.56% | 1.16 |
| | | | | (b) | Medium | n.a. | 48 | 0.40% | 1.56 | 1.33% * | 2.85 |
| | | | | (c) | Small | 5 | 47 | 2.50% * | 5.22 | 2.66% * | 3.71 |

[a] Other banks are banks that are in the same geographical area as the two banks that intend to merge.

[b] Large banks have at least $10 billion of assets before 1983 and at least $15 billion of assets after 1983; medium banks have assets between $1 and $10 billion before 1983 and between $1.5 and $15 billion after 1983; small banks have at most $1 billion of assets before 1983 and at most $1.5 billion of assets after 1983.

[c] Number of merger announcements; n.a.: not available.

[d] Total number of "other banks" for the N merger announcements.

[e] Average abnormal return during the announcement week (week 0).

[f] Absolute value of the t-statistic or AR[0]. Asterisks indicate significance at the 0.05 level.

[g] Cumulative average abnormal returns from week −1 to week 0.

[h] Absolute value of the t-statistic for CAR[−1,0]. Asterisks indicate significance at the 0.05 level.

reduction in the number of potential bidding banks. Note that we assume that banks in a size group are alternatively targets for banks in the larger size groups and potential bidders for banks in the smaller size groups.

### *10.1. Evidence on the competitive effect: A test of the market-power hypothesis*

The banks in our sample were divided into three size groups according to the following criterion: until 1983, large banks have at least \$10 billion in assets, and after 1983, at least \$15 billion; until 1983, medium banks have at least \$1 billion and at most \$10 billion, and after 1983, at least \$1.5 billion and at most \$15 billion; until 1983, small banks have at most \$1 billion in assets, and after 1983, at most \$1.5 billion.

There are eight possible outcomes of each merger according to size combinations. They are listed in the first three columns of Table 14A. The first case is that of the merger of two large banks that creates a large bank and the last case in that of the merger of two small banks that creates a small bank. For each one of the eight cases we report the market reaction of other banks in the three size groups. These are banks operating in the same geographical areas as the two banks that intend to merge. Capital N indicates the number of merger announcements and lower case n the total number of "other banks" for the N merger announcements. The last four columns on the right-side of Table 14A give the abnormal returns of "other banks" and their corresponding t-statistics.

There are ten cases in Table 14A that are relevant for a test of the market-power hypothesis. Eight of these lessen competition by reducing the number of banks in a market segment and two of these strengthen competition by increasing the number of banks in a market segment. The eight cases where competition is lessened are: case (1) – reduction in the number of large banks; cases (2), (4) and (5) – reduction in the number of medium banks; and cases (3), (6), (7) and (8) – reduction in the number of small banks. The two cases where competition is strengthened are: case (4) – rise in the number of large banks; and case (7) – rise in the number of medium banks. According to the market-power hypothesis, a reduction in the number of rival banks should favor an increase in product prices that should benefit both merging banks and their rivals. Hence the merger announcement should trigger a rise in the stock of rival banks. Looking at table 14A we have:

| Reduction in the number of | Rival banks | Case in Table 14A | Abnormal returns (CAR) |
|---|---|---|---|
| Large banks | Large | (1) (a) | −0.34% |
| Medium | Medium | (2) (b) | −0.39% (sig.) |
| | Medium | (4) (b) | 3.73% (sig.) |
| | Medium | (5) (b) | 1.50% (sig.) |
| Small banks | Small | (3) (c) | 0.00% |
| | Small | (6) (c) | 0.71% (sig.) |
| | Small | (7) (c) | 1.00% |
| | Small | (8) (c) | 2.66% (sig.) |

Of the eight cases above, four have significant (sig.) *positive* abnormal returns (CAR [-1,0]) and are thus consistent with the market-power hypothesis. But the rise in rival stock prices does not provide an unambiguous test of the market-power hypothesis because higher prices for rival banks can be attributed to information effects.

Indeed, suppose that the announced merger is perceived as beneficial to the merging banks because of potential synergetic gains. In this case the stock price of rival banks may rise because the merger signals opportunities for rivals to improve *their* efficiency via synergetic mergers (Eckbo (1983)). And though the data in Table 14A provide some weak support for the market-power hypothesis, it must be noted that we are testing both the market-power hypothesis *and* the hypothesis that the banking market is segmented by bank size.

According to the market-power hypothesis, an increase in the number of rival banks yields a decrease in product prices, which harms rival banks. Hence the merger announcement should trigger a

Table 14B

Geographical effect: Intrastate mergers. Market reaction of other banks [a] when two banks in the same state announce a merger.

| Case | Bank (A) + | (Bank (B) = | Bank (AB) | Size | Reaction of other banks [a] according to their size [b] | | | | | |
|---|---|---|---|---|---|---|---|---|---|---|
| | Size of A [b] | Size of B | Size of AB | | N [c] | n [d] | AR[0] [e] | t(AR) [f] | CAR[−1,0] [g] | t(CAR) [h] |
| (1) | Large | Large | Large | Large | 1 | n.a. | −2.30% | 1.13 | −3.60% | 1.26 |
| (2) | Large | Medium | Large | Medium | 4 | n.a. | 1.27% | 1.39 | 2.14% | 1.57 |
| (3) | Medium | Medium | Large | Medium | 3 | n.a. | 5.17% * | 5.34 | 6.76% * | 4.91 |
| (4) | Medium | Medium | Medium | Medium | 18 | n.a. | 0.89% * | 2.04 | 1.06% | 1.65 |
| | | | | Small | 18 | n.a. | 0.56% | 1.83 | 0.81% | 1.26 |
| (5) | Medium | Small | Medium | Small | 36 | n.a. | 0.62% * | 3.26 | 0.51% * | 2.05 |
| (6) | Small | Small | Small | Small | 5 | n.a. | 1.63% * | 2.61 | 1.13% | 1.37 |

[a] Other banks are banks that are in the same geographical area as the two banks that intend to merge.

[b] Large banks have at least $10 billion of assets before 1983 and at least $15 billion of assets after 1983; medium banks have assets between $1 and $10 billion before 1983 and between $1.5 and $15 billion after 1983; small banks have at most $1 billion of assets before 1983 and at most $1.5 billion of assets after 1983.

[c] Number of merger announcements.

[d] Total number of "other banks" for the N merger announcements; n.a.: not available.

[e] Average abnormal return during the announcement week (week 0).

[f] Absolute value of the t-statistic for AR[0]. Asterisks indicate significance at the 0.05 level.

[g] Cumulative average abnormal returns from week −1 to week 0.

[h] Absolute value of the t-statistic for CAR[−1,0]. Asterisks indicate significance at the 0.05 level.

Table 14C
Geographical effect: Interstate mergers. Market reaction of other banks [a] when one bank announces a merger with an out-of-state bank.

| Case | Bank (A) + | Bank (B) = | Bank (AB) | Size | Reaction of other banks [a] according to their size [b] | | | | | |
|---|---|---|---|---|---|---|---|---|---|---|
| | Size of A [b] | Size of B | Size of AB | | N [c] | n [d] | AR[0] [e] | t[AR] [f] | CAR[−1,0] [g] | t(CAR) [h] |
| (1) | Large | Large | Large | Large | 2 | n.a. | −1.76% | 1.89 | −0.32% | 0.23 |
| (2) | Large | Medium | Large | Medium | 10 | n.a. | −1.19% * | 3.09 | −1.78% * | 2.92 |
| (3) | Medium | Medium | Large | Medium | 3 | n.a. | 0.77% | 1.61 | 3.19% * | 4.20 |
| (4) | Medium | Medium | Medium | Medium | 16 | n.a. | −0.20% | 1.15 | −0.04% * | 2.00 |
| | | | | Small | 15 | n.a. | 0.79% * | 3.34 | 0.28% | 1.98 |
| (5) | Medium | Small | Medium | Small | 14 | n.a. | −0.06% | 0.11 | −0.58% | 1.41 |
| (6) | Small | Small | Small | Small | – | n.a. | – | – | – | – |

[a] Other banks are banks that are in the same geographical area as the two banks that intend to merge.
[b] Large banks have at least \$10 billion of assets before 1983 and at least \$15 billion of assets after 1983; medium banks have assets between \$1 and \$10 billion before 1983 and between \$1.5 and \$15 billion after 1983; small banks have at most \$1 billion of assets before 1983 and at most \$1.5 billion of assets after 1983.
[c] Number of merger announcements.
[d] Total number of "other banks" for the N merger announcements; n.a.: not available.
[e] Average abnormal return during the announcement week (week 0).
[f] Absolute value of the t-statistic for AR[0]. Asterisks indicate significance at the 0.05 level.
[g] Cumulative average abnormal returns from week −1 to week 0.
[h] Absolute value of the t-statistic for CAR[−1,0]. Asterisks indicate significance at the 0.05 level.

drop in the stock price of rival banks. Looking at Table 14A we have:

| Reduction in the number of | Rival banks | Case in Table 14A | Abnormal returns (CAR) |
|---|---|---|---|
| Large banks | Large | (4) (a) | −0.29% |
| Medium banks | Medium | (7) (b) | 1.72% |

In both cases, the market reaction of rivals is insignificantly different from zero, a result that is inconsistent with the market-power hypothesis.

Finally, note that there are cases listed in Table 14A for which there should be no effect on rival banks since the mergers do not change the number of competitors. For example, consider case (1) (b) and case (1) (c). Two large banks merged to form a new large bank. This, however, should not affect medium and small banks since their number has not changed. But a look at Table 14A indicates several cases where rival banks exhibit significant abnormal returns in contradiction with the predictions of the market-power hypothesis. Again, the evidence is inconsistent with this hypothesis.

*Intrastate vs. interstate mergers*. To test the sensitivity of the above conclusion to whether mergers are intrastate or interstate, we divided our sample of bank mergers into two subsamples. One subsample contains intrastate mergers and the other interstate mergers. We then replicated the tests reported in Table 14A on the two subsamples. The results for intrastate mergers are in Table 14B and those for interstate mergers in Table 14C. A look at these two tables indicates that the conclusions reached from the examination of the results in Table 14A are not modified by the results shown in Tables 14B and 14C.

## *10.2. Evidence on the corporate-control effect*

Recall that the corporate-control effect refers to changes in the supply of, and demand for, alternative targets. We have seen that when a merger occurs, the number of banks in a given market segment may change. This, in turn, may change the number of potential bidders and alternative targets.

Let us examine a number of cases listed in Table 14A:

(1) The merging of two large banks to create one large bank reduces the number of *bidders* for medium and small target banks. That is, it reduces the potential demand for these banks. This means that the merger announcement should have a negative effect on medium and small banks. This result is observed for medium banks (case (1) (b)) but not for small banks (case (1) (c)).

(2) The merging of two medium banks to create one large bank reduces the number of potential medium targets for large bidders and should have a positive effect on medium banks. This is in fact observed in Table 14A (case (4) (b)). The merger also reduces the number of potential medium bidders for small targets and should have a negative effect on small target banks. However, this result is not observed in Table 14A (case (4) (c)).

(3) The merging of two medium banks into one medium bank reduces the number of alternative medium targets for large bidders and should have a positive effect on medium banks, as observed in Table 14A (case (5) (b)). The merger also reduces the number of medium bidders for small targets and should have a negative effect on small target banks. However, this result is not observed in Table 14A (case (5) (c)).

(4) The merging of two small banks into one small bank reduces the number of alternative small targets for potential medium bidders and should have a positive effect on small banks, as observed in Table 14A (case (8) (c)).

As shown above, the evidence is mixed. There is some support for the hypothesis that a reduction in the number of alternative targets via mergers has a positive effect on the remaining potential target banks. But there is no evidence that a reduction in the number of potential bidders for a group of alternative target banks affects these banks negatively. Again recall that we are performing a joint test: a test of implications of the market for corporate control and a test of the segmentation of the banking industry according to size.

### *10.3. Regulatory effects*

What happens to rivals, alternative bidders and potential targets when the Federal Reserve releases its approval or denial order? The evidence is summarized in Tables 14D and 14E for those merger proposals that were subsequently approved by the Federal Reserve, and in Tables 14F and 14G for those merger proposals that were either subsequently denied by the Federal Reserve or cancelled by the bidder.

*Approved mergers*. Table 14D reports the market reaction of rivals, potential bidders and alternative targets for the subsample of merger announcements that were subsequently approved by regulators. The market reaction of that subsample is consistent with that of the entire sample reported in Table 14A.

The market reaction of the "other" banks is reported in Table 14E. In principle, we should expect little reaction since we know that the market generally anticipates approval (see Chapter V, Section 5). This is indeed what we observe in Table 14E, except for the case of the merger of two small banks into one small bank. We know that in this case the reduction in the number of small banks has positive implications for the other small banks in the same market area for two reasons: the lessening of competitive pressures (the competitive effect) and the decline in the number of potential targets (the corporate-control effect). But the positive market reaction occurs mostly during the announcement week of the regulator's approval order rather than during the preceding announcement of the merger proposal.

*Denied and cancelled mergers*. Table 14F reports the market reaction of rivals, potential bidders and alternative targets for the subsample of merger announcements that were subsequently either denied by the regulator or cancelled by the bidder. As in the case of approved mergers, the market reaction of the subsample of mergers that were subsequently either denied or cancelled is consistent with that of the entire sample reported in Table 14A. It is also consistent with the subsample of approved mergers reported in Table 14D.

Table 14D

Regulatory effect: Market reaction of other banks [a] when bank (A) announces a merger with bank (B) for the subsample of mergers that were subsequently approved by regulators.

| Case | Bank (A) + Bank (B) = Bank (AB) | | | Size | Reaction of other banks [a] according to their size [b] | | | | | |
|---|---|---|---|---|---|---|---|---|---|---|
| | Size of A [b] | Size of B | Size of AB | | N [c] | n [d] | AR[0] [e] | t(AR) [f] | CAR[−1,0] [g] | t(CAR) [h] |
| (1) | Large | Large | Large | Large | 3 | n.a. | −1.94% * | 2.13 | −1.42% | 0.92 |
| (2) | Large | Medium | Large | Medium | 7 | n.a. | −0.32% | 1.33 | −0.43% | 1.11 |
| (3) | Medium | Medium | Large | Medium | 3 | n.a. | 4.57% * | 5.42 | 6.85% * | 6.47 |
| (4) | Medium | Medium | Medium | Medium | 19 | n.a. | 0.52% | 1.67 | 0.18% | 1.10 |
| | | | | Small | 19 | n.a. | 0.81% * | 3.20 | 0.69% * | 2.61 |
| (5) | Medium | Small | Medium | Small | 26 | n.a. | 0.77% * | 3.20 | 0.47% | 1.69 |
| (6) | Small | Small | Small | Small | 3 | n.a. | 1.19% | 1.04 | 0.40% | 0.23 |

[a] Other banks are banks that are in the same geographical area as the two banks that intend to merge.

[b] Large banks have at least $10 billion of assets before 1983 and at most $15 billion of assets after 1983; medium banks have assets between $1 and $10 billion before 1983 and between $1.5 and $15 billion after 1983; small banks have at most $1 billion of assets before 1983 and at most $1.5 billion of assets after 1983.

[c] Number of merger announcements.

[d] Total number of "other banks" for the N merger announcements; n.a.: not available.

[e] Average abnormal return during the announcement week (week 0).

[f] Absolute value of the t-statistic for AR[0]. Asterisks indicate significance at the 0.05 level.

[g] Cumulative average abnormal returns from week −1 to week 0.

[h] Absolute value of the t-statistic for CAR[−1,0]. Asterisks indicate significance at the 0.05 level.

Table 14E
Regulatory effect: Market reaction of other banks [a] when regulators announce the approval of a merger.

| Case | Bank (A) + | Bank (B) = | Bank (AB) | Size | Reaction of other banks [a] according to their size [b] | | | | | |
|---|---|---|---|---|---|---|---|---|---|---|
| | Size of A [b] | Size of B | Size of AB | | N [c] | n [d] | AR[0] [e] | t(AR) [f] | CAR[−1,0] [g] | t(CAR) [h] |
| (1) | Large | Large | Large | Large | 3 | 13 | 0.70% | 0.25 | 1.73% | 0.58 |
| (2) | Large | Medium | Large | Medium | 7 | 178 | 0.03% | 0.03 | −0.20% | 0.50 |
| (3) | Medium | Medium | Large | Medium | 3 | 54 | −0.85% | 0.73 | −1.78% | 0.97 |
| (4) | Medium | Medium | Medium | Medium | 19 | 295 | 0.04% | 0.27 | 0.63% | 1.28 |
| | | | | Small | 19 | 276 | −0.37% | 0.93 | −0.00% | 0.29 |
| (5) | Medium | Small | Medium | Small | 26 | 465 | −0.45% | 1.39 | −0.51% | 1.15 |
| (6) | Small | Small | Small | Small | 4 | 34 | 1.91% * | 3.07 | 2.95% * | 2.96 |

[a] Other banks are banks that are in the same geographical area as the two banks that intend to merge.
[b] Large banks have at least $10 billion of assets before 1983 and at most $15 billion of assets after 1983; medium banks have assets between $1 and $10 billion before 1983 and between $1.5 and $15 billion after 1983; small banks have at most $1 billion of assets before 1983 and at most $1.5 billion of assets after 1983.
[c] Number of merger announcements.
[d] Total number of “other banks” for the N merger announcements.
[e] Average abnormal return during the announcement week (week 0).
[f] Absolute value of the t-statistic for AR[0]. Asterisks indicate significance at the 0.05 level.
[g] Cumulative average abnormal returns from week −1 to week 0.
[h] Absolute value of the t-statistic for CAR[−1,0]. Asterisks indicate significance at the 0.05 level.

Table 14F

Denial and cancellation effects: Market reaction of other banks [a] when bank (A) announced a merger with bank (B) for the subsample of mergers that were subsequently either denied by regulators or cancelled.

| Case | Bank (A) + Bank (B) = Bank (AB) | | | Size | Reaction of other banks [a] according to their size [b] | | | | | |
|---|---|---|---|---|---|---|---|---|---|---|
| | Size of A [b] | Size of B | Size of AB | | N [c] | n [d] | AR[0] [e] | t(AR) [f] | CAR[−1,0] [g] | t(CAR) [h] |
| (1) | Large | Medium | Large | Medium | 2 | n.a. | −0.28% | 0.30 | 0.62% | 0.19 |
| (2) | Medium | Medium | Large | Medium | 1 | n.a. | 3.96% * | 2.28 | 6.45% * | 2.63 |
| (3) | Medium | Medium | Medium | Medium | 4 | n.a. | −0.09% | 0.05 | 0.33% | 0.48 |
| | | | | Small | 4 | n.a. | 0.33% | 0.50 | −1.75% | 1.40 |
| (4) | Medium | Small | Medium | Small | 2 | n.a. | 3.00% * | 2.37 | 3.10% | 1.68 |
| (5) | Small | Small | Small | Small | 2 | n.a. | 2.17% | 1.73 | 1.67% | 1.17 |

[a] Other banks are banks that are in the same geographical area as the two banks that intend to merge.

[b] Large banks have at least $10 billion of assets before 1983 and at least $15 billion of assets after 1983; medium banks have assets between $1 and $10 billion before 1983 and between $1.5 and $15 billion after 1983; small banks have at most $1 billion of assets before 1983 and at most $1.5 billion of assets after 1983.

[c] Number of merger announcements.

[d] Total number of "other banks" for the N merger announcements; n.a.: not available.

[e] Average abnormal return during the announcement week (week 0).

[f] Absolute value of the t-statistic for AR[0]. Asterisks indicate significance at the 0.05 level.

[g] Cumulative average abnormal returns from week −1 to week 0.

[h] Absolute value of the t-statistic for CAR[−1,0]. Asterisks indicate significance at the 0.05 level.

Table 14G

Denial and cancellation effects: Market reaction of other banks [a] when it is announced that a merger was denied by regulators or cancelled.

| Case | Bank (A) + | Bank (B) = | Bank (AB) | Size | Reaction of other banks [a] according to their size [b] | | | | | |
|---|---|---|---|---|---|---|---|---|---|---|
| | Size of A [b] | Size of B | Size of AB | | N [c] | n [d] | AR[0] [e] | t(AR) [f] | CAR[−1,0] [g] | t(CAR) [h] |
| (1) | Large | Large | Large | Medium | 2 | n.a. | −0.13% | 0.09 | −0.17% | 0.10 |
| (2) | Medium | Medium | Large | Medium | 1 | n.a. | −3.55% * | 1.92 | −4.49% | 1.72 |
| (3) | Medium | Medium | Medium | Medium | 4 | n.a. | −0.02% | 0.05 | 1.10% | 1.03 |
| | | | | Small | 4 | n.a. | −0.36% | 0.85 | −1.88% | 1.69 |
| (4) | Medium | Small | Medium | Small | 2 | n.a. | −0.47% | 0.43 | −0.83% | 0.42 |
| (5) | Small | Small | Small | Small | 3 | n.a. | −0.93% | 1.42 | −1.24% | 1.42 |

[a] Other banks are banks that are in the same geographical area as the two banks that intend to merge.

[b] Large banks have at least $10 billion of assets before 1983 and at least $15 billion of assets after 1983; medium banks have assets between $1 and $10 billion before 1983 and between $1.5 and $15 billion after 1983; small banks have at most $1 billion of assets before 1983 and at most $1.5 billion of assets after 1983.

[c] Number of merger announcements.

[d] Total number of “other banks” for the N merger announcements; n.a.: not available.

[e] Average abnormal return during the announcement week (week 0).

[f] Absolute value of the t-statistic for AR[0]. Asterisks indicate significance at the 0.05 level.

[g] Cumulative average abnormal returns from week −1 to week 0.

[h] Absolute value of the t-statistic for CAR[−1,0]. Asterisks indicate significance at the 0.05 level.

The market reaction of "other" banks is reported in Table 14G. In principle we should observe a reversal of the earlier market reaction (as we have seen in Chapter V, Section 5). A look at the results in Table 14G indicates that we do have negative market reactions for those cases that exhibited positive market reactions at the time of the announcement of the merger proposals. But in some cases the magnitudes of these negative effects are not strong enough to completely offset the earlier positive effects. This is also true for mergers between a medium and a small bank into one medium bank and for mergers between two small banks into one small bank. In both cases the negative effect at the time of the release of the denial order or the decision to cancel is smaller than the earlier positive effect associated with the announcement of the merger proposals. We cannot, however, conclude that in these two cases there are permanent net aggregate gains because market reactions are not measured over sufficiently long periods of time.

## 11. Summary and concluding remarks

In this chapter we examined the cross-sectional behavior of abnormal returns associated with merger announcements in order to explain why target and bidding banks react differently to merger announcements. We have also examined the market reaction of rival banks, potential bidders and alternative targets triggered by merger announcements in order to examine whether banks *not* involved in a merger react to the announcement of the merger proposals between two other banks, and if so, how this reaction can be explained.

We were able to identify a number of exogenous variables that can partly explain the differences in the market reaction of target and bidding banks to the announcements of merger proposals. We have also shown that banks *not* directly involved in a merger do react to merger announcements and we tested a number of hypotheses that can explain why "other" banks react to merger announcements which *do* not directly involve them.

A summary of the major findings is found below:

(1) The market reaction associated with mergers which will be paid for in cash is significantly higher than that associated with mergers which will be paid for in securities. This result is consistent with that reported in previous studies of non-financial mergers. This phenomenon is observed for both target and bidding banks and can be explained by the differential impact that the two means of payment have on personal taxes, agency costs and information signalling. However, when we adjust for differences in bank size, pre-merger target bank performance, and the effect of interstate banking legislation, the difference between the abnormal returns associated with cash offers and those associated with security offers is no longer significant.

(2) Interstate mergers do not create net aggregate wealth to shareholders whereas intrastate mergers do. The market rewards intrastate mergers but does not reward interstate mergers. One would expect, *a priori*, that interstate mergers would create more wealth for shareholders than intrastate mergers on the premise that interstate mergers provide shareholders with the opportunity to diversify their activities geographically. They also widen the number of targets with which a bidder may find synergetic gains via combinations. But we found the opposite to be true. This phenomenon can be explained by noting that synergetic gains may be better exploited if merging banks operate in the same market and that interstate mergers do not, on average, provide superior diversification opportunities in comparison to intrastate mergers.

(3) Mergers that occurred *before* the enactment of interstate banking legislation (mainly intrastate mergers and some interstate mergers which were exceptionally approved by regulators, see Chapter I) created net aggregate wealth to shareholders, whereas those which occurred after did not. This finding is consistent with the previous one. It also indicates that, as the number of bank mergers increases, they become, on average, less profitable.

(4) The exploitation of potential synergies via combinations is often cited as a major incentive for firms to merge. The synergy hypothesis can be verified indirectly by testing two proposi-

tions. The first is that the smaller a target bank relative to its bidder, the higher the potential synergetic gains. The second is that the smaller the bidder (irrespective of the target bank's size), the higher the potential synergetic gains. We found evidence consistent with both the relative-size proposition and the absolute-size proposition and concluded that empirical findings are consistent with the synergy hypothesis of mergers.

(5) An extension of the synergy hypothesis is the inefficient-management hypothesis according to which takeovers involving poorly-managed target banks should create more net aggregate wealth than those involving well-managed targets. The difficulty in testing this hypothesis is the identification of poorly-managed banks. Managerial quality was measured by: (a) the equity-to-total assets ratio, (b) the ratio of the target bank's return-on-equity to that of the average of all banks operating in the state where the target is located, and (c) the market performance of the target bank prior to the merger announcement. Using these measures we found that higher abnormal returns are associated with mergers involving a poorly-managed target than with mergers involving a well-managed target. This finding is consistent with the hypothesis that inefficiently-managed target banks provide an opportunity or gains if acquired and transformed into well-managed banks.

(6) We found that the pre-merger performance of bidding banks affects the magnitude of the stock market reaction to their shares during the period of the time surrounding the announcement of merger proposals. The bidder's stock price reacts positively to merger announcements when the bidder is a poor market performer prior to the merger announcement and reacts negatively when it is a good pre-merger market performer. We do not have a satisfactory explanation for this phenomenon.

(7) There is tentative evidence that abnormal returns associated with mergers between two banks with low stock-return correlations are higher than those associated with mergers between two banks with high stock-return correlations. This finding is consistent with the diversification hypothesis of mergers. Low correlation coefficients indicate larger potential risk-reduction

benefits via diversification and provide an incentive for banks to merge.

(8) A multiple-variable cross-sectional regression analysis indicates that *target* bank abnormal returns associated with merger announcements are inversely related to both the size of the target bank relative to that of its bidder and to the pre-merger performance of the target bank. Mergers which occurred before the enactment of interstate banking legislation generated higher abnormal returns to targets than post-legislation mergers.

(9) A multiple-variable cross-sectional regression analysis indicates that *bidding* bank abnormal returns associated with merger announcements are *inversely related to the number of potential bidders*. Intrastate mergers and mergers which occurred before the enactment of interstate banking legislation generated higher abnormal returns to bidders than interstate and post-legislation mergers.

(10) Merger announcements affect not only the stock price of the two merging banks but also the stock price of other banks in their market area not directly related to the announced merger. Specifically, rival banks as well as potential bidders and alternative targets react to merger announcements not involving them directly. There is weak evidence showing that rivals react positively (market-power hypothesis). There is also a positive reaction of alternative targets when the merger reduces the number of available alternative targets (the corporate-control hypothesis). No clear pattern emerged from the analysis of changes in the number of potential bidders.

## Appendix I: Provisions of the Basle Accord

(Reproduced from "International Convergence of Capital Measurement and Capital Standards", Basle Committee on Banking Regulations and Supervisory Practices, July 1988)

I. Definition of Capital Included in the Capital Base
(to apply at year-end 1992, see Part IV for transitional arrangements)

A. Capital Elements

Tier I (a) Paid-up share capital/common stock

(b) Disclosed reserves

Tier II (a) Undisclosed reserves

(b) Asset revaluation reserves

(c) General provisions/general loan-loss reserves

(d) Hybrid (debt/equity) capital instruments

(e) Subordinated term debt

The sum of Tier I and Tier II elements will be eligible for inclusion in the capital base, subject to the following limits.

B. Limits and Restrictions

(i) The total of Tier II (supplementary) elements will be limited to a maximum of 100 percent of the total of Tier I elements.

(ii) Subordinated-term debt will be limited to a maximum of 50 percent of Tier I elements.

(iii) Where general provisions/general loan-loss reserves include amounts reflecting lower valuations of assets or latent but unidentified losses present in the balance sheet, the amount of such provisions or reserves will be limited to a maximum of 1.25 percentage points, or exceptionally and temporarily up to 2.0 percentage points, of risk assets. [1]

(iv) Asset revaluation reserves that take the form of latent gains on unrealized securities (see below) will be subject to a discount of 55 percent.

C. Deductions from the Capital Base

From Tier I: (i) Goodwill.

From total capital: (i) Investments in unconsolidated banking and financial subsidiary companies.

[1] This limit would apply only in the event that no agreement is reached on a consistent basis for including unencumbered provisions or reserves in capital (see paragraphs 20 and 21).

N.B. The presumption is that the framework would be applied on a consolidated basis to banking groups.

(ii) Investments in the capital of other banks and financial institutions (at the discretion of national authorities).

D. Definition of Capital Elements

(i) Tier I. Includes only *permanent shareholders' equity* (issued and fully-paid ordinary shares/common stock and perpetual, non-cumulative preference shares) and *disclosed reserves* (created or increased by appropriations of retained earnings or other surplus; for example, share premiums, retained profit, [2] general reserves, and legal reserves). In the case of consolidated accounts, this also includes minority interests in the equity of subsidiaries that are less than wholly owned. This basic definition of capital excludes revaluation reserves and cumulative preference shares.

(ii) Tier II. (a) Undisclosed reserves are eligible for inclusion within supplementary elements provided these reserves are accepted by the supervisor. Such reserves consist of that part of the accumulated after-tax surplus of retained profits that banks in some countries may be permitted to maintain as an undisclosed reserve. Apart from the fact that the reserve is not identified in the published balance sheet, it should have the same high quality and character as a disclosed capital reserve; as such, it should not be encumbered by any provision or other known liability, but should be freely and immediately available to meet unforeseen future losses. This definition of undisclosed reserves excludes hidden values arising from holdings of

[2] Including, at national discretion, allocations during the course of the year to or from reserves from current year's retained profit.

securities in the balance sheet at below current market prices (see below).

(b) Revaluation reserves arise in two ways. First, in some countries, banks (and other commercial companies) are permitted to revalue fixed assets (normally their own premises) from time to time, in line with the change in market values. In some of these countries, the amount of such revaluations is determined by law. Revaluations of this kind are reflected on the face of the balance sheet as a revaluation reserve.

Second, hidden values or "latent" revaluation reserves may be present as a result of long-term holdings of equity securities valued in the balance sheet at the historical cost of acquisition.

Both types of revaluation reserves may be included in Tier II provided that the assets are prudently valued, fully reflecting the possibility of price fluctuation and forced sale. In the case of latent revaluation reserves, a discount of 55 percent will be applied to the difference between historical cost book value and market value to reflect the potential volatility of this form of unrealized capital and the notional tax charge on it.

(c) General provisions/general loan-loss reserves held against future, presently unidentified losses are freely available to meet losses that subsequently materialize and therefore qualify for inclusion within supplementary elements. Provisions ascribed to impairment of particular assets or known liabilities should be excluded. Furthermore, where general provisions/general loan-loss reserves include amounts reflecting lower valuations of assets or latent but unidentified losses already present in the balance sheet, the amount of such provisions or reserves eligible for inclusion will be limited to a maximum of 1.25 percentage points, or exceptionally and temporarily up to 2.0 percentage points. [3]

(d) Hybrid (debt/equity) capital instruments combine characteristics of equity capital and debt. Their precise specifications differ from country to country, but they should meet the following requirements:

- they are *unsecured, subordinated*, and *fully paid up*;
- they are not *redeemable* at the initiative of the holder or without the prior consent of the supervisory authority;
- they are *available* to *participate in losses* without the bank being obliged to cease trading (unlike conventional subordinated debt); and
- although the capital instrument may carry an obligation to pay interest that cannot permanently be reduced or waived (unlike dividends on ordinary shareholders' equity), *it should allow service obligations to be deferred (as with cumulative preference shares)* where the profitability of the bank would not support payment.

Cumulative preference shares with these characteristics would be eligible for inclusion in this category. In addition, the following are examples of instruments that may be eligible for inclusion: long-term preferred shares in Canada, *titres participatifs and titres subordonnés à durée indéterminée* in France, *Genussscheine* in Germany, perpetual subordinated debt and preference shares in the United Kingdom, and mandatory convertible debt instruments in the United States. Debt capital instruments that do not meet these criteria may be eligible for inclusion in item (e).

[3] This limit would apply only in the event that no agreement is reached on a consistent basis for including unencumbered provisions or reserves in capital (see paragraphs 20 and 21).

(e) Subordinated-term debt includes conventional unsecured subordinated debt capital instruments with a minimum original fixed term to maturity of more than five years and limited life redeemable preference shares. During the last five years to maturity, a cumulative discount (or amortization) factor of 20 percent per year will be applied to reflect the diminishing value of these instruments as a continuing source of strength. Unlike instruments included in item (d), these instruments are not normally available to participate in the losses of a bank that continues trading. For this reason, these instruments will be limited to a maximum of 50 percent of Tier 1.

II. Risk Weights by Category of On-Balance-Sheet Assets

0 percent
(a) Cash. [4]
(b) Claims on central governments and central banks denominated in national currency and funded in that currency.
(c) Other claims on OECD [5] central governments [6] and central banks.
(d) Claims collateralized by cash or OECD central government securities [6] or guaranteed by OECD central governments. [7]

[4] Includes (at national discretion) gold bullion held in own vaults or on an allocated basis to the extent backed by bullion liabilities.

[5] The OECD countries that are full members of the OECD or that have concluded special lending arrangements with the IMF associated with the Fund's General Arrangements to Borrow.

[6] Some member countries intend to apply weights to securities issued by OECD central governments to take account of investment risk. These weights would, for example, be 10 percent for all securities or 10 percent for those maturing in up to one year and 20 percent for those maturing in more than one year.

[7] Commercial loans partially guaranteed by these bodies will attract equivalent low weights on the part of the loan that is fully covered. Similarly, loans partially collateralized by cash or securities issued by OECD central governments and multilateral development banks will attract low weights on the part of the loan that is fully covered.

0, 10, 20 or 50 percent (at national discretion) (a) Claims on domestic public sector entities, excluding central government, and loans guaranteed [7] by such entities.

20 percent (a) Claims on multilateral development banks (IBRD, IADB, AsDB, AfDB, EIB) [8] and claims guaranteed by or collateralized by securities issued by such banks. [7]

(b) Claims on banks incorporated in the OECD and loans guaranteed [7] by OECD incorporated banks.

(c) Claims on banks incorporated in countries outside the OECD with a residual maturity of up to one year, and loans with a residual maturity of up to one year guaranteed by banks incorporated in countries outside the OECD.

(d) Claims on non-domestic OECD public sector entities, excluding central government, and loans guaranteed [7] by such entities.

(e) Cash items in process of collection.

50 percent (a) Loans fully secured by mortgage on residential property that is or will be occupied by the borrower or that is rented.

100 percent (a) Claims on the private sector.

(b) Claims on banks incorporated outside the OECD with a residual maturity of more than one year.

(c) Claims on central governments outside the OECD (unless denominated in national currency – and funded in that currency – see above).

(d) Claims on commercial companies owned by the public sector.

(e) Premises, plant and equipment, and other fixed assets.

[8] Claims on other multilateral development banks in which G-10 countries are shareholding members may, at national discretion, also attract a 20 percent weight.

(f) Real estate and other investments (including non-consolidated investment participations in other companies).
(g) Capital instruments issued by other banks (unless deducted from capital).
(h) All other assets.

## III. Credit Conversion Factors for Off-Balance-Sheet Items

The framework takes account of the credit risk on off-balance-sheet exposures by applying credit conversion factors to the different types of off-balance-sheet instruments or transactions. With the exception of foreign exchange and interest rate related contingencies, the credit conversion factors are set out in the table below. They are derived from the estimated size and likely occurrence of the credit exposure, as well as the relative degree of credit risk as identified in the Committee's paper, *The Management of Banks' Off-Balance-Sheet Exposures: A Supervisory Perspective*, issued in March 1986. The credit conversion factors would be multiplied by the weights applicable to the category of the counterparty for an on-balance-sheet transaction (see Part II).

| Instruments | Credit conversion factors |
|---|---|
| 1. Direct credit substitutes, for example, general guarantees of indebtedness (including standby letters of credit serving as financial guarantees for loans and securities) and acceptances (including endorsements with the character of acceptances) | 100 percent |
| 2. Certain transaction-related contingent items (e.g., performance bonds, bid bonds, warranties, and standby letters of credit related to particular transactions) | 50 percent |
| 3. Short-term self-liquidating trade-related contingencies (such as documentary credits collateralized by the underlying shipments) | 20 percent |
| 4. Sales and repurchase agreements and asset sales with recourse,[9] where the credit risk remains with the bank | 100 percent |
| 5. Forward asset purchases, forward deposits, and partly-paid shares and securities,[9] which represent commitments with certain drawdown | 100 percent |

| Instruments | Credit conversion factors |
|---|---|
| 6. Note issuance facilities and revolving underwriting facilities | 50 percent |
| 7. Other commitments (e.g., formal standby facilities and credit lines) with an original [10] maturity of more than one year | 50 percent |
| 8. Similar commitments with an original maturity of up to one year, or that can be unconditionally canceled at any time | 0 percent |

(N.B. member countries will have some limited discretion to allocate particular instruments into items 1 to 8 above according to the characteristics of the instrument in the national market.)

*Foreign Exchange and Interest Rate Related Contingencies*

The treatment of foreign exchange and interest rate related items needs special attention because banks are not exposed to credit risk for the full face value of their contracts; their risk is limited to the potential cost of replacing the cash flow (on contracts showing positive value) if the counterparty defaults. The credit equivalent amounts will depend *inter alia* on the maturity of the contract and the volatility of the rates underlying that type of instrument.

Despite the wide range of instruments in the market, the theoretical basis for assessing the credit risk on all of them has been the

[9] These items are to be weighted according to the type of asset and not according to the type of counterparty with whom the transaction has been entered into. Reverse repos (i.e., purchase and resale agreements – where the bank is the receiver of the asset) are to be treated as collateralized loans, reflecting the economic reality of the transaction. The risk is therefore to be measured as an exposure on the counterparty. Where the asset temporarily acquired is a security that attracts a preferential risk weighting, this would be recognized as collateral and the risk weighting would be reduced accordingly.

[10] In order to facilitate data collection, during the transitional period to year-end 1992, but not beyond, national supervisory authorities will have discretion to apply residual maturity as a basis for measuring commitments.

same. It has consisted of an analysis of the behavior of matched pairs of swaps under different volatility assumptions. Since exchange rate contracts involve an exchange of principal on maturity as well as being generally more volatile, higher conversion factors are proposed for those instruments that feature exchange rate risk. Interest rate contracts [11] are defined to include single-currency interest rate swaps, basis swaps, forward rate agreements, interest rate futures, interest rate options purchased, and similar instruments. Exchange rate contracts [11] include cross-country interest rate swaps, forward foreign exchange contracts, currency futures, currency options purchased, and similar instruments. Exchange rate contracts with an original maturity of 14 calendar days or less are excluded.

A majority of G-10 supervisory authorities are of the view that the best way to assess the credit risk on these items is to ask banks to calculate the current replacement cost by marking contracts to market, thus capturing the current exposure without any need for estimation, and then adding a factor (the 'add-on') to reflect the potential future exposure over the remaining life of the contract. It has been agreed that, in order to calculate the credit equivalent amount of its off-balance-sheet interest rate and foreign exchange rate instruments under this current exposure method, a bank would sum (1) the total replacement cost (obtained by 'marking to market') of all its contracts with positive value and (2) an amount for potential future credit exposure calculated on the basis of the total notional principal amount of its book, split by residual maturity as follows:

| Residual maturity | Interest rate contracts | Exchange rate contracts |
|---|---|---|
| Less than one year | Nil | 1.0 percent |
| One year and more | 0.5 percent | 5.0 percent |

[11] Instruments traded on exchanges may be excluded where they are subject to daily margining requirements. Options purchased over the counter are included with the same conversion factors as other instruments, but this decision might be reviewed in light of future experience.

No potential credit exposure would be calculated for single currency floating/floating interest rate swaps; the credit exposure on these contracts would be evaluated solely on the basis of their mark-to-market value.

A few G-10 supervisors believe that this two-step approach, incorporating a mark-to-market element, is not consistent with the remainder of the capital framework. They favor a simpler method whereby the potential credit exposure is estimated against each type of contract and a national capital weight allotted, no matter what the market value of the contract might be at a particular reporting date. It has therefore been agreed that supervisory authorities should have discretion [12] to apply the alternative method of calculation described below, in which credit conversion factors are derived without reference to the current market price of the instruments. In deciding on what those national credit conversion factors should be, it has been agreed that a slightly more cautious bias is justified since the current exposure is not being calculated on a regular basis.

In order to arrive at the credit equivalent amount using this original exposure method, a bank would simply apply one of the following two sets of conversion factors to the notional principal amounts of each instrument according to the nature of the instrument and its maturity:

| Maturity [a] | Interest rate contracts | Exchange rate contracts |
|---|---|---|
| Less than one year | 0.5 percent | 2.0 percent |
| One year and less than two years | 1.0 percent | 5.0 percent [b] |
| For each additional year | 1.0 percent | 3.0 percent |

[a] For interest rate contracts, there is national discretion as to whether the conversion factors are to be based on original or residual maturity. For exchange rate contracts, the conversion factors are to be calculated according to the original maturity of the instrument.

[b] I.e., 2 percent + 3 percent.

[12] Some national authorities may permit individual banks to choose what method to adopt, it being understood that once a bank had chosen to apply the current exposure method, it would not be allowed to switch back to the original exposure method.

It is emphasized that the above conversion factors, as well as the additions for the current exposure method, should be regarded as provisional and may be subject to amendment as a result of changes in the volatility of exchange rates and interest rates.

Careful consideration has been given to the arguments put forward for recognizing netting (i.e., for weighting the net rather than the gross claims arising out of swaps and similar contracts with the same counterparties). The criterion on which a decision has been based is the status of a netting contract under national bankruptcy regulations. If a liquidator of a failed counterparty has (or may have) the right to unbundle the netted contracts, demanding performance on those contracts favorable to his client and defaulting on unfavorable contracts, there is no reduction in counterparty risk. Accordingly, it has been agreed that:

- Banks may net contracts subject to novation, [13] since it appears that counterparty risk is genuinely reduced by the substitution of a novated contract that legally extinguishes the previous obligation. However, since under some national bankruptcy laws liquidators may have the right to unbundle transactions undertaken within a given period under a charge of fraudulent preference, supervisory authorities will have national discretion to require a phase-in period before a novation agreement can be recognized in the weighting framework.
- Banks may not, for the time being, net contracts subject to closeout clauses. [14] The effectiveness of such agreements in an insolvency has not yet been tested in the courts, nor has it been possible to obtain satisfactory legal opinion that liquidators would not be able to overturn them. However, the Committee does not wish to discourage market participants from employing clauses

[13] Netting by novation as defined in this context is a bilateral contract between two counterparties under which any obligation to each other to deliver a given currency on a given date is automatically amalgamated with all other obligations for the same currency and value date, legally substituting one single net amount for the previous gross obligations.

[14] Closeout as defined in this context refers to a bilateral contract that provides that if one of the counterparties is wound up, the outstanding obligations between the two are accelerated and netted to determine the counterparty's net exposure.

that might well afford protection in certain circumstances in some national jurisdictions and would be prepared to reverse its conclusion if subsequent decisions in the courts support the integrity of closeout netting agreements. [15]

Once a bank has calculated the credit equivalent amounts, whether according to the current or the original exposure method, they are to be weighted according to the category of counterparty in the same way as in the main framework, including concessionary weighting in respect of exposures backed by eligible guarantees and collateral. In addition, since most counterparties in these markets, particularly for long-term contracts, tend to be first-class names, it has been agreed that a 50 percent weight will be applied in respect of counterparties that would otherwise attract a 100 percent weight. [16] However, the Committee will keep a close eye on the credit quality of participants in these markets and reserves the right to raise the weights if average credit quality deteriorates or if loss experience increases.

## IV. Transitional Arrangements

| | Initial | Year-end 1990 | Year-end 1992 |
|---|---|---|---|
| 1. Minimum standard | The level prevailing at year-end 1987 | 7.25 percent | 8.0 percent |
| 2. Measurement formula | Core elements plus 100 percent | Core elements plus 100 percent (3.625% plus 3.625%) | Core element plus 100 percent (4% plus 4%) |

[15] The other principal form of netting, payments netting, which is designed to reduce the counterparty risk arising out of daily settlements, will not be recognized in the capital framework since the counterparty's gross obligations are not in any way affected.

[16] Some member countries reserve the right to apply the full 100 percent weight.

| | Initial | Year-end 1990 | Year-end 1992 |
|---|---|---|---|
| 3. Supplementary elements included in core | Maximum 25 percent of total core | Maximum 10 percent of total core (i.e., 0,36%) | None |
| 4. Limit on general loan-loss reserves in supplementary elements (a) | No limit | 1.5 percentage points, or exceptionally up to 2.0 percentage points | 1.25 percentage points, or exceptionally up to 2.0 percentage points |
| 5. Limit on term subordinated elements | No limit (at discretion) | No limit (at discretion) | Maximum of 50 percent of Tier I |
| 6. Deduction for goodwill | Deducted from Tier I (at discretion) | Deducted from Tier I (at discretion) | Deducted from Tier I |

[a] This limit would apply only in the event that no agreement is reached on a consistent basis for including unencumbered provisions or reserves in capital (see paragraphs 20 and 21).

## Appendix II: Role of current primary capital guidelines

(Reproduced from Staff Memorandum to the Board of Governors, Federal Reserve System, August 1, 1988)

The Basle Accord provides a transition period through the end of 1992, during which a risk-based capital measure and a minimum ratio standard would be phased into existing national supervisory systems. In issuing the framework for comment in March, the federal banking agencies indicated their intention to retain existing primary capital and total capital-to-total asset ratios (leverage ratios) in conjunction with the risk-based framework. The reason for this was that the risk-based minimum standard did not take effect until the end of 1990, and the risk-based standard, unlike current ratios that relate capital to total assets, does not place a limit on total leverage. The retention of the existing capital standard, at least initially, does not mean that well-capitalized banking organizations would gain no benefits from the introduction of a risk-based standard. Indeed, organizations in sound condition with strong risk-based capital ratios could, with the concurrence of their primary regulator, be allowed to reduce their primary and total capital ratios (that is, increase their leverage) closer to the existing 5.5 percent and 6.0 percent minimums – levels that most institutions are currently well above.

At the same time, the federal agencies recognized that different capital definitions could be confusing. For this reason, the agencies indicated that prior to the end of 1990, they would determine whether a leverage constraint (that is, a minimum capital-to-*total assets* ratio) would continue to be applied in conjunction with the risk-based capital standard. If such a leverage constraint were deemed appropriate, the agencies would adopt (for leverage ratio purposes) capital definitions consistent with those contained in the risk-based capital framework.

The majority favored abandoning the use of existing leverage ratios because they could be confusing and deemed unnecessary in light of the risk-based framework. However, several respondents, including the Independent Bankers Association of America, supported retention of the ratios. Some supported retention of leverage ratios out of concern that the risk-based standard was too lenient; others argued that it was appropriate until greater experience was gained using the risk-based ratio.

*Staff-recommendation*. The staff recommends that the Board retain the existing primary and total capital-to-total assets leverage ratios, at least initially. Some capital standard would appear to be appropriate until the interim risk-based ratio takes effect in 1990. Retention of the existing ratios would also provide an element of continuity as transition is made to a risk-based framework. More critically, the assignment of a significant volume of assets to the 0 percent risk category, such as all short-term claims on central governments of the OECD-based defined group of countries, as well as all claims guaranteed by these entities or collateralized by their securities, means that the risk-based capital ratio by itself establishes *no limit on total leverage* involving these types of assets. Thus, it would appear prudent, at least initially, to retain some maximum leverage constraint. Moreover, the staffs of the Federal banking agencies believe that, for this reason, a leverage constraint of some kind may be appropriate for the longer term, although not necessarily at the current levels of 5.5 percent or 6.0 percent.

Thus, the staff recommends that the Federal banking agencies (1) retain the existing capital standards initially; (2) review as soon as possible, in any event before 1990, the need for a total leverage constraint; and, if such a constraint is deemed appropriate; (3) bring the definition of capital for this purpose into line with the Basle framework.

CHAPTER VII

# CAPITAL MARKET REACTION TO THE ANNOUNCEMENT OF INTERSTATE BANKING LEGISLATION: THE CASES OF TEXAS, ARIZONA AND VIRGINIA

## 1. Introduction

In the previous chapters, we examined the reaction of bank stock prices to the announcement of merger proposals. We have shown that these announcements affect both target and bidding banks. The former react, on average, positively and the latter react, on average, negatively. We have also found that stock price changes associated with intrastate merger announcements were, on average, significantly higher than those associated with interstate merger announcements (see Chapter VI).

We provided in Chapter VI a possible explanation for why the stock price reaction of banks should be weaker in the case of interstate announcements (essentially because synergetic gains may be more difficult to achieve via interstate mergers than via intrastate mergers, see Chapter VI, Section 4). Another possible explanation, particularly for the case of target banks, is that the stock price of those banks which would benefit most from being acquired by an out-of-state bank may have risen long before the merger proposal is announced. Consider a state that unexpectedly announces the introduction of legislation that will permit out-of-state banks to unconditionally acquire any bank in that state. The removal of all legal barriers should trigger a rise in the stock price of those banks which are potential targets for out-of-state banks. By the time interstate legislation is enacted and a specific out-of-state bank makes a bid on a given target bank, most of the potential merger gains that usually accrue to the target may have already been reflected in the target bank's stock price. In other words, the market price of target banks would already have adjusted in anticipation of the merger, as found by Cornett and De (1989).

This chapter examines the price reaction of bank stocks to a sequence of announcements related to interstate banking legislation in three states that opened up their borders to out-of-state banks. These are Arizona, Texas and Virginia. Arizona enacted legislation in 1985 that allowed unrestricted, nationwide interstate banking beginning October 1, 1986. Texas enacted the same legislation in 1986 that became effective on January 1, 1987, and Virginia enacted regional reciprocal interstate banking legislation in 1985 that became effective on January 1, 1986. According to the argument we have developed above, the stock price of banks in these states should have risen when interstate banking legislation was first suggested. The reaction should have been stronger in the cases of Arizona and Texas than in the case of Virginia since the first two enacted unrestricted, nationwide interstate legislation (that is, banks in any other state can acquire in-state banks even if that state does not permit interstate banking) whereas Virginia enacted restrictive interstate banking legislation based on regional reciprocity (that is, Virginia banks can only be acquired by banks located in a limited number of states that have themselves opened up their borders to Virginia banks).

The following three sections examine the reaction of banks to the announcement of interstate banking legislation in Texas, Arizona and Virginia. The last section contains a summary of our findings and some concluding remarks.

## 2. Reaction of bank stock prices to announcements related to interstate banking legislation in Texas

Texas is a particularly interesting case to analyze because interstate banking legislation was proposed rather unexpectedly and enacted relatively quickly. Unanticipation and swiftness are two desirable characteristics if we wish to examine the stock price reaction of banks in response to interstate banking legislation. If an

Exhibit A
Sequence of events leading to the enactment of interstate banking legislation in Texas.

| Date | Event |
|---|---|
| Sat. July 26, 1986 | Texas banking commissioner James Sexton urges legislation allowing interstate banking. He has the support of both the State Governor and the House Speaker. The commissioner asks the legislature to consider both an interstate and a branch banking proposal in its special session called for August 6, 1986 (*Houston Post*: 07/26/86). |
| Fri. August 1, 1986 | The uncertain outlook of Texas banks is shaping unusual consensus among bankers to allow interstate banking; bankers fear that some banks may soon need help from larger and better capitalized institutions outside the state (*Wall Street Journal*: 08/01/86. |
| Fri. August 8, 1986 | Consumer groups charge that legislative committees are set to consider within the next week measures that would open Texas to interstate banking but none of the legislation has been seen by the public (*Houston Post*: 08/09/86). |
| Wed. August 20, 1986 | The Texas senate approves legislation that would allow both interstate and limited branch banking. The two bills and the proposed constitutional change pass 26-2 and are sent to the House for approval (*Houston Post*: 08/21/86). |
| Thur. August 21, 1986 | Stock prices of most major bank holding companies in Texas rise sharply in active trading, as the Texas senate approves a sweeping interstate banking measure (*Wall Street Journal*: 08/21/86). |
| Fri. August 22, 1986 | The House Financial Institution's Committee approves and sends to the floor of the House a bill legalizing interstate banking and a proposed constitutional amendment allowing branch banking. The interstate banking bill is approved 8-1 and the branch banking proposal is unanimously approved (*Houston Post*: 08/23/86). |
| Thur. August 28, 1986 | Senators accept the House-passed version of the interstate banking and branching bills, sending the legislation to the governor for his signature. If signed, the new legislation becomes effective on January 1, 1987 (*Houston Post*: 08/29/86. |
| Tues. Sept. 23, 1986 | Governor Mark White signs into law the bill that allows out-of-state banks to purchase Texas banks without reciprocal measures from other states (*Houston Post*: 09/24/86). |

event is unexpected, the stock price reaction to that event should be sharper since no prior adjustment has taken place. If the sequence of events that led to the enactment of interstate banking legislation occurred over a relatively short period of time, then we can more easily identify the exact dates when particularly relevant events took place by thoroughly examining press reports during that period.

### *2.1. Chronology of events*

The earliest press reports regarding the possible introduction of interstate banking legislation in Texas appeared late July 1986. Interstate banking legislation was approved by both the Texas Senate and House late August 1986. The final version of the bill was signed into law by the state governor on September 23, 1986 and became effective on January 1, 1987. Less than two months separated the initiation of the provision from actual enactment. The key dates related to this sequence of events are reported in Exhibit A.

Late July 1986, the *Houston Post* reported that Texas banking commissioner James Sexton was urging for legislation that would permit Texas banks to engage in interstate banking and to expand within the state via branch banking. Both activities were at that time prohibited by state law. Earlier attempts to allow state banks to branch out within the state and to permit out-of-state banks to acquire Texas banks had met strong opposition from bank associations and consumer organizations. This resistance began to subside as the number of failing banks rose sharply. In 1985, 12 Texas banks failed, with the same number collapsing during the first six months of 1986. Faced with a rising number of bank failures and a depressed economy, Texas needed out-of-state banks to rescue the increasing number of weak banks operating in that state.

According to the September 1986 issue of *The Banker*, "in the first seven months of 1986, the average Texas bank stock lost 37 percent of its value, as mounting bad energy and real estate loans have depressed earnings and pushed a few banks into the red. The Texas legislature, which would not normally have met until January 1987, was called into a special one-month session on August 6 to solve the fiscal crisis caused by dwindling oil and gas tax revenues. Pressure to use the opportunity to amend restrictive banking laws began building up in July, but governor Mark White said he wanted to see some progress on closing the projected $3.5 billion budget gap before he included banking issues on the agenda. When he did, halfway through the session, the Senate moved with almost indecent haste and there were none of the previously mooted intermediate steps, such as demanding interstate reciprocity or excluding banks from California and New York".

On August 20, the Texas Senate approved legislation that would allow both interstate and branch banking. The two bills passed 26-2 and were sent to the House Financial Institutions Committee, which approved them. A bill legalizing interstate banking and a proposed constitutional amendment allowing branch banking was approved by the House on August 22. On August 28, senators accepted the House-passed version of the interstate banking and branching bills. The interstate banking bill was signed into law by the state governor on September 23, 1986.

The price reaction of bank stocks to the sequence of events that led to the enactment of interstate banking legislation in Texas can be examined using a time-series regression analysis. The methodology and the empirical results are reported below.

### *2.2. Regression analysis results*

*Methodology*. The sample of banks is first divided into two groups: Texas banks and out-of-state banks. Texas banks are then assigned to one of three equally-weighted portfolios of banks constructed according to bank size (see Chapter VI for details regarding size cut-off points). The large-bank portfolio contains 4 banks, the medium-bank portfolio 7 banks, and the small-bank portfolio 5 banks. Out-of-state banks are assigned to one of four equally-weighted portfolios also constructed according to bank size. The money-center-bank portfolio contains 15 banks, the large-bank portfolio 4 banks, the medium-bank portfolio 149 banks and the small-bank portfolio 172 banks. This approach yields a total of seven portfolios.

To estimate the market reaction of a given group of banks to certain events, we used a simultaneous equations, multivariate regression framework as suggested by Binder (1985a, 1985b). Two characteristics associated with regulatory changes called for the use of this approach:

(a) multiple announcements of regulatory changes, and
(b) high cross-sectional correlations in the security return residuals of affected banks.

The following regressions were run:

$$R_{pt} = \alpha_p + \beta_p \cdot R_{mt} + \sum_{k=1}^{4} u_{pk} \cdot D_k + e_{pt},$$

where $R_{pt}$, the dependent variable, is the weekly return on portfolio p (p = 1, 2, ..., 7) during the year 1986 (t = 1, 2, ..., 52). The independent variables are:

$R_m$ = weekly return on the CRSP value weighted index,

$D_1$ = a dummy variable that takes the value of one during the 3 weeks surrounding press reports that the state commissioner is urging the legislature to adopt interstate banking legislation (from the week beginning July 25, to the week ending August 14), and zero otherwise,

$D_2$ = a dummy variable that takes the value of one during the 2 weeks surrounding press reports that the Texas Senate, the Financial Institutions Committee and the Texas House approved a bill allowing interstate banking (from the week beginning August 15 to the week ending August 28) and zero otherwise,

$D_3$ = a dummy variable that takes the value of one during a 2-week interim period in which no specific events related to interstate legislation (from the week beginning August 29 to the week ending September 11) and zero otherwise,

$D_4$ = a dummy variable that takes the value of one during the 2 weeks surrounding press reports that the bill allowing interstate banking was signed by the state governor (from the week beginning September 12 to the week ending September 25) and zero otherwise.

The sum of the first two terms on the right-hand side of the regression equation is the standard market model presented in Chapter III. The four following terms (the dummy variables) are measures of the abnormal returns of portfolio p due to specific events surrounding the introduction and enactment of interstate banking legislation in Texas.

The coefficient of the first independent variable ($\beta_p$) captures the changes in bank stock prices due to the movements of the market as a whole. These price changes would have occurred irrespective of announcements related to interstate banking legislation and hence should be accounted for and neutralized by introducing the market model term, $\alpha_p + \beta_p \cdot R_{mt}$.

The multivariate regression approach allows for discrimination on the differential effects of announcements across portfolios of banks and for contemporaneous correlations among individual portfolio returns. This is accomplished by use of the zero-one dummy variable for market model equations. The coefficients of the equation measure the impact of an event on stock return prices. The estimate of the coefficients ($u_{pk}$) are similar to residual returns obtained from the market model. Moreover, it permits the evaluation of many different events (announcements) during the time period examined. Finally, the t-statistic on the regression coefficients is used to test the significance of the estimated abnormal returns.

The coefficients $u_{pk}$ ($k = 1, 2, 3, 4$) capture the effect that a specific event (or non-event) may have on the value of portfolio p. The coefficients $u_{p1}$, $u_{p2}$ and $u_{p4}$ are expected, *a priori*, to be positive and the coefficients $u_{p3}$ to be zero (non-event) for Texas banks. In the case of out-of-state banks, the coefficients $u_{p1}$, $u_{p2}$ and $u_{p4}$ may take any value. The sequence of events occurring in Texas may or may not be of great significance to out-of-state banks. The coefficient $u_{p3}$ should, *a priori*, be equal to zero.

*Empirical evidence and interpretation*. The estimated coefficients of the seven regression equations are reported in Table 15A. The upper part of the table gives the estimated coefficients for the three size portfolios of Texas banks. The lower part gives the estimated coefficients for the four size portfolios of out-of-state banks. Below each estimated coefficient is its corresponding t-statistic.

Note that the estimated value of the constant coefficients are significantly negative for Texas banks of all sizes. They are not significantly different from zero for out-of-state banks, except for the case of the small-size portfolio in which the estimated value of the constant coefficient is significantly positive. The results indicate that the stock price of Texas banks dropped significantly during the year 1986 (by a weekly average of about 1.39 percent for large banks, 1.32 percent for medium-size banks and 0.72 percent for small banks) after adjusting for the general market movements and the effects of the announcements related to interstate banking legislation. This finding is not surprising given the weakness of the Texas economy in 1986 and the mounting difficulties encountered by Texas banks during that period of time. Regarding out-of-state banks, an insignificant constant coefficient is expected. The significant positive constant coefficient for small banks can be explained by an underestimation of the beta coefficient ($\beta_p$) due to nonsynchronous trading between the small-size portfolio and the market index (Cohen et al. (1983)). It may also be the manifestation of the small-firm effect in the banking industry. The small-firm effect refers to the finding that firms with relatively smaller market capitalization outperform their larger counterparts on a risk-adjusted basis (Banz (1981)).

Finally, note that the beta coefficients of the bank portfolios are significantly positive in all but two cases: small Texas banks and large out-of-state banks. This is in contrast to the expectation of significantly positive beta coefficients in all cases. The insignificance of the beta coefficient of small Texas banks and large out-of-state banks can be explained by the very small number of banks in these two portfolios and by the nonsynchronous bias suffered by the portfolio of small Texas banks. The following four null hypotheses are tested:

Hypothesis 1 (H1). The event parameters $u_{p1}$, $u_{p2}$ and $u_{p4}$ are equal to zero for Texas banks irrespective of their size.

Hypothesis 2 (H2). The non-event parameter $u_{p3}$ is different from zero for Texas banks irrespective of their size.
Hypothesis 3 (H3). The event parameters $u_{p1}$, $u_{p2}$ and $u_{p4}$ are different from zero for out-of-state banks irrespective of their size.
Hypothesis 4 (H4). The non-event parameter $u_{p3}$ is different from zero for out-of-state banks irrespective of their size.

As shown by the results reported in Table 15A, H1 is rejected for large and medium-size banks but not for small banks. The stock price of large and medium-size banks reacted positively to the sequence of announcements related to interstate banking legislation. The magnitude of that response is significant. The stock price of large banks rose by 5.58 percent, on average, during the 3 weeks surrounding press reports that interstate banking legislation would soon be presented to the legislature. They rose by 7.26 percent during the 2 weeks surrounding the approval by the legislature and by 5.32 percent during the 2 weeks surrounding the signing of the bill by the state governor. Similar results are reported for medium-size banks. Small banks exhibit a positive response only during the 2-week period surrounding the passage of the bill. During that period, the price reaction of small banks is weaker than that of large and medium-size banks (4.38 percent versus 7.26 percent and 8.75 percent). In the next section, we examine whether these stock price reactions are significantly different from one another.

Since there is no stock price reaction by Texas banks during the 2-week interim period separating the passage of the interstate banking bill through the legislature and the signing of this bill into law by the state governor, H2 is rejected. H3 is rejected for out-of-state banks irrespective of their size. The sequence of events occurring in Texas does not, on average, affect the stock price of out-of-state banks. H4 is rejected for money-center and large banks but not for medium-size and small out-of-state banks. It is not clear why medium-size and small out-of-state banks should exhibit a significant drop in their stock price during the 2-week interim period (a non-event period for Texas banks).

Table 15A

Reaction of bank stock to announcements related to interstate banking legislation in Texas: Regression analysis [a]

| *Dependent variable* [b] Return on a portfolio of | Constant coefficient [d] | Independent variables [c] | | | | | F[i] statistics |
|---|---|---|---|---|---|---|---|
| | | Market return | Dummy [e] 1 | Dummy [f] 2 | Dummy [g] 3 | Dummy [h] 4 | |
| *Texas banks* | | | | | | | |
| Large banks (4) [c] | −0.0139 * | 0.9800 * | 0.0558 * | 0.0726 * | −0.0083 | 0.0532 | 4.19 * |
| | (2.85) | (3.86) | (2.54) | (2.72) | (0.28) | (1.96) | |
| Medium banks (7) | −0.0132 * | 0.5588 * | 0.0482 * | 0.0875 * | −0.0049 | 0.0425 | 4.55 * |
| | (2.78) | (2.27) | (2.27) | (3.38) | (0.17) | (1.65) | |
| Small banks (5) | −0.0072 * | 0.1532 | −0.0131 | 0.0438 * | 0.0188 | 0.0092 | 1.92 |
| | (2.15) | (0.87) | (0.86) | (2.38) | (0.94) | (0.50) | |
| *Out-of-state banks* | | | | | | | |
| Money center banks (15) | −0.0010 | 1.2742 * | −0.0027 | −0.0054 | 0.0064 | −0.0045 | 0.17 |
| | (0.49) | (11.38) | (0.28) | (0.46) | (0.50) | (0.38) | |
| Large banks (4) | 0.0015 | 1.1892 | −0.0078 | −0.0143 | −0.0135 | 0.0040 | 0.66 |
| | (0.62) | (0.46) | (0.72) | (1.08) | (0.94) | (0.30) | |

| | | | | | | | |
|---|---|---|---|---|---|---|---|
| Medium banks (149) | 0.0019 | 0.7387 * | 0.0043 | 0.0035 | −0.0253 * | 0.0137 | 2.38 * |
| | (1.15) | (8.60) | (0.58) | (0.39) | (2.56) | (1.52) | |
| Small banks (172) | 0.0046 * | 0.4647 * | −0.0022 | −0.0096 | −0.0172 * | −0.0011 | 1.63 |
| | (3.48) | (6.74) | (0.36) | (1.33) | (2.17) | (0.15) | |

[a] Estimated coefficients for time-series regressions relating the returns on a portfolio of banks (grouped by size and whether banks are in Texas or out-of-state) to the returns on a market index and three dummy variables, each variable taking the value of one during weeks of particular events (identified below) and the value of zero otherwise.

[b] Return on an equally-weighted portfolio of banks grouped by size and whether banks are in Texas or out-of-state.

[c] Number of banks in the portfolio.

[d] Absolute values of t-statistics are in parentheses below the corresponding estimated coefficient. Asterisks indicate significance at the 0.05 level.

[e] Dummy one takes the value of one during the three weeks surrounding press reports that Texas banking commissioner will push for legislation allowing interstate banking (last week of July 1986).

[f] Dummy two takes the value of one during the two weeks surrounding press reports that the Texas Senate, the Texas House Committee and the Texas House have approved a bill allowing interstate banking (third and fourth weeks of August 1986).

[g] Dummy three takes the value of one during a two-week interim period with no specific events related to interstate legislation (first two weeks of September 1986).

[h] Dummy four takes the value of one during the two weeks surrounding press reports that the bill allowing interstate banking has been signed into law by the Governor of Texas (last two weeks of September 1986).

[i] F-statistics; asterisks indicate significance at the 0.05 level.

The results reported in Table 15A indicate that there may be significant differences in the stock price reaction of banks to the announcements of interstate banking legislation. There seems to be differences both among Texas banks and among non-Texas banks. There also seems to be differences between Texas and non-Texas banks. These issues are examined below.

## 2.3. *Differences in stock price reaction*

This section examines whether there exist differential market reactions to the announcements related to interstate banking legislation in Texas.

In order to answer this question the following five *null* hypotheses were tested.

Hypothesis 5 (H5). The event parameters $u_{pk}$ are equal across all Texas banks in the sample ($u_{1k} = u_{2k} = u_{3k}$).

Hypothesis 6 (H6). The event parameters $u_{pk}$ are equal across all non-Texas banks in the sample ($u_{4k} = u_{5k} = u_{6k} = u_{7k}$).

Hypothesis 7 (H7). The event parameters $u_{pk}$ for large Texas banks are the same as those for large out-of-state banks ($u_{p1} = u_{p5}$).

Hypothesis 8 (H8). The event parameters $u_{pk}$ for medium-size Texas banks are the same as those for medium-size out-of-state banks ($u_{p2} = u_{p6}$).

Hypothesis 9 (H9). The event parameters $u_{pk}$ for small Texas banks are the same as those for small out-of-state banks ($u_{p3} = u_{p7}$).

The results of an F-test for each hypothesis and for each type of dummy ($k = 1, 2, 3, 4$) are reported in Table 15B. This table provides the value of the F-statistic and, below it, the corresponding probability that the null hypothesis is accepted.

Table 15B indicates that H5 is rejected for $k = 1, 2$, but not for $k = 3, 4$, at the 5 percent level of significance. The event parameters are *not* the same for all Texas banks during the 3-week pre-legislation period ($D_1$) and the 2-week legislature period ($D_2$). They are the

Table 15B

Testing for differences in the reaction of bank stock prices to announcements related to interstate banking legislation in Texas.

| Null hypothesis [a] | Dummy 1 | Dummy 2 | Dummy 3 | Dummy 4 |
|---|---|---|---|---|
| | F-statistic (probability > F) [b] | F-statistic (probability > F) [b] | F-statistic (probability > F) [b] | F-statistic (probability > F) [b] |
| (1) Dummy coefficients are the same for all Texas banks | 3.3858 * (0.0180) | 4.4966 * (0.0042) | 0.2974 (0.8288) | 1.4974 (0.2130) |
| (2) Dummy coefficients are the same for all non-Texas banks | 0.7991 (0.4504) | 1.6136 (0.2003) | 0.5428 (0.5815) | 1.5677 (0.2096) |
| (3) Dummy coefficient for large banks in Texas is the same as that for out-of-state large banks | 6.0044 * (0.0146) | 7.5639 * (0.0062) | 0.0234 (0.8786) | 2.4394 (0.1190) |
| (4) Dummy coefficient for medium banks in Texas is the same as that for out-of-state medium banks | 4.6354 * (0.0318) | 11.4865 * (0.0008) | 0.5699 (0.4507) | 1.3555 (0.2449) |
| (5) Dummy coefficient for small banks in Texas is the same as that for out-of-state small banks | 0.4168 (0.5189) | 6.7736 * (0.0096) | 2.5789 (0.1090) | 0.2538 (0.6146) |

[a] The null hypotheses are based on the estimated coefficients of the dummy variables reported in Table 15A.
[b] This is the probability that the null hypothesis is accepted. Asterisks indicate significance at the 0.05 level.

same during the 2-week enactment period ($D_4$). It can therefore be concluded that the stock price reaction of Texas banks to announcements related to the introduction and passage of legislation allowing interstate banking depends on bank size, with *smaller* banks reacting less strongly than medium-size and larger banks (see the magnitude of the event parameters reported in Table 15A). This reaction is not surprising since large and medium-size Texas banks are more likely than small banks to become candidates for an acquisition by out-of-state banks which are looking for a significant presence in the Texas banking market. In other words, the bidder-competition hypothesis is more significant for these banks than for small banks.

H6 cannot be rejected since the event parameters are the same (insignificantly different from zero) for all non-Texas banks. Both H7 and H8 are rejected during the 3-week pre-legislation period ($D_1$) and the 2-week legislature period ($D_2$) but not during the interim and enactment periods ($D_3$ and $D_4$). H9 is rejected for the 2-week legislature period but not for the other 3 periods. Globally, these results indicate that Texas banks reacted differently from out-of-state banks to announcements related to interstate banking legislation. Since Texas banks are most likely to become targets, and out-of-state banks most likely to become bidders, this finding is consistent with the earlier common observation that target-bank shareholders reap most of the value created by an acquisition, and that target-bank shareholder gains are directly related to the number of potential bidders.

### 3. Reaction of bank stock prices to the announcement of interstate banking legislation in Arizona

Arizona is the third state that opened up its borders unconditionally to out-of-state banks. In 1984, both Alaska and Maine enacted legislation permitting unrestricted, nationwide interstate banking. In April 1985, the Arizona legislature voted to admit banks from any other state, as of October 1, 1986, without a reciprocal agreement from the outsider's home state. However, this unconditionality will be in effect only until June 30, 1992. After that date, out-of-state banks may only enter the state with *de novo* operations.

The same tests performed on portfolios of Texas banks were performed on Arizona banks. The results are described below.

### *3.1. Regression analysis results*

The methodology is identical to that presented in the case of Texas banks (Section 2.1). However, there is only a single dummy variable that takes the value of one during the two weeks (beginning April 6 and ending April 19, 1985) surrounding press reports that Arizona would allow unrestricted, nationwide interstate banking. The regression results are reported in Table 15C. The upper part of the table gives the estimated coefficients and their corresponding t-statistic for Arizona banks. The lower part gives the same information for out-of-state banks. In the case of Arizona banks, there is only one medium-size bank and a small-bank portfolio because no bank in Arizona was large enough to qualify as a "large bank" according to our size criteria (a bank must have at least $15 billion in assets to be considered a large bank).

The estimated constant coefficient is significantly positive in three out of the five cases reported in Table 15C, a result that can be attributed to: (1) an underestimation of the beta coefficient of these portfolios, (2) the small-firm effect, or (3) a combination of these two phenomena. Note that the estimated beta coefficients are all significantly positive with money-center banks having the highest betas and small banks the lowest betas. The estimated event parameter is significantly positive only for medium-size banks located inside and outside Arizona. The stock price of the medium-size Arizona bank rose by 4.67 percent during the 2-week period surrounding press reports that Arizona would allow interstate banking. The stock price of medium-size banks outside Arizona rose by 1.22 percent during that period. These price increases can be attributed to the information about the change in the state law, excluding any effect due to the general market movement during that 2-week period.

Table 15C

Reaction of bank stock prices to the announcement of interstate banking legislation in Arizona: Regression analysis. [a]

| *Dependent variable* [b] Return on a portfolio of | Constant coefficient [d] | *Independent variables* | |
|---|---|---|---|
| | | Market return [d] | Dummy variable [d] |
| *Arizona banks* | | | |
| Medium banks (1) [c] | 0.0057 | 0.478 * | 0.0467 * |
| | (1.64) | (2.61) | (2.36) |
| Small banks (2) | 0.0068 * | 0.5833 * | −0.0041 |
| | (2.37) | (3.90) | (0.26) |
| *Out-of-state banks* | | | |
| Money center banks (15) | −0.0002 | 1.3132 * | 0.0142 |
| | (0.06) | (8.88) | (0.91) |
| Large banks (8) | −0.0013 | 0.7850 * | −0.0009 |
| | (0.57) | (6.46) | (0.07) |
| Medium banks (155) | 0.0045 * | 0.3966 * | 0.0122 * |
| | (4.48) | (7.50) | (2.18) |
| Small banks (175) | 0.0036 * | 0.1501 * | 0.0004 |
| | (5.07) | (4.06) | (0.11) |

[a] Estimated coefficients for time-series regressions relating the returns on a portfolio of banks (grouped by size and whether banks are in Arizona or out-of-state) to the returns on a market index and a dummy variable that takes the value of one during the two weeks (from April 6 to April 19, 1985) surrounding press reports that Arizona will allow unrestricted interstate banking and the value of zero otherwise. Actual event date is April 18, 1985.

[b] Return on an equally-weighted portfolio of banks grouped by size and whether banks are in Arizona or our-of-state.

[c] Number of banks in the portfolio.

[d] Absolute value of t-statistics are in parentheses below the corresponding estimated coefficients. Asterisks indicate significance at the 0.05 level.

As in the case of Texas, it seems that it is the largest banks in the state which respond positively to the announcement of the forthcoming removal of barriers against interstate banking. This is because it is the largest banks that are most likely to become candidates for a takeover by an out-of-state bank.

### 3.2. *Cumulative abnormal returns*

We report in Table 15D the cumulative average abnormal returns of both Arizona and non-Arizona banks over the 3-week period centered on the event week (April 18, 1985). The column in Table 15D gives the corresponding t-statistic. The results in Table 15D confirm those reported in Table 15C. Medium-size banks, both inside and outside Arizona, react favorably to the announcement of interstate banking legislation with the Arizona bank displaying the highest rise in stock price during the 3-week period (12.17 percent).

### 3.3. *Differences in stock price reaction*

The results are summarized in Table 15E. We have seen that the medium-size bank in Arizona reacted positively to the announcement whereas small banks did not exhibit any significant reaction (see Table 15C). The results in Table 15E indicate that there is a

Table 15D
Reaction of bank stock prices to the announcement of interstate banking legislation in Arizona: Cumulative average abnormal returns.

| Type of banks | CAR[−1, +1] [b] | t(CAR) [c] |
|---|---|---|
| *Arizona banks* | | |
| Medium banks (1) [a] | 12.17% * | 3.26 |
| Small banks (2) | 4.69% | 1.40 |
| *Out-of-state banks* | | |
| Money center banks (15) | 4.56% | 1.16 |
| Large banks (8) | 0.08% | 0.03 |
| Medium banks (155) | 3.28% * | 2.36 |
| Small banks (175) | −0.11% | 0.12 |

[a] Number of banks in portfolio.
[b] Cumulative average abnormal returns on the portfolio of banks over a three-week period centered on the event week. Actual event date is April 18, 1985. Asterisks indicate significance at the 0.05 level.
[c] Absolute value of t-statistic for the corresponding CAR.

Table 15E
Testing for differences in the reaction of banks to the announcement of interstate banking legislation in Arizona.

| Null hypothesis [a] | F-statistics (probability > F) [b] | Outcome |
|---|---|---|
| (1) Dummy coefficients are the same for all Arizona banks | 3.6749 (0.0031) | Reject at the 0.010 level |
| (2) Dummy coefficients are the same for all non-Arizona banks | 5.0445 (0.0069) | Reject at the 0.010 level |
| (3) Dummy coefficient for medium banks in Arizona is the same as that for out-of-state medium banks | 3.2152 (0.0738) | Reject at the 0.075 level |

[a] The null hypotheses are based on the estimated coefficients of the dummy variable reported in Table 15C.
[b] This is the probability that the null hypothesis is accepted.

significant difference between the reaction of the medium-size bank portfolio and the small-bank portfolio. We reject the hypothesis that these two categories of banks have the same stock price reaction (at the 1 percent level of significance).

The hypothesis that the stock price reaction of out-of-state banks is the same is also rejected since there is also a size effect among non-Arizona banks. Finally, the hypothesis that the medium-size bank in Arizona has the same price reaction as the out-of-state medium-size banks is also rejected. The Arizona bank displays a stronger reaction to the announcement of interstate banking legislation.

## 4. Reaction of bank stock prices to the announcement of regional banking legislation in Virginia

We conclude with an examination of the case of Virginia. Contrary to the previous two cases, Virginia allows only regional, reciprocal interstate banking. Reports that Virginia will allow interstate banking only on a regional, reciprocal basis appeared in the press during the second half of March 1985.

The estimated coefficients of six size-related regression equations are reported in Table 15F. There is a single dummy variable that

Table 15F
Reaction of bank stock prices to the announcement of regional banking legislation in Virginia: Regression analysis. [a]

| *Dependent variable* [b] Return on a portfolio of | Constant coefficient [d] | *Independent variables* | |
|---|---|---|---|
| | | Market return [d] | Dummy variable [d] |
| *Virginia banks* | | | |
| Medium banks (7) [c] | 0.0059 * | 0.6710 * | −0.0151 |
| | (3.24) | (6.92) | (1.49) |
| Small banks (6) | 0.0068 * | 0.2147 | −0.0126 |
| | (3.19) | (1.90) | (1.06) |
| *Out-of-state banks* | | | |
| Money center banks (15) | 0.0001 | 1.2864 * | −0.0097 |
| | (0.04) | (8.41) | (0.61) |
| Large banks (8) | −0.0016 | 0.7616 * | −0.0133 |
| | (0.69) | (6.19) | (1.03) |
| Medium banks (149) | 0.0046 * | 0.3833 * | −0.0068 |
| | (4.36) | (6.78) | (1.14) |
| Small banks (171) | 0.0032 * | 0.1481 * | −0.0012 |
| | (4.62) | (4.02) | (0.31) |

[a] Estimated coefficients for time-series regressions relating the returns on a portfolio of banks (grouped by size and whether banks are in Virginia or out-of-state) to the returns on a market index and a dummy variable that takes the value of one during the two weeks (March 15 to March 19, 1985) surrounding press reports that Virginia will allow interstate banking only on a reciprocal basis and the value of zero otherwise. Actual event date is April 24, 1985.

[b] Return on an equally-weighted portfolio of banks grouped by size and whether banks are in Virginia or out-of-state.

[c] Number of banks in the portfolio.

[d] Absolute values of t-statistics are in parentheses below the corresponding estimated coefficient. Asterisks indicate significance at the 0.05 level.

takes the value of one during the 2-week period from March 15 to March 29, 1985 and zero otherwise.

There is no significant stock price reaction to the announcement of legislation allowing only restrictive interstate banking by either Virginia banks or banks located outside Virginia, irrespective of bank size. It seems that restricted, regional and reciprocal interstate banking legislation does not provide new opportunities for banks (at least in the case of Virginia), hence the lack of significant market response. It is also possible that this event was fully anticipated by the market before the 2-week period in March 1985.

## 5. Summary and concluding remarks

This chapter examined the stock price reaction of banks to the announcement of interstate banking legislation. As expected, this announcement was greeted favorably by the capital markets and led to a rise in the stock price of banks which reflected the new opportunities offered by the removal of barriers to interstate banking.

Three cases were analyzed: Texas, Arizona and Virginia. The first two states enacted legislation that permits unrestricted, nationwide interstate banking. The third enacted legislation that allows only regional, reciprocal interstate banking. Since unrestricted, nationwide interstate banking offers more potential bidders than regional, reciprocal interstate banking, the stock price reaction of banks in the former case was, as expected, stronger than in the latter case.

The findings were consistent with our expectations. They are summarized below:

(1) Texas banks reacted favorably to the sequence of events that led to the enactment of interstate banking legislation. Out-of-state banks, however, did not react to the announcements. A possible explanation of this phenomenon is that the removal of interstate banking barriers made Texas banks prime candidates for a takeover

by out-of-state banks. Since target bank shareholders seem to reap most of the benefit accruing from mergers, it is not surprising that Texas banks reacted positively to the announcements of interstate banking legislation.

(2) Not all Texas banks reacted to the announcement of interstate banking legislation in the same fashion. Small banks reacted, on average, less strongly than medium-size and large banks. This finding is consistent with the argument that medium-size and large banks are more likely than small banks to become candidates for an acquisition by out-of-state banks looking for a significant presence in the Texas banking market.

(3) Medium-size banks located inside and outside Arizona reacted positively to the announcement that Arizona may adopt unrestricted, nationwide interstate banking. The price reaction of Arizona banks was significantly stronger than that of out-of-state banks. Small banks, both inside and outside Arizona, did not exhibit any significant price reaction to the announcements. These findings are consistent with those reported in the case of Texas.

(4) No significant stock price reaction was observed for either Virginia banks or banks located outside Virginia when that state adopted legislation allowing regional, reciprocal interstate banking. This result can be attributed to the fact that regional, reciprocal interstate banking does not offer the same market-extension opportunities as those presented by unrestricted, nationwide interstate banking.

CHAPTER VIII

# CONCLUDING REMARKS

Since the early 1980s, the merger activities of banks in the U.S. have increased dramatically. Beatty, Santomero and Smirlock (1987) showed that the average annual number of bank mergers in the 1970s was 143, while in 1987 and 1988 it reached almost 600. As regional banking agreements become more of a reality, many more such mergers are likely to occur in the near future. There is little doubt that dramatic changes in the U.S. banking industry can be expected soon.

This trend toward greater bank merger activity is primarily the result of a number of key economic, legal and business developments. Since the beginning of the 1980s, the banking industry has been the subject of major regulatory and operational changes including:

(1) *Deregulation*. The Depository Institutions and Deregulation and Monetary Control Act of March 1980 is widely considered to be the most significant piece of bank legislation since the Banking Act of 1933 (see Aharony, Saunders and Swary (1988)). A key component of the Act was the removal of interest rate ceilings and entry barriers facing those thrift institutions wishing to provide financial services previously reserved for commercial banks. Thus, the Act has increased both competition and risk in banking.

(2) *Relaxation of restrictions on geographic expansion*. The relaxation of both intrastate and interstate geographic restrictions on bank operations has encouraged greater merger activity. The limitation of geographic expansion, as spelled out in the McFadden Act and the Douglas Amendment to the Bank Holding Act, prohibit multi-bank holding companies from acquiring a bank in another state unless that state allows such entry. However, since 1982, when New York became the first state to endorse legislation allowing cross-border affiliations, forty-two states (by mid-

1988) have sanctioned some type of interstate expansion provision. And seven states – Alaska, Arizona, Idaho, Maine, New Mexico, Texas and Utah – have enacted legislation permitting unrestricted interstate banking. This development, with its potential for further changes in the structure of the banking industry, has increased the number of alternative target and bidding banks, thereby adding new dimensions and opportunities to the market for bank mergers.

(3) *Bank failures*. Since the beginning of the 1980s there has been a sharp and steady increase in bank failures. The number of bank failures grew from 10 closures in 1981, to 200 closures and 21 assistance transactions in 1988. In that same year, the FDIC reported the *first operating loss* in its history.

(4) *Capital Adequacy Requirements*. In January 1989, the Federal Reserve Board required that banks adopt a risk-based capital structure. This new capital structure takes into account different types of off-balance sheet exposures in assessing capital adequacy. These requirements should substantially affect the management of bank assets and capital.

All these developments, taken together, have led to increased competition among banks and between banks and other financial institutions. This, in turn, has created a climate that is more favorable to bank mergers.

Our study of mergers and acquisitions in the U.S. banking industry has used capital market data to examine the effects of several aspects of bank merger activity on stockholder wealth. The study employed a standard event-study methodology and a considerably updated and enlarged sample of publicly traded bank stocks.

The major findings are summarized below.

(a) The rate of bank failures in recent years differs significantly among states. Furthermore, the percentage of bank failure in a given state is negatively correlated with economic conditions in that state.

(b) Interstate banking may provide valuable diversification opportunities for banks operating in states with poorly diversified economies (such as Texas and the Southwest region). In contrast, interstate banking is less valuable for banks operating in states with well-diversified economies (such as California). Poor management, *per se*, cannot fully explain why banks fail.

(c) The share price of target banks increased on average by 11.50 percent during the week of the announcement of an intended acquisition, for a sample of 118 cases which took place between 1970 and 1987. Bidding bank share prices, however, decreased, on average, by about 1.50 percent. There is evidence that bank mergers create *net aggregate wealth* to shareholders. The dollar gains realized by the shareholders of target banks exceeded the dollar losses incurred by the shareholders of bidding banks.

(d) The share price of target banks whose merger has been approved by the Federal Reserve increased, on average, by 1.70 percent during the week the approval order was announced. The share price of target banks whose merger has been denied, by contrast, declined, on average, by 7.30 percent during the week the denial order was issued. The share price of bidding banks were not significantly affected by Federal Reserve decisions.

(e) The magnitude of target-bank abnormal returns is positively correlated to the size of the bidding bank relative to that of the target bank, the absolute size of the bidding bank, the term of payment (cash versus securities), intrastate merger, poorly-managed target and low stock-return correlation (between bidders and targets). In a multiple-variable, cross-sectional regression, variables which consider the combined effect of all the above variables as well as other independent variables indicate that target bank abnormal returns associated with merger announcements are inversely related to both the size of the target bank relative to that of its bidder and to the pre-merger performance of the target bank. A multiple-variable, cross-sectional regression analysis indicates that bidding bank abnormal returns associated with merger announcements are inversely related to the number of potential bidders.

(f) Merger announcements affect both rival banks and potential bidders as well as alternative targets not directly involved in the merger. We found weak evidence that rivals react positively to the announcement of mergers (a decrease in the number of competitors may be favorable to rival banks). Similarly, there is a positive reaction by potential targets when the merger reduces the number of alternative targets (a smaller supply of target banks is favorable to potential targets). No clear pattern emerged from the analysis of changes in the number of potential bidders.

(g) The stock price reaction of banks in Texas and Arizona to the announcement of interstate banking legislation was found to be positive, reflecting the new opportunities created by the removal of barriers to interstate banking. Texas banks, for example, reacted favorably to the sequence of events that led to the enactment of interstate banking legislation which made banks in that state, especially large and medium-size banks, prime candidates for takeover by out-of-state banks.

We report evidence that *intrastate* mergers create net value to the stockholders of target banks. The acquiring bank shareholders experience negative abnormal returns, except in the case of emergency mergers. *Interstate* mergers, however, do not create net gains, but rather result in a transfer of wealth from the shareholders of bidding banks to those of target banks. This wealth transfer is greater, the larger the number of potential bidders. It seems, therefore, that the recent relaxation of geographic restrictions has not produced, on average, synergetic gains that are recognized by the capital market.

The effect of interstate banking varies across individual states. It depends on the level of diversification of each state's economy activity. Accordingly, it is not surprising that those states which enacted legislation permitting unrestricted national interstate banking were states characterized by adverse economic conditions (such as Arizona, Texas, Maine and Utah). The positive market reaction associated with such legislation reflects the market expectation of the potential value of interstate banking in those states.

*Policy Implication*

The economic rationale for interstate banking regulation is somewhat unclear. The economic root of the implementation of the McFadden Act could be best explained by the pressure exercised by local bankers on state regulators and legislators to enact legislation that protects their market area. However, since the enactment of the McFadden Act, major developments in the U.S. banking industry have made it necessary to reconsider the cost and benefits of this Act. In addition, the enforcement of this Act during a period characterized by the globalization of the banking industry is placing U.S. banks at a competitive disadvantage vis-à-vis their foreign counterparts.

The major recent developments in the U.S. banking industry which indicate a need for abolishing the restriction on bank geographic expansion and for liberalizing state branching laws include:

(a) *Nonbank competition*. The increased competition with banks from non-bank financial intermediaries (which can operate in different states with no restriction) has led to unfair competition for banks. In other words, the same rationale which led regulators to the process of deregulation in the early 1980s is sufficient cause to justify the call for the repeal of the McFadden Act.

(b) *Bank failures*. Since the beginning of the 1980s, a sharp and steady increase in bank failures has been observed. The findings of this study indicate that the number of bank failures differs appreciably from state to state. In addition, we have shown that the number of bank failures is negatively correlated with state economic activity (as measured by the rate of growth in Gross State Product and the rate of state unemployment). Hence, bank geographical diversification may reduce the probability of bank failures.

(c) *Capital adequacy requirements*. The recent imposition of risk-based capital adequacy requirements is expected to be binding for at least part of the U.S. banking industry. The potential adjustments for a bank that lacks sufficient equity could be asset sale, equity issuance, dividend cut or a merger with a bank with a high equity ratio.

The potential benefits and economic value produced by bank mergers is reflected in the positive reaction of capital markets to this type of activity. The current segmentation of the U.S. banking industry can no longer be justified. Bank mergers can provide an efficient mechanism for integrating a segmented banking market. For this reason, bank mergers should not be restricted by legislation except in the cases where it can be shown that they are anti-competitive and detrimental to bank customers.

# REFERENCES

Aharony, Joseph, Anthony Saunders and Itzhak Swary, 1988, "The Effects of DIDMCA on Bank Stockholders' Return and Risk", *Journal of Banking and Finance*, 12, (September), 317–331.

Alexander, Donald, 1985, "An Empirical Test of the Mutual Forbearance Hypothesis: The Case of the Bank Holding Companies", *Southern Economic Journal*, 52, (July), 122–140.

Amihud, Yakov and Baruch Lev, 1981, "Risk Reduction as a Managerial Motive for Conglomerate Merger", *Bell Journal of Economics*, (Autumn), 605–617.

Amihud, Yakov, Peter Dodd and Mark Weinstein, 1986, "Conglomerate Mergers, Managerial Motives and Stockholders Wealth", *Journal of Banking and Finance*, 10, 401–410.

Asquith Paul, Robert F. Bruner and David W. Mullins, 1983, "The Gains to Bidding Firms from Merger", *Journal of Financial Economics*, 11, 121–139.

Bain, Joe S., 1959, *Industrial Organization*, John Wiley and Sons Inc., New York.

Banz, Rolf W., 1981, "The Relationship between Return and Market Value of Common Stocks", *Journal of Financial Economies*, 9, 3–18.

Baumol, William J., 1967, *Business Behavior, Value and Growth*, Mac Millan, New York.

Beatty, Randolph P., Anthony M. Santomero and Michael L. Smirlock, 1987, "Bank Merger Premiums: Analysis and Evidence", *Monograph Series in Finance and Economics 1987-3, Salomon Brothers Center*, Graduate School of Business Administration, New York University.

Benston, George, Allen Berger, Gerald Hanweck and David Humphrey, 1983, "Economies of Scale and Scope in Banking". *Proceedings of a Conference on Bank Structure and Competition*, Federal Reserve Bank of Chicago, (May).

Berger, Allen, Gerald Hanweck and David Humphrey, 1987, "Competitive Viability in Banking: Scale, Scope, and Product Mix Economies", *Journal of Monetary Economics*, 20, 501–520.

Bernanka, Ben, 1983, "Nonmonetary Effects of the Financial Crisis in the Propagation of the Great Depression", *American Economic Review*, 73, (June), 257–276.

Binder, John, 1985a, "Measuring the Effects of Regulation with Stock Price Data", *Rand Journal of Economics*, 16, (Summer), 167–183.

Binder, John, 1985b, "On the Use of the Multivariate Regression Model in Event Studies", *Journal of Accounting Research*, 23, (Spring), 370–383.

Blair, Roger D. and Arnold A. Heggestad, 1978, "Bank Portfolio Regulation and the Probability of Bank Failure", *Journal of Money Credit and Banking*, 10, (February), 88–93.

Born, Jeffrey A., Robert A. Eisenbeis and Robert Harris, 1988, "The Benefits of Geographical and Product Expansion in the Financial Services Industry", *Journal of Financial Services Research*, 1, (January), 161–182.

Bradley, Michael, 1980, "Interfirm Tender Offers and the Market for Corporate Control", *Journal of Business*, 54, (October), 345–376.

Bradley, Michael, Anand Desai and E. Han Kim, 1983, "The Rationale Behind Interfirm Tender Offers: Information or Synergy", *Journal of Financial Economics*, 11, (April), 183–206.

Bradley, Michael, Anand Desai and E. Han Kim, 1988, "Synergistic Gains from Corporate Acquisitions and their Division Between the Stockholders Target and Acquiring Firms", *Journal of Financial Economics*, 21, (May), 3–40.

Brown, Stephen J. and Jerold B. Warner, 1980, "Measuring Security Price Performance", *Journal of Financial Economics*, 8, (September), 205–258.

Brown, Stephen J. and Jerold B. Warner, 1985, "Using Daily Stock Returns: The Case of Event Studies", *Journal of Financial Economics*, 14, (March), 3–31.

Buser, Stephen A., Andrew H. Chen and Edward J. Kane, 1981, "Federal Deposit Insurance Regulatory Policy and Optimal Bank Capital", *Journal of Finance*, 36, (March), 51–60.

Carleton, Willard T., David K. Guilkey and Robert S. Harris, 1983, "An Empirical Analysis of the Role of the Medium of Exchange in Mergers", *Journal of Finance*, 38, (June), 813–826.

Clark, Jeffrey A., 1984, "Estimation of Economies of Scale in Banking Using A Generalized Functional Form", *Journal of Money, Credit and Banking*, 16, (February), 53–68.

Clark, Jeffrey A., 1988, "Economies of Scale and Scope at Depository Financial Institutions: A Review of the Literature", *Economic Review* (Federal Reserve Bank of Kansas City), 73, (September/October), 16–33.

Cohen, Kalman, Gabriel Hawawini, Steven Maier, Robert Schwartz and David Whitcomb, 1983, "Friction in the Trading Process and the Estimation of Systematic Risk", *Journal of Financial Economics*, 12, (August), 263–278.

Cornett, Milton M. and Sankar De, 1989, "Bidder Returns in Corporate Takeover Bids: Evidence from Interstate Bank mergers", *Working Paper Series 89-8, Southern Methodist University.*

Dahl, Drew and Ronald E. Shrieves, 1989, "Evidence on the Role of Holding Company Acquisition in the Management of Bank Capital", *Journal of Financial Services Research*, 2, (February), 21–37.

de Cossio, Francisco, Jack W. Trifts and Kevin P. Scanlon, 1987, "Bank Returns: The Difference Between Intrastate and Interstate Bank Mergers", Proceedings of a Conference on Bank Structure and Competition (Merging Commercial and Investment Banking: Risks, Benefits, Challenges). Federal Reserve Bank of Chicago.

Dennis, Debra K. and John J. McConnell, 1986, "Corporate Mergers and Securities Returns", *Journal of Financial Economics*, 16, (June), 143–187.

Diamond, Douglas, W. and Philip H. Dybvig, 1983, "Bank Runs, Deposit Insurance and Liquidity", *Journal of Political Economy*, 91, (June), 401–419.

DiClemente, John J. and Diana L. Fortier, 1984, "Antitrust and Banking – Written and Revealed Standards", *Issues in Bank Regulation*, (Winter), 11–19.

Dodd, Peter and Richard Ruback, 1977, "Tender Offers and Stockholder Returns: An Empirical Analysis", *Journal of Financial Economics*, 5, 351–373.

Eckbo, Espen B., 1983, "Horizontal Mergers, Collusion, and Stockholder Wealth", *Journal of Financial Economics*, 11, (April), 241–273.

Eckbo, Espen B., 1985, "Mergers and the Market Concentration Doctrine: Evidence from the Capital Market", *Journal of Business*, 58, (July), 325–349.

Eckbo, Espen B. and Peggy Wier, 1985, "Antimerger Policy under the Hart-Scott-Rodino Act: A Reexamination of the Market Power Hypothesis", *Journal Law and Economics*, 28, (April), 119–149.

Edwards, Franklin R., 1964, "Concentration in Banking and its Effect on Business Loan Rates", *The Review of Economics and Statistics*, 46, (August), 294–300.

Eger, Carol Ellen, 1983, "An Empirical Test of the Redistribution Effect in Pure Exchange Mergers", *Journal of Financial and Quantitative Analyses*, 18, (December), 547–572.

Eisenbeis, Robert A., 1975, "Differences in Federal Regulatory Agencies' Bank Merger Policies", *Journal of Money Credit and Banking*, 7, (February), 93–104.

Eisenbeis, Robert A., Robert S. Harris and Josef Lakonishok, 1984, "Benefits of Bank Diversification: The Evidence from Shareholder Returns", *Journal of Finance*, 39, (July), 881–894.

Ellert, James C., 1976, "Mergers, Antitrust Law Enforcement, and Stockholder Returns", *Journal of Finance*, 31, (May) 715–732.

Evanoff, Douglas D. and Diana L. Fortier, 1988, "Reevaluation of the Structure-Conduct-Performance Paradigm in Banking", *Journal of Financial Services Research*, 1, (June), 277–294.

Fama, Eugene F., Lawrence Fisher, Michael C. Jensen and Richard Roll, 1969, "The Adjustment of Stock Prices to New Information", *International Economic Review*, 10, (February), 1–21.

Fama, Eugene F., 1976, *Foundations of Finance Portfolio Decisions and Securities Prices*, Basic Books, New York.

Federal Reserve Bank of Chicago, 1986, *Toward a Nationwide Banking: A Guide to the Issues*, Edited by Herbert Bear and Sue Gregorash.

Feinberg, Robert M., 1985, "'Sales at Risk': A Test of the Mutual Forbearance Theory of Conglomerate Behavior", *Journal of Business, 58*, (April), 225–241.

Firth, Michael, 1980, "Takeovers, Shareholder Returns and the Theory of the Firm", *Quarterly Journal of Economics*, March, 235–260.

Frieder, Larry A., 1980, *Commercial Banking and Holding Company Acquisitions: New Dimensions in Theory Evaluation, and Practice*, UMI Research Press, Ann Arbor, Michigan.

Gilberto, Michael, S. and Nikhil P. Varaiya, 1989, "The Winner's Curse and Bidder Competition in Acquisitions: Evidence from Failed Bank Auctions", *Journal of Finance*, 44, (March), 59–76.

Gilligan, Thomas, Michael Smirlock, 1984, "An Empirical Study of Joint Production and Scale Economies in Commercial Banking", *Journal of Banking and Finance*, 8, (March), 67–77.

Gilligan, Thomas, Michael Smirlock and William Marshall, 1984, "Scale and Scope Economies in Multi-product Banking Firms", *Journal of Monetary Economics*, 13, (May), 393–405.

Graddy, Duane B., and Reuben Kyle III, 1979, "The Simultaneity of Bank Decision Making, Market Structure, and Bank Performance", *The Journal of Finance*, 34, (March), 1–17.

Hannan, Timothy H. and Stephen A. Rhoades, 1987, "Acquisition Targets and Motives: The Case of the Banking Industry", *The Review of Economics Statistics*, 69, (February), 67–74.

Hansen, Robert G., 1987, "A Theory for the Choice of Exchange Medium in Mergers and Acquisitions", *Journal of Business*, 60, (January), 75–95.

Harris, Robert S., Julian Franks and Colin Mayer, 1987, "Means of Payment in Takeovers: Results for the U.K. and the U.S.", Working Paper No 2456 (National Bureau of Economic Research), December, 64 pages.

Harris, Milton and Artur Raviv, 1978, "Some Results on Incentive Contracts with Applications to Education and Employment, Health Insurance and Enforcement", *American Economic Review*, 68, (March), 20–30.

Harris, Milton and Artur Raviv, 1979, "Optimal Incentive Contracts with Imperfect Information", *Journal of Economic Theory*, 20, (April), 231–259.

Hobson, Hugh A., John T. Masten and Jacobus T. Severiens, 1978, "Holding Company Acquisitions and Bank Performance: A Comparative Study", *Journal of Bank Research*, 9, (Summer), 116–20.

Huang, Yen-Sheng and Ralph A. Walkling, 1987, "Target Abnormal Returns Associated with Acquisition Announcements: Payment, Acquisition Form and Managerial Resistance", *Journal of Financial Economics*, 19, (December), 329–349.

Jacklin, Charles J. and Sudipto Bhattacharya, 1988, "Distinguishing Panics and Information-Based Banks Runs: Welfare and Policy Implications", *Journal of Political Economy*, 96, (June), 568–592.

James, Christopher and Peggy Wier, 1987a, "Returns to Acquirers and Competition in the Acquisition Market: The Case of Banking", *Journal of Political Economy*, 95, (April), 355–370.

James, Christopher and Peggy Wier, 1987b, "An Analysis of FDIC Failed Bank Auctions", *Journal of Monetary Economics*, 20, (July), 141–153.

Jarell, Gregg A., James A. Brickley and Jeffry M. Netter, 1988, "The Market for Corporate Control: The Empirical Evidence Since 1980," *Journal of Economic Perspectives*, 2, (Winter), 49–68.

Jensen, Michael C., 1986, "Agency Costs of Free Cash Flow, Corporate Finance and Takeovers", *American Economic Review*, 76, (May), 323–329.

Jensen, Michael C. and Richard S. Ruback, 1983, "The Market for Corporate Control: The Scientific Evidence", *Journal of Financial Economics*, 11, (April), 5–50.

Jensen, Michael C. and William H. Meckling, 1976, "Theory of the Firm: Managerial Behavior, Agency Costs and Ownership Structure", *Journal of Financial Economics*, 3, (October), 305–360.

Johnson, Rodney and David Meinster, 1975, "The Performance of Bank Holding Company Acquisitions: A Multivariate Analysis", *Journal of Business*, 48, (April), 204–212.

Kahane, Yehuda, 1977, "Capital Adequacy and the Regulation of Financial Intermediaries", *Journal of Banking and Finance*, 1 (October), 207–218.

Kaufman, George, G., 1966, "Bank Market Structure and Performance; The Evidence from Iowa", *Southern Economic Journal*, 32, (April), 429–439.

Keenan, Michael, 1982, "Valuation Problems in Service-Sector Mergers", in *Mergers and Acquisitions*, edited by Michael Keenan and Lawrence J. White, Lexington Books, 29–40.

Klein, Michael A., 1971, "A Theory of the Banking Firm", *Journal of Money Credit and Banking*, 3, (May), 205–218.

Lobue, Marie, 1984, "Categorial Bank Acquisition", *Journal of Bank Research*, 14, (Winter), 274–282.

Loeys, Jan G., 1986, "Bank Acquisitions: The Mitigating Factors Defense", *Banking Law Journal*, 103, (September/October), 427–449.

Long, John B. Jr., 1974, "On the Pricing of Corporate Debt: The Risk Structure of Interest Rates, Discussion", *Journal of Finance*, 29, (May), 485–488.

Marshall, William, Edward Greenberg and Jess Yawitz, 1984, "Incentives for Diversification and the Structure of the Conglomerate Firm", *Southern Economic Journal*, 51, (July), 1–23.

Meltzer, Allen, H., 1967 "Major Issues in the Regulation of Financial Institutions", *Journal of Political Economy*, 75, (Supplement: August), pp. 482–502.

Mester, Loretta J., 1987, "Efficient Production of Financial Services: Scale and Scope Economies", *Business Review*, (Federal Reserve Bank of Philadelphia), (January/February), 15–25.

Myers, Stewart C. and Nicholas S. Majluf, 1984, "Corporate Financing and Investment Decisions when Firms Have Information That Investors Do Not Have", *Journal of Financial Economics*, 13, (June), 187–221.

Neely, Walter P., 1987, "Banking Acquisitions: Acquirer and Target Shareholders Returns", *Financial Management*, 16, (Winter), 66–74.

Penrose, Edith, 1959, *The Theory of the Growth of the Firm*, Oxford Blackwell.

Pettway, Richard and Jack W. Trifts, 1985, "Do Banks Overbid When Acquiring Failed Banks", *Financial Management*, 14, 5–15.

Piper, Thomas R., and Steven J. Weiss, 1971, "The Profitability of Bank Acquisitions by Multi-Bank Holding Companies", *New England Economic Review*, Federal Reserve Bank of Boston, (September/October), 2–12.

Pyle, David H., 1972, "Descriptive Theories of Financial Institutions Under Uncertainty", *Journal of Financial and Quantitative Analysis*, 7, (December), 2009–29.

Rhoades Stephen A., 1982, "Structure-Performance Studies in Banking: An Update Summary and Evaluation", Washington, Federal Reserve System, *Staff Studies*, No 119, (August).

Rhoades Stephen A., 1985a, Market Share as a Source of Market Power: Implications and Some Evidence", *Journal of Economics and Business*, 37, (December), 343–363.

Rhoades Stephen A., 1985b, "Mergers and Acquisitions by Commercial Banks, 1960–1983", Washington, Federal Reserve System, *Staff Studies*, No 142, (January).

Rhoades Stephen A., 1986, "Bank Operating Performance of Acquired Firms in Banking Before and After Acquisition", Washington Federal Reserve System, *Staff Studies*, No 149, (May).

Roll, Richard, 1986, "The Hubris Hypothesis of Corporate Takeovers", *Journal of Business*, 59, (April), 197–216.

Roll, Richard, 1988, "Empirical Evidence on Takeover Activity and Shareholder Wealth", in *Knights, Raiders and Targets*, edited by John Coffee, Louis Lowenstein and Susan Rose-Ackerman, New York: Oxford University Press.

Rose, Peter, 1987, "The Impact of Mergers in Banking – Evidence from a Nationwide Sample of Federally Chartered Banks", *Journal of Economics and Business*, 39, (November), 289–312.

Rose, Peter, James Kolari and Kenneth W. Riener, 1985, "A National Survey Study of Bank Services and Bank Prices Arrayed by Size and Structure", *Journal of Bank Research*, 16, (Summer), 72–85.

Ross, Stephen A., 1978, "A Simple Approach to the Valuation of Risky Streams", *Journal of Business*, 51, (July), 453–475.

Savage, Donald, T. 1987, "Interstate Banking Developments", *Federal Reserve Bulletin*, 73, (February), 79–92.

Saunders, Anthony, Elizabeth Strock and Nickolaos Travlos, 1987, "Ownership Structure, Deregulation and Bank Risk Taking", Working Paper Series, York University Graduate School of Business Administration.

Schwert, William G., 1981, "Using Financial Data to Measure Effects of Regulation", *Journal of Law and Economics*, 24, (April), 121–158.

Shavel, Steven, 1979, "Risk Sharing and Incentives in the Principal and Agent Relationship", *Bell Journal of Economics*, 10, (Spring), 55–73.

Shull Bernard, 1974, "Bank Expansion: The New Competition and the Old Predatory Practices", *Banking Law Journal*, 91, (September), 726–747.

Smith David, 1971, "The Performance of Merging Banks", *Journal of Business*, 44, (April), 184–192.

Stigler, George J., 1964, "A Theory of Oligopoly", *Journal of Political Economy*, 72, (February), 44–61.

Stillman, Robert, 1983, "Examining Antitrust Policy Towards Horizontal Mergers", *Journal of Financial Economics*, 11, (April), 225–240.

Sushka, Marie E. and Yvette Bendeck, 1988, "Bank Acquisitions and Stockholders' Wealth", *Journal of Banking and Finance*, 12 (December), 551–562.

Swary, Itzhak, 1986, "Stock Market Reaction to Regulatory Action in the Continental Illinois Crisis", *Journal of Business*, 59, (July), 451–473.

Swary, Itzhak, 1983, "Bank Acquisition of Non-Bank Firms: An Empirical Analysis of Administrative Decisions", *Journal of Banking and Finance*, 7, (June), 213–230.

Swary, Itzhak, 1980, *Capital Adequacy Requirements and Bank Holding Companies*, UMI Research Press, Ann Arbor, Michigan.

Travlos, Nickolaos G., 1987, "Corporate Takeover Bids, Methods of Payment, and Bidding Firms' Stock Returns", *Journal of Finance*, 42, (September), 943–963.

Trifts, Jack W. and Kevin P. Scanlon, 1987, "Interstate Bank Mergers: The Early Evidence", *Journal of Financial Research*, 10, (Winter), 305–311.

Varvel, Walter A., 1975, "A Valuation Approach to Bank Holding Company Acquisitions", *Economic Review*, Federal Reserve Bank of Richmond, 61, (July/August), 9–15.

Wansley, James W., William R. Lane and Ho C. Yang, 1983, "Abnormal Returns to Acquired Firms by Type of Acquisition and Method of Payment", *Financial Management*, 12, (Autumn), 16–22.

Ware, Robert F., 1972, "Banking Structure and Performance Some Evidence from Ohio", *Economic Review*, Federal Reserve Bank of Cleveland, 294–300.

Whalem, Gary, W. and Richard L. Mugel, 1986, "Rival Stock Price Reactions to Large BHC Acquisition Announcements Evidence on Linked Oligopoly", *Proceedings of a Conference on Bank Structure and Competition, Federal Reserve Bank of Chicago*, (May).

Whitehead David D. and Jan Luytjes, 1984, "Can Interstate Banking Increase Competitive Market Performance? An Empirical Test", *Economic Review*, Federal Reserve Bank of Atlanta, 69, (January), 4–10.

Wier, Peggy, 1983, "The Costs of Antimerger Lawsuits: Evidence from the Stock Market", *Journal of Financial Economics*, 11, (April), 207–224.

# INDEX OF SUBJECTS

# INDEX OF NAMES